P9-AGD-047

CREATING WEB PAGES
Simplified®

Visual™

by Mike Wooldridge

WILEY

Wiley Publishing, Inc.

CREATING WEB PAGES SIMPLIFIED®

Published by
Wiley Publishing, Inc.
10475 Crosspoint Boulevard
Indianapolis, IN 46256

www.wiley.com

Published simultaneously in Canada

Copyright © 2009 by Wiley Publishing, Inc., Indianapolis, Indiana

No part of this publication may be reproduced, stored in a retrieval system or transmitted in any form or by any means, electronic, mechanical, photocopying, recording, scanning or otherwise, except as permitted under Sections 107 or 108 of the 1976 United States Copyright Act, without either the prior written permission of the Publisher, or authorization through payment of the appropriate per-copy fee to the Copyright Clearance Center, 222 Rosewood Drive, Danvers, MA 01923, 978-750-8400, fax 978-646-8600. Requests to the Publisher for permission should be addressed to the Permissions Department, John Wiley & Sons, Inc., 111 River Street, Hoboken, NJ 07030, 201-748-6011, fax 201-748-6008, or online at www.wiley.com/go/permissions.

Library of Congress Control Number: 2009925426

ISBN: 978-0-470-48192-9

Manufactured in the United States of America

10 9 8 7 6 5 4 3 2 1

Trademark Acknowledgments

Wiley, the Wiley Publishing logo, Visual, the Visual logo, Simplified, Read Less - Learn More and related trade dress are trademarks or registered trademarks of John Wiley & Sons, Inc. and/or its affiliates in the United States and other countries, and may not be used without written permission. All other trademarks are the property of their respective owners. Wiley Publishing, Inc. is not associated with any product or vendor mentioned in this book.

LIMIT OF LIABILITY/DISCLAIMER OF WARRANTY: THE PUBLISHER AND THE AUTHOR MAKE NO REPRESENTATIONS OR WARRANTIES WITH RESPECT TO THE ACCURACY OR COMPLETENESS OF THE CONTENTS OF THIS WORK AND SPECIFICALLY DISCLAIM ALL WARRANTIES, INCLUDING WITHOUT LIMITATION WARRANTIES OF FITNESS FOR A PARTICULAR PURPOSE. NO WARRANTY MAY BE CREATED OR EXTENDED BY SALES OR PROMOTIONAL MATERIALS. THE ADVICE AND STRATEGIES CONTAINED HEREIN MAY NOT BE SUITABLE FOR EVERY SITUATION. THIS WORK IS SOLD WITH THE UNDERSTANDING THAT THE PUBLISHER IS NOT ENGAGED IN RENDERING LEGAL, ACCOUNTING, OR OTHER PROFESSIONAL SERVICES. IF PROFESSIONAL ASSISTANCE IS REQUIRED, THE SERVICES OF A COMPETENT PROFESSIONAL PERSON SHOULD BE SOUGHT. NEITHER THE PUBLISHER NOR THE AUTHOR SHALL BE LIABLE FOR DAMAGES ARISING HEREFROM. THE FACT THAT AN ORGANIZATION OR WEBSITE IS REFERRED TO IN THIS WORK AS A CITATION AND/OR A POTENTIAL SOURCE OF FURTHER INFORMATION DOES NOT MEAN THAT THE AUTHOR OR THE PUBLISHER ENDORSES THE INFORMATION THE ORGANIZATION OR WEBSITE MAY PROVIDE OR RECOMMENDATIONS IT MAY MAKE. FURTHER, READERS SHOULD BE AWARE THAT INTERNET WEBSITES LISTED IN THIS WORK MAY HAVE CHANGED OR DISAPPEARED BETWEEN WHEN THIS WORK WAS WRITTEN AND WHEN IT IS READ.

FOR PURPOSES OF ILLUSTRATING THE CONCEPTS AND TECHNIQUES DESCRIBED IN THIS BOOK, THE AUTHOR HAS CREATED VARIOUS NAMES, COMPANY NAMES, MAILING, E-MAIL AND INTERNET ADDRESSES, PHONE AND FAX NUMBERS AND SIMILAR INFORMATION, ALL OF WHICH ARE FICTITIOUS. ANY RESEMBLANCE OF THESE FICTITIOUS NAMES, ADDRESSES, PHONE AND FAX NUMBERS AND SIMILAR INFORMATION TO ANY ACTUAL PERSON, COMPANY AND/OR ORGANIZATION IS UNINTENTIONAL AND PURELY COINCIDENTAL.

Contact Us

For general information on our other products and services please contact our Customer Care Department within the U.S. at 877-762-2974, outside the U.S. at 317-572-3993, or fax 317-572-4002.

For technical support please visit www.wiley.com/techsupport.

Permissions

Artville/Getty Images
Corbis Digital Stock
Digital Vision
ImageState
PhotoDisc, Inc.
PhotoDisc/Getty Images
Purestock
Ryan McVay/PhotoDisc/Getty Images
Steve Rawlings/Digital Vision

The following Wikimedia images were used under free licenses:
Everest kalapatthar crop.jpg (Creative Commons Attribution ShareAlike 2.5, Pavel Novak)
Cathedral square Santiago de Compostela.jpg (Creative Commons Attribution ShareAlike 3.0 Unported, Niels Bosboom)
Great Pyramid of Giza edge.jpg (GNU Free Documentation License, Mgiganteus1)

WILEY
Wiley Publishing, Inc.

Sales

Contact Wiley
at (877) 762-2974 or
fax (317) 572-4002.

Praise for Visual Books

"Like a lot of other people, I understand things best when I see them visually. Your books really make learning easy and life more fun."

John T. Frey (Cadillac, MI)

"I have quite a few of your Visual books and have been very pleased with all of them. I love the way the lessons are presented!"

Mary Jane Newman (Yorba Linda, CA)

"I just purchased my third Visual book (my first two are dog-eared now!), and, once again, your product has surpassed my expectations."

Tracey Moore (Memphis, TN)

"I am an avid fan of your Visual books. If I need to learn anything, I just buy one of your books and learn the topic in no time. Wonders! I have even trained my friends to give me Visual books as gifts."

Illona Bergstrom (Aventura, FL)

"Thank you for making it so clear. I appreciate it. I will buy many more Visual books."

J.P. Sangdong (North York, Ontario, Canada)

"I have several books from the Visual series and have always found them to be valuable resources."

Stephen P. Miller (Ballston Spa, NY)

"Thank you for the wonderful books you produce. It wasn't until I was an adult that I discovered how I learn — visually. Nothing compares to Visual books. I love the simple layout. I can just grab a book and use it at my computer, lesson by lesson. And I understand the material! You really know the way I think and learn. Thanks so much!"

Stacey Han (Avondale, AZ)

"I absolutely admire your company's work. Your books are terrific. The format is perfect, especially for visual learners like me. Keep them coming!"

Frederick A. Taylor, Jr. (New Port Richey, FL)

"I have several of your Visual books and they are the best I have ever used."

Stanley Clark (Crawfordville, FL)

"I bought my first Visual book last month. Wow. Now I want to learn everything in this easy format!"

Tom Vial (New York, NY)

"Thank you, thank you, thank you...for making it so easy for me to break into this high-tech world. I now own four of your books. I recommend them to anyone who is a beginner like myself."

Gay O'Donnell (Calgary, Alberta, Canada)

"I write to extend my thanks and appreciation for your books. They are clear, easy to follow, and straight to the point. Keep up the good work! I bought several of your books and they are just right! No regrets! I will always buy your books because they are the best."

Seward Kollie (Dakar, Senegal)

"Compliments to the chef!! Your books are extraordinary! Or, simply put, extra-ordinary, meaning way above the rest! THANK YOU THANK YOU THANK YOU! I buy them for friends, family, and colleagues."

Christine J. Manfrin (Castle Rock, CO)

"What fantastic teaching books you have produced! Congratulations to you and your staff. You deserve the Nobel Prize in Education in the Software category. Thanks for helping me understand computers."

Bruno Tonon (Melbourne, Australia)

"Over time, I have bought a number of your 'Read Less - Learn More' books. For me, they are THE way to learn anything easily. I learn easiest using your method of teaching."

José A. Mazón (Cuba, NY)

"I am an avid purchaser and reader of the Visual series, and they are the greatest computer books I've seen. The Visual books are perfect for people like myself who enjoy the computer, but want to know how to use it more efficiently. Your books have definitely given me a greater understanding of my computer, and have taught me to use it more effectively. Thank you very much for the hard work, effort, and dedication that you put into this series."

Alex Diaz (Las Vegas, NV)

Credits

Sr. Acquisitions Editor
Jody Lefevere

Project Editor
Sarah Hellert

Technical Editor
Vince Averello

Copy Editor
Scott Tullis

Editorial Director
Robyn Siesky

Editorial Manager
Cricket Krengel

Business Manager
Amy Knies

Sr. Marketing Manager
Sandy Smith

Vice President and Executive Group Publisher
Richard Swadley

Vice President and Executive Publisher
Barry Pruett

Sr. Project Coordinator
Kristie Rees

Graphics and Production Specialists
Carrie Cesavice
Andrea Hornberger
Jennifer Mayberry

Screen Artists
Ana Carrillo
Ronda David-Burroughs
Jill A. Proll

Quality Control
Melissa Cossell

Proofreader
Cynthia Fields

Indexer
Broccoli Information Mgt.

Special Help
Kim Heusel
Tobin Wilkerson

About the Author

Mike Wooldridge is a Web developer based in the San Francisco Bay area. He has authored more than 20 books for the Visual series.

Author's Acknowledgments

Mike thanks Sarah Hellert once again for her top-notch project editing, Vince Averello for his knowledgeable technical editing, and Scott Tullis for his careful copy editing. This book is dedicated to Mike's nine-year-old son and his classmates, who are learning HTML. He hopes this book will help them and others turn their ideas into Web pages.

Table of Contents

3

Adding Text

```
headings.html - WordPad
File  Edit  View  Insert  Format  Help
<HTML>
<HEAD>
<TITLE>M and L's Travel Agency: Common Cont
</HEAD>
<BODY>

<H1>Duffel Bag</H1>
<H2>Suitcase</H2>
<H3>Backpack</H3>
<H4>Briefcase</H4>
<H5>Laptop bag</H5>
<H6>Fannypack</H6>

</BODY>
</HTML>
```

M and L's Travel Agency: Common Containers - Windows Internet Explorer
C:\Users\Mike\Documents\HTML Pages\ch03\headings.html
File Edit View Favorites Tools Help
M and L's Travel Agency: Common Containers

Duffel Bag
Suitcase
Backpack
Briefcase
Laptop bag
Fannypack

4

Formatting Text

```
<TITLE>M and L's Travel Agency</TITLE>
</HEAD>
<BODY TEXT="#008000">

<H1 ALIGN="center"><FONT COLOR="red">M and L's Trav

<P ALIGN="center"><I>We get you there!</I></P>

<P>For more than 15 years, M and L's Travel Agency
plan exciting adventures to destinations around th
specialize in one-of-a-kind vacation packages for
budgets. Let us help you with your airline tickets,
rental cars, either online or in person.
</P>
```

M and L's Travel Age
We get you there!

For more than 15 years, M and L's Travel Agency has helped custom
adventures to destinations around the world. We specialize in one-o
packages for all interests and budgets. Let us help you with your airl
bookings, and rental cars, either online or in person.

Popular destinations:

- Pyramids of Giza, Egypt
- Machu Picchu, Peru
- Ambergris Caye, Belize
- Great Wall, China

Table of Contents

5

Adding Images

6

Adding Links

7

Working with Tables

8

Creating Forms

Table of Contents

9

Creating Style Sheets

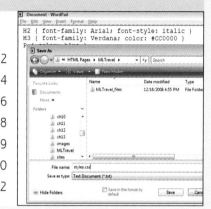

10

Formatting Text with Style Sheets

11

Controlling Layout with Style Sheets

12

Adding Multimedia and Other Features

Table of Contents

13

Publishing Your Web Pages

14

Creating a Google Site

15

Creating a Blog on Blogger

16

Creating a Facebook Page

How to Use This Book

Do you look at the pictures in a book before anything else on a page? Would you rather see an image instead of read about how to do something? Search no further. This book is for you. Opening *Creating Web Pages Simplified* allows you to read less and learn more about publishing text, images, video, and other media online.

Who Needs This Book

This book is for a reader who has limited experience with creating Web pages and wants to learn more. It is also for readers who want to expand or refresh their knowledge of HTML and other methods for publishing content on the Web.

Book Organization

Creating Web Pages Simplified has 16 chapters.

Chapter 1, **Getting Familiar with Web Pages**, introduces you to the Internet, HTML, and Web browsers.

In Chapter 2, **Creating Your First Web Page**, you learn how to quickly create a page using HTML and view the page.

Chapter 3, **Adding Text**, covers how to organize words and paragraphs on your pages.

In Chapter 4, **Formatting Text**, you learn how to highlight, resize, and apply other formatting to text on a page.

Chapter 5, **Adding Images**, shows you how to insert photos and illustrations on your pages.

Chapter 6, **Adding Links**, explains how to turn text, images, and other page elements into clickable links to other pages.

In Chapter 7, **Working with Tables**, you learn how to organize information into rows and columns on a page.

Chapter 8, **Creating Forms**, helps you build forms so your visitors can submit information using your pages.

In Chapter 9, **Creating Style Sheets**, you learn the basics about applying advanced styles to pages.

Chapter 10, **Formatting Text with Style Sheets**, teaches you to organize words and paragraphs on Web pages using style rules.

In Chapter 11, **Controlling Layout with Style Sheets**, you learn how to precisely resize, align, and overlap elements on a page.

Chapter 12, **Adding Multimedia and Other Features**, shows you how to integrate video, audio, and interactive media onto your pages.

In Chapter 13, **Publishing Your Web Pages**, you learn how to move your content to a Web server so others can view it.

Chapter 14, **Creating a Google Site**, introduces you to an easy-to-use service for creating Web pages run by Google.

Chapter 15, **Creating a Blog on Blogger**, shows you how to set up an online diary where you can post your thoughts and opinions.

Chapter 16, **Creating a Facebook Page**, teaches you about online social networks and how to set up an account on Facebook.

Chapter Organization

This book consists of sections, all listed in the book's table of contents. A *section* is a set of steps that show you how to complete a specific technique. Each section, usually contained on two facing pages, has an introduction, a set of full-color screen shots and steps that walk you through the task, and a tip. This format allows you to quickly look at a topic of interest and learn it instantly.

What You Need to Use This Book

- A computer running Windows Vista or XP, or a Mac running OS X.

- For a dialup Internet connection, you need either an internal or external dialup modem connected to your computer.

- For a high-speed Internet connection, you need a broadband modem (usually provided by your Internet service provider).

- To share an Internet connection, you need a network router.

Using the Mouse

This book uses the following conventions to describe the actions you perform when using the mouse:

Click

Press your left mouse button once. You generally click your mouse on something to select something on the screen.

Double-click

Press your left mouse button twice. Double-clicking something on the computer screen generally opens whatever item you have double-clicked.

Right-click

Press your right mouse button. When you right-click anything on the computer screen, the program displays a shortcut menu containing commands specific to the selected item.

Click and Drag, and Release the Mouse

Move your mouse pointer and position it over an item on the screen. Press and hold down the left mouse button. Now, move the mouse to where you want to place the item and then release the button. You use this method to move an item from one area of the computer screen to another.

The Conventions in This Book

A number of typographic and layout styles have been used throughout *Creating Web Pages Simplified* to distinguish different types of information.

Bold

Bold type represents the names of commands and options that you interact with. Bold type also indicates text and numbers that you must type into a dialog box or window.

Italics

Italic words introduce a new term and are followed by a definition.

Numbered Steps

You must perform the instructions in numbered steps in order to successfully complete a section and achieve the final results.

Bulleted Steps

These steps point out various optional features. You do not have to perform these steps; they simply give additional information about a feature. Steps without bullets tell you what the program does in response to your following a numbered step. For example, if you click a menu command, a dialog box may appear or a window may open. The step text may also tell you what the final result is when you follow a set of numbered steps.

Notes

Notes give additional information. They may describe special conditions that may occur during an operation. They may warn you of a situation that you want to avoid — for example, the loss of data. A note may also cross-reference a related area of the book. A cross-reference may guide you to another chapter or another section in the current chapter.

You can easily identify the tips in any section by looking for the Simplify It icon. Tips offer additional information, including tips, hints, and tricks. You can use the tip information to go beyond what you have learned in the steps.

Chapter 1

Getting Familiar with Web Pages

Are you interested in building your own Web pages? This chapter introduces you to the Internet, where Web pages are stored and accessed, and to HTML, the language used to create Web pages. It also explains the basics behind HTML editors and Web browsers, which you use to design and view your Web content.

With a Web browser, you can view the HTML for any page on the Web and save the HTML to your computer. This can serve as a starting point for creating your pages.

Later chapters cover writing HTML to create your Web pages from scratch as well as using online services to set up blogs, social-network pages, and more.

Internet Basics

The Internet is a worldwide collection of interconnected computer networks that enables businesses, organizations, governments, and individuals to communicate in a variety of ways. One of the most popular ways users communicate on the Internet is by publishing and interacting with Web pages. You can create Web pages from scratch using HTML or set them up using various online services. You can also use the Internet to send and receive e-mail, chat with other users, and transfer files between computers.

The Internet began as a military research project in the late 1960s. In 2008, the number of Internet users around the globe topped 1.6 billion.

Types of Connections

Users connect to the Internet through a variety of methods. A relatively inexpensive but slow way to connect is with dial-up service, which involves using a modem and a phone line. Faster ways to connect include DSL (Digital Subscriber Line), cable modem, satellite, and fiber-optic access. Networks include special wireless transmitters that allow computers to access the Internet wirelessly. Companies that help you connect to the Internet are known as *Internet service providers*, or ISPs.

Connection Speeds

Connection speeds play an important part in a user's Internet experience because slower connections result in slower file transfers and Web page viewing. Dial-up connections offer the slowest access to the Internet at up to 56 kilobits per second, or Kbps. DSL usually offers connection speeds of up to 3 megabits per second, or Mbps, whereas cable modems can achieve speeds of up to 30 Mbps. A Web page that takes about 20 seconds to download via dial-up can take less than a second using a cable modem.

Communication Standards

The Internet infrastructure relies on a variety of protocols that dictate how computers and networks talk to each other. For example, *Transmission Control Protocol/Internet Protocol*, or TCP/IP, is a set of rules that control how Internet messages flow between computers. *Hypertext Transfer Protocol*, or HTTP (●), is a set of rules that determine how browsers should request Web pages and how server computers should deliver them. Agreed-upon protocols allow seamless communication among the many different types of computers that connect to the Internet.

The World Wide Web

The World Wide Web is a giant collection of documents, or pages, stored on computers around the globe. Commonly called *the Web*, this collection of pages represents a wealth of text, images, audio, and video available to anyone with a computer and an Internet connection. Web pages are stored on *servers*, which are Internet-connected computers running software that allows them to serve up information to other computers. When you place a text file, image, or other document in a special Web directory on a server, that information is available for other Web users to view. Chapter 13 talks about how to transfer information to a Web server.

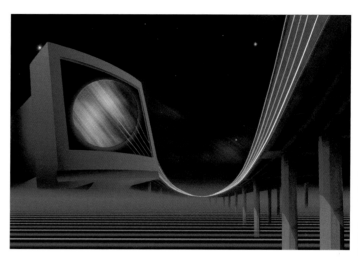

URLs and Links

Every page on the Web has a unique address called a URL, which is short for *Uniform Resource Locator*. A URL looks like this:

http://www.example.com/index.html

If you know a page's URL, you can type it into a Web browser to view that page over the Internet. You can also view pages by way of hyperlinks, or *links*, which are clickable words or images on Web pages. Every link on a Web page is associated with a URL that connects it to another page, media file, or other resource on the Internet. Users can jump from one Web page to another by clicking links. Chapter 6 discusses how to create links with HTML.

Browsers

A Web browser is software that allows you to view and interact with Web pages. When you type a URL or click a link in a Web browser, the browser retrieves the appropriate page from a server on the Internet and displays that page. Microsoft Internet Explorer, Mozilla Firefox, and Apple Safari are the three most popular browsers in use today. Each program has evolved through a number of versions, with newer versions supporting more recent Web features. As you build your pages using HTML code, remember that different browsers may display your pages slightly differently depending on the version.

An Introduction to HTML

You can build Web pages using HTML, which is short for *Hypertext Markup Language*. HTML documents are made up of text content and special codes known as *tags* that tell Web browsers how to display the content. HTML documents are identified by their .html or .htm file extensions. You can edit the code in an HTML document by opening the document in a text editor.

For the most part, HTML is platform independent, which means you can view Web pages on any computer operating system, including Windows, Mac, and Linux.

HTML Tags

HTML consists of text interspersed with special instructions known as *tags*. Surrounded by brackets, < >, HTML tags tell a browser how to organize and present text, images, and other Web page content. Many tags are written using an opening tag and a closing tag that surround content that appears on the page. When writing HTML tags, you can use upper- or lowercase letters. To make the coding easy to distinguish from other text in the page, you can type tag names in uppercase. For details, see the section "Understanding HTML Syntax."

```
<LI>Duffel Bag</LI>
    <UL>
    <LI>Camping Equipment</LI>
    <LI>Tent</LI>
    </UL>
<LI>Suitcase</LI>
    <UL>
    <LI>Clothing</LI>
    <LI>Toiletries</LI>
    </UL>
<LI>Laptop Bag</LI>
    <UL>
    <LI>Computer</LI>
    <LI>Power cord</LI>
    <LI>Mouse</LI>
    </UL>
```

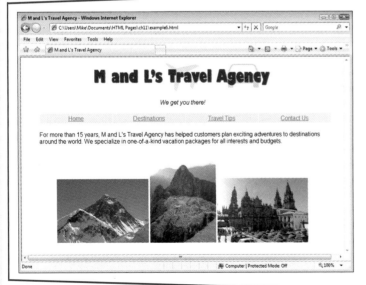

Rendering HTML

When a browser displays a Web page, it retrieves the HTML file for that page from a server, parses the HTML tags to determine how the content should be formatted, and renders the page. The HTML tags tell the browser what images, video, audio, and other content need to be downloaded and integrated into the page. The HTML may also tell the browser to download style sheets and interactive scripts to further enhance the page. To view the HTML underlying a Web page, see the section "View HTML Code in a Browser."

HTML Standards

The World Wide Web Consortium, or W3C, is the primary group guiding the evolution of the HTML language. The W3C is made up of hundreds of companies and organizations including Web industry leaders such as Microsoft, Apple, and Google. The standards developed by the W3C give developers of Web servers and browsers a set of common guidelines with which to develop their products. You can visit the W3C's Web site at www.w3.org.

HTML Versions

The most recent version of HTML is 4.01. Version 4.01 includes rules for using more than 90 different HTML tags, most of which are covered in this book. It improves on previous versions by adding better support for multimedia, scripting, and style sheets. Support for style sheets is especially important because it allows developers to apply more precise formatting to Web pages. It also allows developers to keep complex styling information separate from the rest of the HTML. Style sheets are covered in Chapters 9, 10, and 11.

XHTML

XHTML, or *Extensible Hypertext Markup Language*, is an alternative language for coding Web pages that conforms to the stricter standards of XML, or *Extensible Markup Language*. XHTML is tag-based and uses many of the same tags as in HTML. However, in XHTML, all tags must be closed, tag names and attributes must be coded in lowercase, and attribute values for tags must be surrounded by quotes. Most modern browsers can read both HTML and XHTML. Although XHTML is not covered in this book, you can read more about it at the W3C site at www.w3.org.

```
<p>This is an example of an
<abbr title="Extensible HyperText Markup Language">
Strict document.<br />
<img id="validation-icon"
   src="http://www.w3.org/Icons/valid-xhtml10"
   alt="Valid XHTML 1.0 Strict" /><br />
<object id="pdf-object"
   name="pdf-object"
   type="application/pdf"
   data="http://www.w3.org/TR/xhtml1/xhtml1.pdf"
   width="100%"
   height="500">
</object>
```

Next Generation of HTML

As this book is being published, the W3C is developing the specifications for HTML 5, the next version of HTML. This version introduces features to help Web designers more easily create and maintain the dynamic pages seen in many of today's Web sites. HTML 5 will include tags for defining headers, footers, and navigation sections, along with tags for adding interactive elements such as editable and sortable tables. For more information, see www.whatwg.org/html5.

Explore Web Browsers

A Web browser is software that can retrieve HTML documents from the Web, parse the HTML instructions, and display the resulting Web pages. In addition to retrieving the HTML, the browser takes care of downloading all the associated images, style sheets, scripts, and other information needed for the page to appear and function properly.

You can also use a browser to display HTML documents you save locally on your computer. When coding your HTML, you can use a Web browser to test your work.

Finding a Browser

Most computer operating systems come with a Web browser already installed. Microsoft Windows Vista computers include the Internet Explorer browser, whereas Apple Mac computers include the Safari browser. (The examples in this book use Internet Explorer.) Mozilla Firefox is another Web browser that has become increasingly popular in recent years. You can learn more about Firefox and download it for free at www.mozilla.com/firefox. For more information about the Web browsers in use today, see the Wikipedia entry at http://wikipedia.org/wiki/Web_browser.

Browser Discrepancies

There are many Web browsers in use today, and numerous versions of each. Although most of them interpret HTML essentially the same way, slight differences in interpretation mean that not all of them display Web pages exactly the same way. Also, some more recent browser versions recognize newer HTML features that older browsers do not. You can avoid surprises by writing clean, well-formed HTML code and testing your pages in different browsers as you work. Wikipedia offers a detailed comparison of Web browser features at http://wikipedia.org/wiki/Comparison_of_web_browsers.

Explore
HTML Editors

Because HTML documents are plain-text documents, you can use any text-editing program to code HTML and create a Web page. All computer operating systems come with some sort of text editor installed. You can also use a variety of Web-specific coding

environments that write your HTML code, validate it, and upload it to a Web server. Higher-end editing tools help you write style sheets, scripts, and other types of code in addition to HTML.

Simple Text Editors

Simple text editors, also called plain-text editors, are easy to find. Microsoft Windows Vista comes with Notepad, whereas Apple Mac computers come with TextEdit. Simple text editors offer no-frills word processing and are often the best choice when you are learning to write HTML. This book uses the Windows WordPad and Notepad text editors in its examples. Wikipedia has a list of free and commercial text editors at http://wikipedia.org/wiki/List_of_text_editors.

HTML Editors

HTML editors, such as Adobe Dreamweaver and Microsoft Expression, are dedicated programs for writing HTML code and managing Web pages. These programs can shield you from having to write HTML code by offering a graphical environment for building Web pages as well as a text-based environment. Most HTML editors also color your HTML tags for easier viewing, validate your code, and help you upload finished pages to a server.

Word Processing Programs

You can also use word processing programs, such as Microsoft Word, to write HTML. In Word, you can select HTML as the file type when you save a document, and the program automatically adds the appropriate HTML tags. However, commercial word processors tend to store lots of extra information with your HTML, which can make it a challenge to edit the files in other editors.

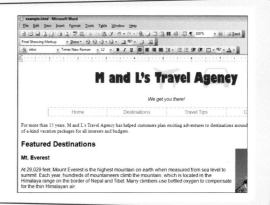

Understanding HTML Syntax

HTML is a language for describing Web page content. HTML rules, or *syntax*, govern the way in which code is written and how Web browsers interpret it. HTML with incorrect syntax can result in words, images, and other elements on your Web page showing up in unexpected places or not at all. It can also result in your pages appearing differently in different Web browsers. Learning the correct way to write your code can save you time and confusion later and ensure that Web users see your pages as you intended them to be seen.

Writing HTML

In HTML, tags determine how page content is organized and formatted. Tags consist of words or abbreviations surrounded by angle brackets, < >. This HTML code creates a paragraph in your page:

```
<P>Hello, world!</P>
```

Tags can be written using upper- or lowercase letters. The following are all legal versions of the line break tag:

```
<BR> <br> <Br>
```

You can type tag names in uppercase to distinguish the code from other text. Uppercase tag names is the convention used in this book. Because Web browsers read the tags as instructions rather than page content, the bracketed information does not appear in the browser window when the page is rendered.

Tag Structure

Certain structural HTML tags identify different parts of your HTML document. For example, the <BODY> and </BODY> tags surround the main body content that appears in the browser window. The <HEAD> and </HEAD> tags surround accessory information, including references to style sheets and metadata, that does not appear directly in the browser window. The <HTML> and </HTML> tags appear at the very beginning and very end of the document, respectively. Many tags, such as the paragraph tag <P> and </P>, are written using an opening tag and a closing tag, whereas others, such as the image tag (<IMG>), stand alone. Closing tags must always include a slash (/) before the tag name.

Text Formatting

HTML includes a variety of tags for formatting text. You can surround text with <B> and </B> tags to turn text bold and <I> and </I> tags to turn it italic. You can label passages of text with heading tags, which create bold text set off on a separate line. There are six sizes of headings, with <H1> headings being the largest and <H6> headings being the smallest. Text formatting tags are covered in Chapters 3 and 4.

M and L's Travel Agency

Featured Destinations

Mt. Everest

At 29,029 feet, Mount Everest is the *highest mountain on earth* when measured from sea level to summit. Each year, hundreds of mountaineers climb the mountain, which is located in the Himalaya range on the border of Nepal and Tibet. Many climbers use bottled oxygen to compensate for the thin Himalayan air.

Machu Picchu

Located in the Peruvian Andes, the ancient Inca city of Machu Picchu was constructed in the 1400s at the height of the Inca Empire. It was abandoned less than 100 years later when the Inca empire collapsed under Spanish conquest. Today Machu Picchu is the most visited tourist attraction in Peru.

Santiago de Compostela

Located in the Galicia region of northwest Spain, Santiago de Compostela marks the end of the famous medieval pilgrimage route, the Way of St. James. Each year, tens of thousands of Christian pilgrims spend weeks or months traveling by foot, bicycle and even donkey along the route from the south of France. They finish at Santiago's cathedral where, legend has it, the remains of St. James are buried.

Other Tags

Among the central features of Web pages are the hyperlinks that allow you to navigate from one page to another and one site to another. The <A>, or anchor, tag lets you define text or other page elements as clickable hyperlinks (see Chapter 6). You can organize page content into rows and columns using table tags, which include <TABLE>, <TR>, <TD>, and others (see Chapter 7).

Attributes and Values

Each HTML tag has specific attributes that you can assign to customize its behavior. Most attributes work by setting a numeric or descriptive value. For example, you can set a paragraph's alignment using the ALIGN attribute and a type of alignment: left, right, center, or justify. The code for a centered paragraph:

```
<P ALIGN="center">My centered text.</P>
```

Some attributes are required for an HTML tag to function properly. Attributes always go inside the opening HTML tag, and it is good form to enclose attribute values in quotation marks. The <IMG> tag requires a SRC attribute so that the browser can insert the correct image file on the page:

```
<IMG SRC="myphoto.jpg">
```

Entities

You can add special characters to a page, such as a copyright symbol or a fraction, by using special codes called *entities*. Entities represent characters not readily available on the keyboard. All entities are preceded by an ampersand (&) and followed by a semicolon (;). For example, the following code adds a copyright symbol to your page:

```
&copy;
```

Entities are also useful for displaying characters that have special meaning in HTML. For example, to create a less-than symbol on your Web page, you use the following code:

```
&lt;
```

You cannot use a plain less-than symbol (<) because in HTML it is used to start a tag. For more about entities and special characters, see Chapter 3.

Avoiding Syntax Errors

To avoid HTML errors, proofread your code. Most HTML editors have features that highlight bad syntax. Make sure your tags have brackets, your closing tags include a slash, and your attribute values are surrounded by quotation marks. Multiple HTML tags should be properly nested, meaning your closing tags should be in the reverse order of the opening tags. For example:

```
<P><B>My text.</B></P>
```

To help make your HTML readable, consider using new lines to type code instead of running everything together on one long line. Doing so will not affect how your page is displayed because Web browsers ignore extra white space. Testing your Web pages in multiple Web browsers can also be a good way to discover syntax errors because browsers can vary in their leniency to certain types of errors.

View HTML Code in a Browser

You can view the HTML code for any Web page that you have loaded into your Web browser. Viewing HTML from different Web sites is a good way to learn how to write your own code and can spawn new ideas for your own pages. You can also save a Web page locally for use as a template or to study later.

In Microsoft Windows Vista, Internet Explorer opens the HTML code in the Notepad text editor. To view an HTML page that you have saved locally, see Chapter 2.

View HTML Code in a Browser

VIEW THE SOURCE CODE

① Open a Web page in your browser window.

② Click **View**.

③ Click **Source**.

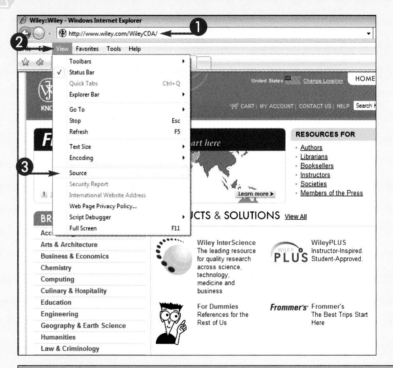

A Notepad window appears displaying the HTML source code for the page.

④ Click the **Close** button (⊠) when finished.

The window closes.

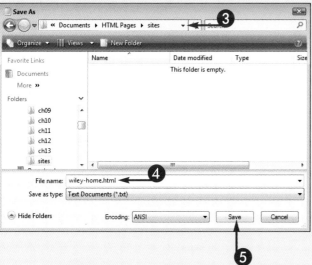

SAVE THE SOURCE CODE

① In the Notepad window that displays the source code, click **File**.

② Click **Save As**.

The Save As dialog box appears.

③ Click here to navigate to the folder where you want to store the page.

④ Type a name for the page.

HTML pages must have an .html or .htm file extension to display correctly in a browser.

⑤ Click **Save**.

Notepad saves the page.

Simplify It

Will the HTML documents that I save to my computer work when I open them in a browser?
Possibly. It depends on how the HTML is coded. In addition to the HTML, you may have to download images, style sheets, scripts, and other external content separately and then edit the HTML so that the page references them correctly. For more about referencing content using absolute and relative links, see Chapter 6.

How else can I save a Web page in my browser?
In Internet Explorer, you can click **File** and then **Save As**. The browser gives you several ways to save your page. Complete saves the HTML and embedded content, HTML Only saves just the HTML, and Web Archive saves the HTML and other content as a single file.

Chapter 2

Creating Your First Web Page

Are you ready to begin creating a Web page? This chapter shows you how to get started with a basic HTML document.

HTML includes a number of basic structural tags that appear in almost every HTML page. Becoming familiar with these tags is a good first step to creating your pages.

This chapter also teaches you how to save an HTML document in a text editor and open the document in a Web browser, so you can see the results of your work.

Understanding HTML Document Structure

Although Web pages can differ widely in terms of content and layout, all pages have certain HTML tags that give them the same basic structure. These tags tell a Web browser where the HTML for a page begins and ends, what content is displayed in the browser window, and where to find metadata, references to style sheets and scripts, and other important elements. Understanding this structure helps you correctly organize the content in your HTML pages. It is a good idea to add these structural tags to your page before anything else.

HTML Tags

The <HTML> and </HTML> tags at the beginning and end of a text document identify it as HTML code. When a browser encounters these tags, it knows that anything within the two tags defines a Web page. Older Web browsers expect to see the HTML tags; with the latest version of HTML and newer versions of browsers, the tags are not always necessary, but adding them is always good form.

Document Type Declaration

You can add a DOCTYPE declaration to specify which tags a browser can expect to see in your HTML document. In HTML 4.01, there are three document types: HTML 4.01 Transitional, HTML 4.01 Strict, and HTML 4.01 Frameset. The Transitional type incorporates both current tags and older tags that have been phased out, or *deprecated*. The Strict type is more pared down and excludes deprecated tags. The Frameset type includes tags for creating framed pages, which are not covered in this book.

Document Header

You use the header of an HTML document to add descriptive and accessory information to your Web page. The document header tags, <HEAD> and </HEAD>, immediately follow the opening <HTML> tag. The document header contains information that does not appear in the browser viewing area, including title information, metadata, scripts, and style sheets. For more about style sheets, see Chapter 9.

Document Title

You can add a title to your HTML document to help people and search engines identify your Web page. For example, if you are building a Web page for a business, you might want to include the company's name and specialization in the title. Most Web browsers display the title in the browser window's title bar. The <TITLE> and </TITLE> tags define a page title and appear inside the document header. It is good form to keep the title to fewer than 64 characters in length.

Metadata

Metadata means "data about data." On a Web page, metadata can include author information, the type of editor used to create the page, a description of the content, relevant keywords, and copyright information. Search engines often use metadata when trying to categorize your page. You place metadata inside the document header.

Body

The visible content that makes up your Web page, including paragraphs, lists, tables, and images, lives in the body of your HTML document. The body of the document is identified by the <BODY> and </BODY> tags. The body of a document comes after the header of a document. Most of the HTML tags covered in this book belong inside the body of the document and determine how its content is formatted. To learn how to begin formatting body text, see Chapter 3.

```
example.html - WordPad
File  Edit  View  Insert  Format  Help

<!DOCTYPE HTML PUBLIC "-//W3C//DTD HTML 4.01 Transitional//EN"
"http://www.w3.org/TR/html4/loose.dtd">
<HTML>
<HEAD>
<TITLE>M and L's Travel Agency</TITLE>

<META NAME="description" CONTENT="A business specializing in travel">

<LINK REL="stylesheet" TYPE="text/css" HREF="styles-hover.css">

</HEAD>
<BODY LEFTMARGIN="100" RIGHTMARGIN="100">

<P ALIGN="center"><IMG SRC="mltravel.gif"></P>
<P ALIGN="center" CLASS="widetext"><I>We get you there!</I></P>

<TABLE ALIGN="center" WIDTH="800" BORDER="0" CELLPADDING="4" CELLSPACING="1">
<TR>
<TD ALIGN="center" WIDTH="25%"><A HREF="index.html">Home</A></TD>
<TD ALIGN="center" WIDTH="25%"><A HREF="dest.html">Destinations</A></TD>
<TD ALIGN="center" WIDTH="25%"><A HREF="tips.html">Travel Tips</A></TD>
<TD ALIGN="center" WIDTH="25%"><A HREF="contact.html">Contact Us</A></TD>
</TR>
</TABLE>

<P CLASS="intro">For more than 15 years, M and L's Travel Agency has helped
customers plan exciting adventures. We specialize in one-of-a-kind vacation
packages for all interests and budgets.</P>
<P>We're available online or in person.</P>

</BODY>
</HTML>
```

Start an HTML Document

You can start an HTML document using a text editor, HTML editor, or word processing program. You use sets of HTML tags to define the basic structure of your page.

The <HTML>, <HEAD>, and <TITLE> tags are basic tags that appear at the beginning of all HTML documents. To save time, you can create a text file that includes these tags and use the file as a template each time you want to create a Web page.

Start an HTML Document

1 Open an editor or word processing program.

Note: The examples in this book use WordPad. See Chapter 1 to learn more about editors.

2 Type <HTML>.

This tag declares the document as HTML.

3 Press Enter.

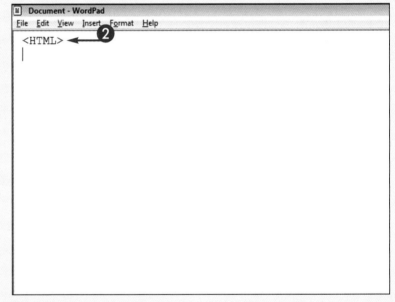

4 Type <HEAD>.

This tag defines where the title, metadata, and other descriptive information appear.

Note: For more about adding metadata to a Web page, see the section "Add Metadata."

5 Press Enter.

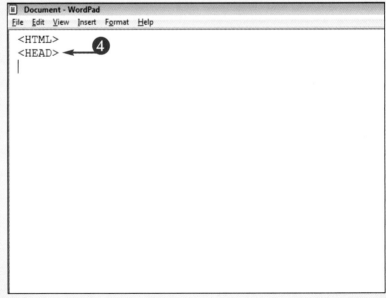

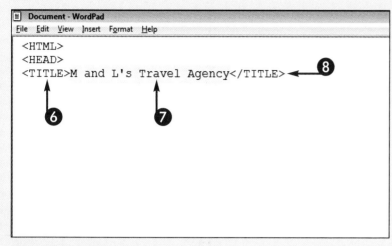

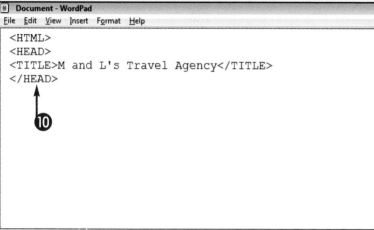

⑥ Type <TITLE>.

⑦ Type title text for your page.

Title text describes the contents of the page and appears in the title bar of the Web browser.

⑧ Type </TITLE>.

⑨ Press Enter.

⑩ Type </HEAD>.

This tag completes the document header information for the page.

⑪ Press Enter.

Note: *You do not need to press* Enter *each time you start a new tag or add a closing tag. However, placing tags on their own lines can help make your code more readable.*

Note: *Browsers ignore extra white space when rendering Web pages.*

Which should I add first to my HTML document, the HTML tags or the page content?
It is usually easier to start your HTML document by typing the basic structural tags, which include the <HTML>, <HEAD>, and <BODY> tags. These tags appear in all HTML documents, and typing them first helps ensure they have valid syntax and are in the correct order. After you add the basic structural tags, you can add the body content and additional HTML tags to format that content.

Does it matter if I type my tags in uppercase, lowercase, or mixed case?
No. The current HTML standard allows for different cases in your HTML text. However, it is good form to format your HTML tags consistently. Also, typing tags in all uppercase letters can make it easier to distinguish HTML code from the page content and to identify errors in your code.

continued

Start an HTML Document *(continued)*

You can use the body tags, <BODY> and </BODY>, to define the content in your Web page. Page content can include lines of text, bulleted and numbered lists, tables, forms, and more. Content added between the body tags appears in the viewing area of a Web browser.

You can add attribute information to the <BODY> tag to change the background color and other overall characteristics of the page. See Chapter 4 for details.

⑫ Type <BODY>.

This tag marks the beginning of the actual content of your Web page.

⑬ Press `Enter`.

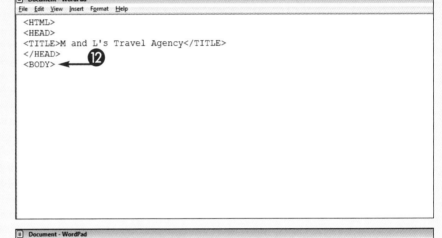

⑭ Type the body text you want to appear on the page.

Body text is the content that appears in the browser window. For practice, you can type a simple paragraph for the body text.

⑮ Press `Enter`.

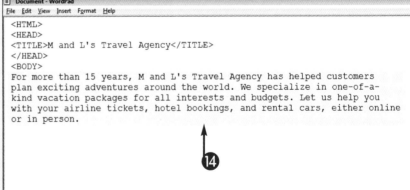

Document - WordPad

File   Edit   View   Insert   Format   Help

```
<HTML>
<HEAD>
<TITLE>M and L's Travel Agency</TITLE>
</HEAD>
<BODY>
For more than 15 years, M and L's Travel Agency has helped customers
plan exciting adventures around the world. We specialize in one-of-a-
kind vacation packages for all interests and budgets. Let us help you
with your airline tickets, hotel bookings, and rental cars, either online
or in person. 16
</BODY>
|
```

16 Type </BODY>.

This tag closes the body portion of the page.

17 Press Enter.

Document - WordPad

File   Edit   View   Insert   Format   Help

```
<HTML>
<HEAD>
<TITLE>M and L's Travel Agency</TITLE>
</HEAD>
<BODY>
For more than 15 years, M and L's Travel Agency has helped customers
plan exciting adventures around the world. We specialize in one-of-a-
kind vacation packages for all interests and budgets. Let us help you
with your airline tickets, hotel bookings, and rental cars, either online
or in person.
</BODY>
</HTML>| 18
```

18 Type </HTML>.

This tag ends the HTML code of your document.

You can save your document and view the page in a Web browser. Remember to save your document with an .html or .htm file extension.

Note: *To learn how to save a file, see the section "Save an HTML Document." To learn how to view the results of your HTML coding, see the section "View an HTML Page."*

Simplify It

How do I turn on WordPad's text wrapping?
It can be annoying when the HTML code in WordPad scrolls off the right side of the screen. You can turn on the text-wrapping feature to keep your code in view at all times. In WordPad, click **View** and then **Options**. In the Options dialog box, click the **Text** tab and then select the **Wrap to Window** option (◯ changes to ◉). This activates text wrapping in the WordPad window.

Save an HTML Document

You can save your Web page as an HTML file so that users can view it in a Web browser. When saving a Web page, you can use either the .html or .htm file extension.

When naming a Web page, it is best not to use spaces and to keep the characters limited to letters, numbers, hyphens (-), and underscores (_). Home pages for Web sites are commonly named index.html or default.htm.

Save an HTML Document

① Click **File**.

Note: *Your text editor may have a different command name for saving files. See your program's documentation for more information.*

② Click **Save**.

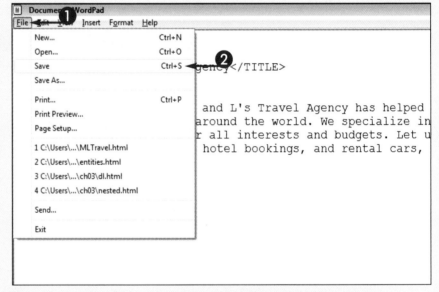

The Save As dialog box appears.

③ Click here to navigate to the folder or drive where you want to store the file.

④ Click here and select Text Document.

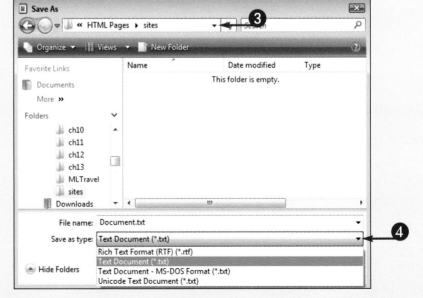

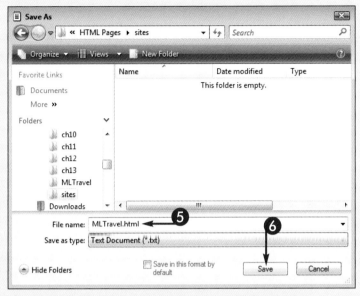

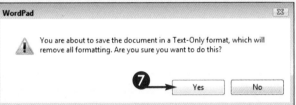

5 Type a name for the file, followed by **.html** or **.htm**.

6 Click **Save**.

A dialog box may appear alerting you that all the formatting will be removed.

7 Click **Yes**.

The editor saves the file.

Simplify It

What is the difference between the .html and .htm extensions?
The shorter .htm extension is left over from the early, pre-Windows days, when file names could have only three-character file extensions. Some Windows-based programs still default to the .htm extension. Today's computers can handle longer file names and extensions, so the three-character limit is no longer an issue. Although Web browsers and servers can read either extension, you probably want to opt for .html because it is more universally used.

What makes a good file name for a Web page?
When naming a file, keep the name simple so that you can easily remember it and locate it again later. In addition, because you need to type file names when creating hyperlinks, use a name that relates to the pages you are designing. For example, if you are creating a page that lists contact information for your company, the file name for that page might be contact.html. Also keep your Web page files in one folder and give the folder a name that clearly identifies the content, such as My Web Pages.

Save a Microsoft Word Document as HTML

You can save a Microsoft Word document as a Web page. Microsoft Word converts the content to HTML and saves it as a text file. Microsoft Word saves HTML documents with a lot of complex style information written in CSS and XML code. This helps ensure that the page

looks exactly as it looked in Word when opened in a Web browser, with the same font styles, margins, and other features. You can see this extra information if you open the saved file in a text editor.

Save a Microsoft Word Document as HTML

1 Create a new document in Microsoft Word.

This example shows a document created in Microsoft Word 2007.

You can use Word's commands to style the text on your page and insert images.

2 Click 📇.

In Microsoft Word 2003, you can click **File** and then **Save**.

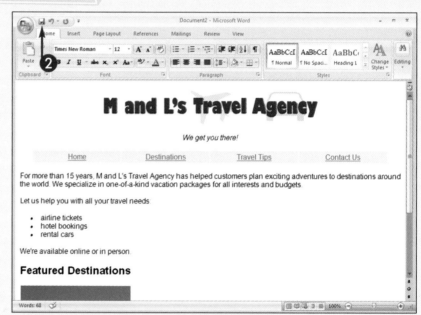

The Save As dialog box appears.

3 Click here to navigate to the folder or drive where you want to store the file.

4 Click here and select **Web Page**.

● To save the file as HTML without the Word-specific XML code, select **Web Page, Filtered**.

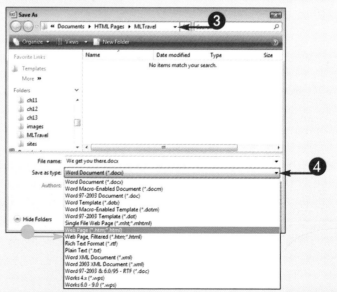

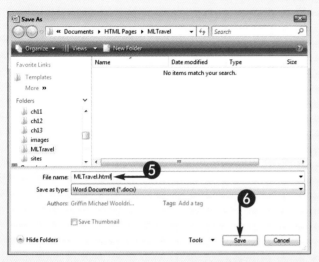

⑤ Type a name for the file, followed by **.html** or **.htm**.

⑥ Click **Save**.

Microsoft Word saves the document as an HTML text file.

Simplify It

How can I create hyperlinks in Microsoft Word?
Click and drag to select the content you want to turn into a link and then click the **Hyperlink** command. In Word 2007, this command is located under the Insert tab. In Word 2003, it is located under the Insert menu. You can define the hyperlink in the dialog box that appears.

How should I edit an HTML page saved in Microsoft Word?
Because Microsoft Word saves its HTML documents with a lot of CSS and XML code, it is often best to edit such pages using Microsoft Word. This keeps you from having to edit the raw code. Instead, you can use Word's formatting menus, toolbars, and other commands.

View an HTML Page

After you create and save an HTML document, you can view it in your Web browser. Your Web browser can view HTML pages that you have saved on your computer as well as pages on the Internet. Opening an HTML page that you are simultaneously editing in a text editor is a useful way to determine if the page is displaying correctly as you add content and tags. When you open a page from your computer in a browser, the file-system path leading to the page appears in the browser address field.

❶ Open your Web browser.

This example uses the Internet Explorer browser.

❷ Click **File**.

❸ Click **Open**.

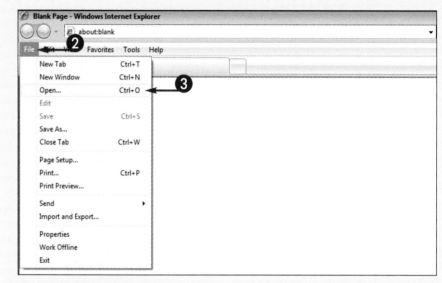

The Open dialog box appears.

❹ Click **Browse**.

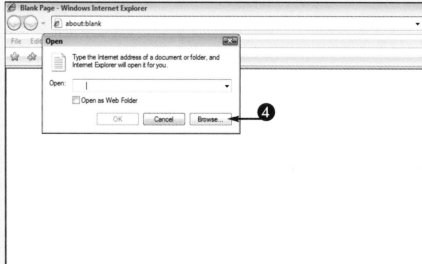

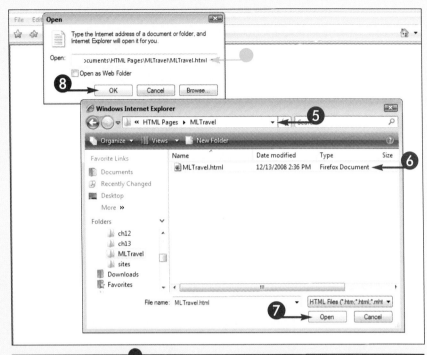

⑤ Click here to navigate to the folder or drive in which your HTML document is stored.

⑥ Click the file name.

⑦ Click **Open**.

○ The Open dialog box displays the path and name of the file.

⑧ In the Open dialog box, click OK.

The Web browser displays the page.

● The title information appears here.

● The body information appears here.

○ The location of the HTML file appears here.

Note: You cannot see metadata in the browser window.

● If you make changes to the HTML of the page that appears in the browser, you can click ⟳ to refresh the page and view the changes.

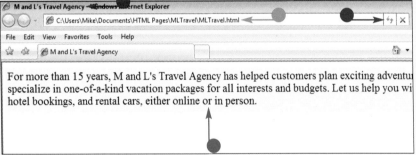

For more than 15 years, M and L's Travel Agency has helped customers plan exciting adventu specialize in one-of-a-kind vacation packages for all interests and budgets. Let us help you wi hotel bookings, and rental cars, either online or in person.

Simplify It

Does it matter what browser I use to view the pages I am building?
No. All popular Web browsers are set up to view HTML pages that you have saved on your computer, also known as *offline pages*. You may need to follow a slightly different set of steps to open an offline HTML document in a browser other than Internet Explorer, such as Mozilla Firefox. Be sure to consult your browser's documentation for more information.

What happens if I cannot view my page?
If you do not see any content for your page, you need to double-check your HTML code for errors. Make sure your document uses correctly paired start and end tags, and proofread your HTML code to make sure everything is correct. Also make sure you named your page with an .html or .htm file extension.

Add a Document Declaration

You can use a document declaration at the top of your Web page to declare which type of HTML tags the browser can expect to see. You can use one of three types: HTML 4.01 Transitional, HTML 4.01 Strict, or HTML 4.01 Frameset.

The Transitional version of HTML includes all the standard structural elements as well as older tags that have been phased out, or *deprecated*. The Strict type includes only currently sanctioned tags. The Frameset type is the same as the Transitional type but includes additional tags for creating frames. HTML frames, which are rarely used in today's Web sites, are not covered in this book.

Add a Document Declaration

1 Open the HTML document you want to edit.

2 Position your cursor before the `<HTML>` tag and press Enter to insert a new line.

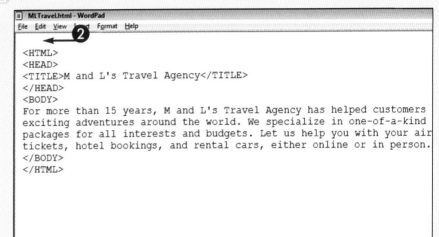

3 Type the DOCTYPE declaration.

● To specify HTML 4.01 Transitional, type:

```
<!DOCTYPE HTML
PUBLIC "-//W3C//
DTD HTML 4.01
Transitional//EN"
"http://www.w3.org/
TR/html4/loose.dtd">
```

You may need to press Enter to continue the coding on a new line.

```
MLTravel.html - WordPad
File  Edit  View  Insert  Format  Help

<!DOCTYPE HTML PUBLIC "-//W3C//DTD HTML 4.01 Strict//EN"
"http://www.w3.org/TR/html4/strict.dtd">
<HTML>
<HEAD>
<TITLE>M and L's Travel Agency</TITLE>
</HEAD>
<BODY>
For more than 15 years, M and L's Travel Agency has helped customers
exciting adventures around the world. We specialize in one-of-a-kind
packages for all interests and budgets. Let us help you with your air
tickets, hotel bookings, and rental cars, either online or in person.
</BODY>
</HTML>
```

```
MLTravel.html - WordPad
File  Edit  View  Insert  Format  Help

<!DOCTYPE HTML PUBLIC "-//W3C//DTD HTML 4.01 Frameset//EN"
"http://www.w3.org/TR/html4/frameset.dtd">
<HTML>
<HEAD>
<TITLE>M and L's Travel Agency</TITLE>
</HEAD>
<BODY>
For more than 15 years, M and L's Travel Agency has helped customers
exciting adventures around the world. We specialize in one-of-a-kind
packages for all interests and budgets. Let us help you with your air
tickets, hotel bookings, and rental cars, either online or in person.
</BODY>
</HTML>
```

● To specify HTML 4.01 Strict,
type:

```
<!DOCTYPE HTML
PUBLIC "-//W3C//
DTD HTML 4.01
Strict//EN" "http://
www.w3.org/TR/html4/
strict.dtd">
```

● To specify HTML 4.01
Frameset, type:

```
<!DOCTYPE HTML
PUBLIC "-//W3C//
DTD HTML 4.01
Frameset//EN"
"http://www.w3.
org/TR/html4/
frameset.dtd">
```

The declaration statement is
complete.

Do I have to include a document declaration?
Most popular browsers can display your page without a DOCTYPE declaration. However, if you are using a validation tool to check your page for proper form, the tool may require that you include a declaration so that it knows what type of HTML it should validate your page against. Including a document declaration is also considered good form.

Which version of HTML should I use?
All Web browsers support HTML Transitional. However, professional developers are moving toward HTML Strict and using it with Cascading Style Sheets (CSS) to control page formatting. Many of the deprecated tags in HTML have been replaced by formatting rules that you apply with CSS. If your page uses frames, which are not covered in this book, then you need to use HTML Frameset because it allows you to add frames to a page. Deciding which version to use really depends on what Web page elements you plan to use and what type of coding you are familiar with.

Add Metadata

You can add metadata to your page to include extra descriptive information that does not appear in the browser window. Metadata can include a page description, author and copyright information, keywords, and more. What you insert in metadata tags can help search engines categorize your page.

You define metadata in the document header using the <META> tag. The <META> tag includes a NAME attribute that determines what type of metadata you are adding with the tag. You add metadata to the document header part of your HTML page, inside the <HEAD> and </HEAD> tags.

Add Metadata

ADD AN AUTHOR NAME

① Click between the <HEAD> and </HEAD> tags and press Enter to start a new line.

In this example, the metadata appears below the <TITLE> tags.

② Type <META NAME= "author" followed by a space.

③ Type CONTENT="My Name">, replacing *My Name* with your name.

④ Press Enter.

ADD A PAGE DESCRIPTION

⑤ Type <META NAME="description" and a blank space.

⑥ Type CONTENT="Page Description">, replacing *Page Description* with your own page description.

⑦ Press Enter.

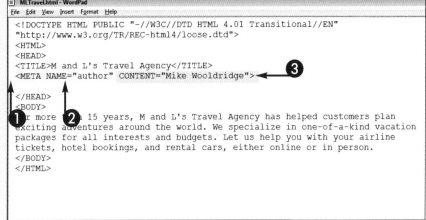

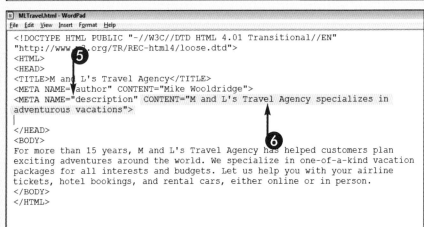

MLTravel.html - WordPad
File   Edit   View   Insert   Format   Help

```
<!DOCTYPE HTML PUBLIC "-//W3C//DTD HTML 4.01 Transitional//EN"
"http://www.w3.org/TR/REC-html4/loose.dtd">
<HTML>
<HEAD>
<TITLE>M and L's Travel Agency</TITLE>
<META NAME="author" CONTENT="Mike Wooldridge">
<META NAME="description" CONTENT="M and L's Travel Agency specializes in
adventurous vacations">
<META NAME="keywords" CONTENT="travel, airlines, hotels, rental cars, jungle
vacations, hiking vacations, tropical vacations">

</HEAD>
<BODY>
For more than 15 years, M and L's Travel Agency has helped customers plan
exciting adventures around the world. We specialize in one-of-a-kind vacation
packages for all interests and budgets. Let us help you with your airline
tickets, hotel bookings, and rental cars, either online or in person.
</BODY>
</HTML>
```

SPECIFY KEYWORDS

⑧ Type <META NAME=
"keywords" and a space.

⑨ Type CONTENT="My
Keywords">, replacing *My
Keywords* with a keyword.

For multiple keywords, use a
comma followed by a space to
separate the keywords.

⑩ Press Enter.

MLTravel.html - WordPad
File   Edit   View   Insert   Format   Help

```
<!DOCTYPE HTML PUBLIC "-//W3C//DTD HTML 4.01 Transitional//EN"
"http://www.w3.org/TR/REC-html4/loose.dtd">
<HTML>
<HEAD>
<TITLE>M and L's Travel Agency</TITLE>
<META NAME="author" CONTENT="Mike Wooldridge">
<META NAME="description" CONTENT="M and L's Travel Agency specializes in
adventurous vacations">
<META NAME="keywords" CONTENT="travel, airlines, hotels, rental cars, jungle
vacations, hiking vacations, tropical vacati   ">
<META NAME="copyright" CONTENT="2009">

</HEAD>
<BODY>
For more th    15 years, M and L's Travel Agency has helped customers plan
exciting adventures around the world. We specialize in one-of-a-kind vacation
packages for all interests and budgets. Let us help you with your airline
tickets, hotel bookings, and rental cars, either online or in person.
</BODY>
</HTML>
```

ADD A COPYRIGHT

⑪ Type <META NAME=
"copyright" and a space.

⑫ Type CONTENT="2009">,
replacing *2009* with your own
numbers or copyright
information.

⑬ Press Enter.

The metadata is now a part of
the HTML document.

Simplify It

**How do I add the name of the
program I used to design my page to
the metadata information?**
To specify an authoring program, type
<META NAME="generator"
CONTENT="Program Name">.
Substitute the name of your program for
the text *Program Name*. Some HTML
editors add this information automatically
when you start a new HTML page.

Who can view my metadata?
The only time users can see your metadata
information is if they view the HTML code
for the page. To view the HTML code of
any page in your browser window, click
View and then **Source**. This opens a text-
editor window displaying the HTML used
to create the page. Any metadata assigned
to the document appears at the top inside
the <HEAD> and </HEAD> tags.

Chapter 3

Adding Text

Are you ready to begin building your Web page by adding text? You can add text by typing words into your HTML document and then surrounding the words with tags. You can create simple paragraphs with <P> tags and differently sized headings with a variety of heading tags. You can create lists using <OL> or <UL> tags in combination with the <LI> tag. This chapter also shows you how to add special characters to your page by typing alphanumeric codes.

Create a New Paragraph

You can use paragraph tags to start new paragraphs in an HTML document. In a word processing program, you press **Enter** or **Return** to separate blocks of text. Web browsers do not read these line breaks. Instead, you must insert a <P> tag in your HTML any time you want to start a new paragraph in your Web page.

Paragraphs are left-aligned by default, but you can choose a different alignment using the align attribute. See the section "Change Paragraph Alignment" to learn more. Paragraph text is normal-sized and unstyled by default. To add bold, italic, and other styles, see Chapter 4.

Create a New Paragraph

① Type <P> to start a new paragraph.

② Type your text.

③ Type </P> at the end of the paragraph.

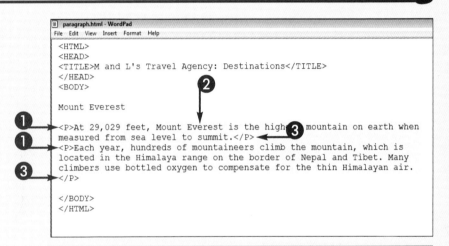

When displayed in a Web browser, the text appears as a paragraph with extra space before and after it.

Note: To create paragraphs that are indented at the sides, see the section "Add Block Quotes."

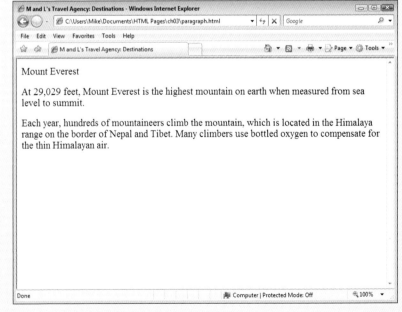

Change Paragraph Alignment

You can control the horizontal positioning, or alignment, of your paragraphs using the ALIGN attribute. You can choose to align a paragraph to the left, right, or center, or justify the text so it is aligned on both the left and

the right. Paragraphs are left-aligned by default. You can also use the ALIGN attribute with headings. It is good form to enclose alignment values in quotes.

Change Paragraph Alignment

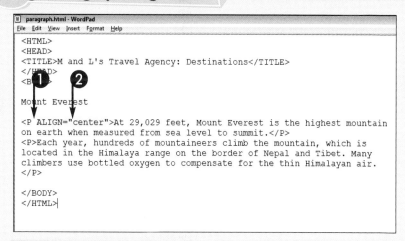

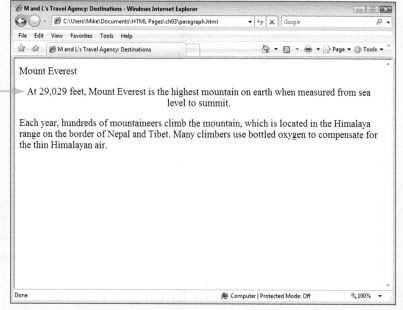

① Click inside the <P> tag in which you want to change the alignment.

② Type ALIGN="?", replacing ? with left, center, right, or justify.

Note: *You can type HTML tag and attribute names in upper- or lowercase letters, or a combination of the two.*

When displayed in a Web browser, the text aligns as specified.

● In this example, the line of text is centered on the page.

Note: *To control the width of a paragraph using style sheets, see Chapter 11.*

Add a Line Break

You can use the line break tag, <BR>, to control where your text breaks. Web browsers normally wrap text automatically; a line of text that reaches the right side of the browser window breaks and continues on the next line. You can insert a line break to instruct the browser to break the text and go to a new line.

You can also use the <BR> tag to add blank lines between paragraphs. This is useful if you want to add extra space above or below a block of text or a heading. By inserting multiple <BR> tags consecutively, you can increase the amount of space.

Add a Line Break

1 Type <BR> in front of the line of text that you want to appear as a new line.

2 Type additional <BR> tags for each line of text where you want a line break.

Note: *You do not need a closing tag for the <BR> tag.*

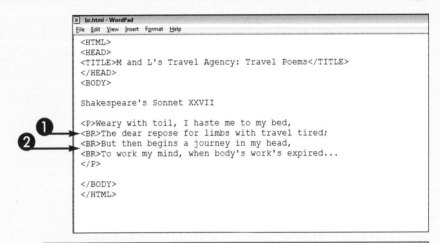

● When a Web browser displays the page, each instance of the tag creates a new text line.

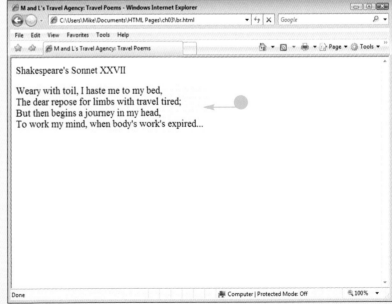

Insert a Blank Space

You can insert blank spaces within a line of text to indent or add emphasis to your text. You can also use blank spaces to help position an element on a line, such as a graphic or photo. The HTML code for adding such spaces is ` `, which stands for *nonbreaking space*.

For details about other special HTML codes, see the "Insert Special Characters" section. Adding a nonbreaking space is an alternative to inserting a line break tag, `<BR>`, which adds space between lines of text.

Insert a Blank Space

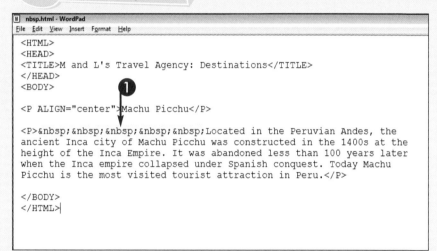

nbsp.html - WordPad
File Edit View Insert Format Help

```
<HTML>
<HEAD>
<TITLE>M and L's Travel Agency: Destinations</TITLE>
</HEAD>
<BODY>

<P ALIGN="center">Machu Picchu</P>

<P>     Located in the Peruvian Andes, the
ancient Inca city of Machu Picchu was constructed in the 1400s at the
height of the Inca Empire. It was abandoned less than 100 years later
when the Inca empire collapsed under Spanish conquest. Today Machu
Picchu is the most visited tourist attraction in Peru.</P>

</BODY>
</HTML>
```

M and L's Travel Agency: Destinations - Windows Internet Explorer

C:\Users\Mike\Documents\HTML Pages\ch03\nbsp.html   Google

File Edit View Favorites Tools Help

M and L's Travel Agency: Destinations   Page ▼ Tools ▼

Machu Picchu

    Located in the Peruvian Andes, the ancient Inca city of Machu Picchu was constructed in the 1400s at the height of the Inca Empire. It was abandoned less than 100 years later when the Inca empire collapsed under Spanish conquest. Today Machu Picchu is the most visited tourist attraction in Peru.

Done   Computer | Protected Mode: Off   100%

1 Type ` ` in the line where you want to add a blank space.

To add multiple spaces, type the code multiple times.

The code stands for *nonbreaking space*. Web browsers do not create a line break where you insert these characters.

The browser displays blank spaces in the line.

● In this example, the blank spaces cause a paragraph to be indented.

Insert Preformatted Text

You can use the preformatted tags, <PRE> and </PRE>, to display the line breaks and spaces you enter for a paragraph or block of text. Web browsers ignore hard returns, line breaks, and extra spaces between words unless you insert the preformatted tags. If you type a paragraph with spacing just the way you want it, you can assign the preformatted tags to keep the spacing in place. Preformatted text is also useful for displaying computer code on a Web page because the exact spacing of such code can be important.

❶ Type <PRE> above the text you want to keep intact.

❷ Type </PRE> below the text.

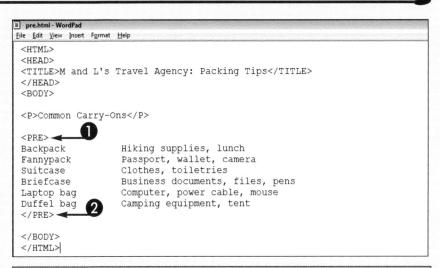

● When displayed in a Web browser, the text retains all your original line breaks and spacing.

Browsers display preformatted text in a monospace font by default. This can help you align elements within the text into columns.

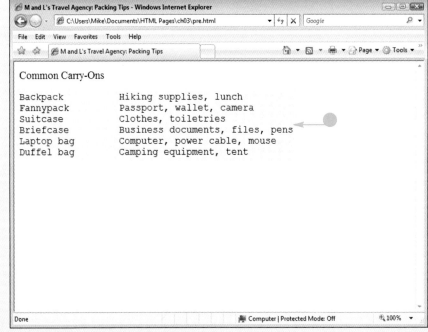

Insert a Heading

You can use headings to help clarify information on a page, organize text, and create visual structure. You can choose from six heading levels for a document, ranging from heading level 1 (`<H1>`), the largest, to heading level 6 (`<H6>`), the smallest. Headings appear as bold text on a Web page with space above and below, similar to paragraphs.

You can use the `ALIGN` attribute to change the horizontal alignment of a heading, such as `<H1 ALIGN="right">`. See the section "Change Paragraph Alignment" to learn more about inserting alignment controls within your text.

Insert a Heading

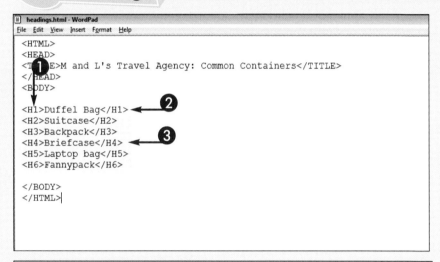

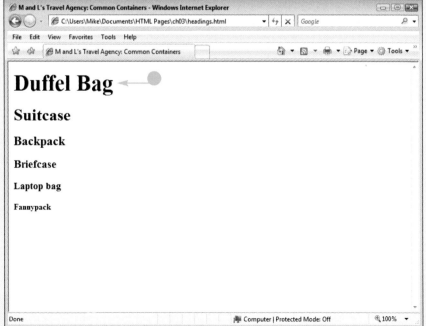

❶ Type `<H?>` in front of the text you want to turn into a heading, replacing *?* with the heading level number you want to assign.

You can set a heading level from 1 to 6.

❷ Type `</H?>` at the end of the heading text, replacing *?* with the corresponding heading level you assign.

❸ Type additional heading tags for any other text that you want to emphasize on the page.

● The heading appears in bold text in the Web browser.

This figure shows an example of each heading size in descending order.

Add Block Quotes

You can use block quotes to set off a paragraph from the rest of the document page. The <BLOCKQUOTE> tag adds the same amount of space on both sides of a paragraph. Block quotes are commonly used with quoted text or excerpts from other sources. You can nest multiple block quote tags around content to increase indentation. Another way to add indenting to blocks of text is with style sheets. See Chapter 11 for details.

Add Block Quotes

❶ Type <BLOCKQUOTE> in front of the text you want to turn into a block quote.

❷ Type </BLOCKQUOTE> at the end of the text.

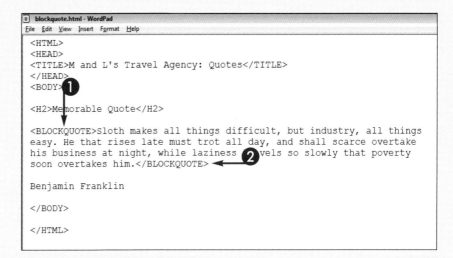

● The Web browser displays the block quote as inset text on the document page.

You can place text inside multiple <BLOCKQUOTE> tags to add more indenting.

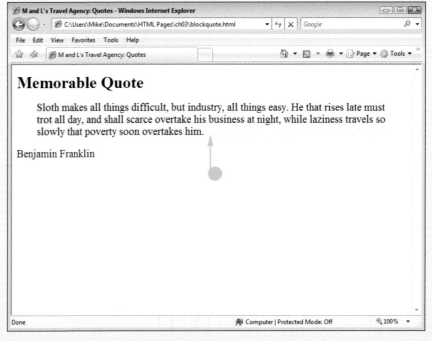

Insert a Comment

You can use comments to write notes to yourself within an HTML document. Comments do not appear when a browser displays a Web page. For example, you might leave a comment about a future editing task or leave a note to other Web developers viewing your HTML source code. Comments can also be useful for

highlighting important sections of HTML code, such as where the header, footer, or navigation section on a page starts and ends.

You can also place comments around HTML code to turn that code off. The browser does not interpret HTML tags inside comments.

Insert a Comment

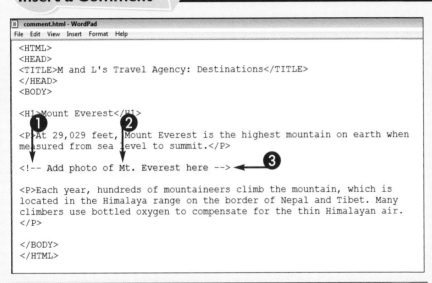

① Type `< ! --` where you want to place a comment.

② Type the comment text.

③ Type `-->`.

● The comment does not appear on the page when viewed in a Web browser.

Create a Numbered List

You can use numbered lists on your Web page to display all kinds of ordered lists. For example, you can use numbered lists to show steps or prioritize items. You create a numbered list by inserting <OL> and </OL> tags around

<LI> and </LI> tags. The <LI> tags specify the list items. You can change the style of the numbers in your list using the STYLE attribute. This allows you to order content using letters or Roman numerals.

Create a Numbered List

PLACE TEXT IN A NUMBERED LIST

① Type <OL> above the text you want to turn into a numbered list.

② Type <LI> in front of each item in the list.

③ Type </LI> after each list item.

④ Type </OL> after the list text.

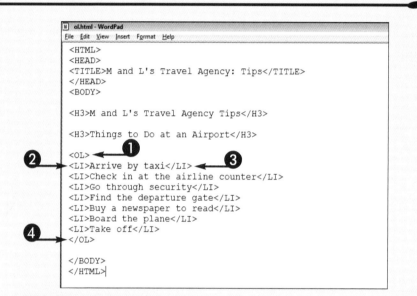

● The text appears as a numbered list on the Web page.

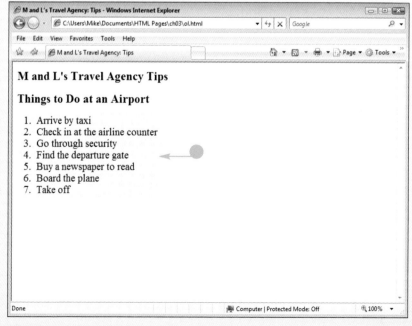

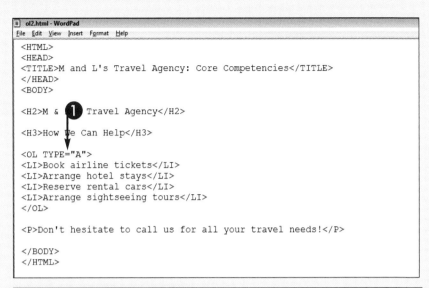

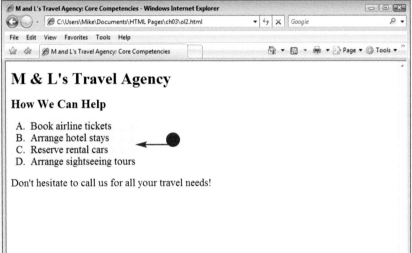

SET A NUMBER STYLE

1 Type `TYPE="?"` within the `<OL>` tag, replacing *?* with a number style code:

A: A, B, C

a: a, b, c

I: I, II, III

i: i, ii, iii

1: 1, 2, 3

The numbered list appears in the style you selected.

● In this example, the list uses letters rather than numbers.

How do I add another item to my numbered list?
Simply insert the text where you want it to appear in the list and add the `<LI>` and `</LI>` tags before and after the text. The Web browser displays the new list order the next time you view the page, rearranging numbers where necessary.

How do I start my numbered list with different numbering from the default numbering?
By default, a Web browser reads your numbered list coding and starts with the number 1. To start with a different number, you must add a `START` attribute to the `<OL>` tag. For example, if the numbering is to start at 5, the coding would read `<OL START="5" TYPE="1">`.

Create a Bulleted List

You can add a bulleted list to your document to set a list of items apart from the rest of the page of text. You can use a bulleted list, also called an unordered list, when you do not need to show the items in a particular order. You create a bulleted list by inserting `<UL>` and `</UL>` tags around `<LI>` and `</LI>` tags. The `<LI>` tags specify the list items.

By default, bullets appear as solid circles. If you want to use another bullet style, you must add a `TYPE` attribute to the `<UL>` tag.

Create a Bulleted List

PLACE TEXT IN A BULLETED LIST

❶ Type `<UL>` above the text you want to turn into a bulleted list.

❷ Type `<LI>` in front of each item in the list.

❸ Type `</LI>` after each list item.

❹ Type `</UL>` after the list text.

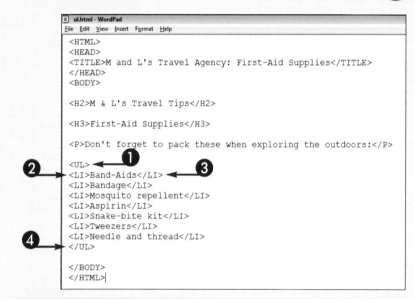

● The text appears as a bulleted list on the Web page.

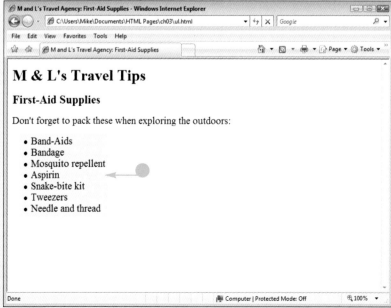

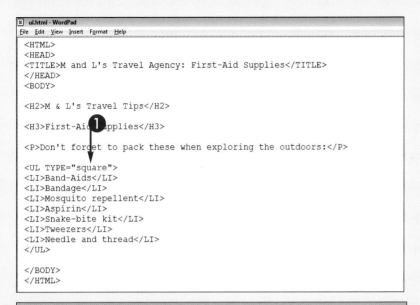

SET A BULLET STYLE

1 Type TYPE="?" within the <UL> tag, replacing *?* with a bullet style code, for example, circle, disc, or square.

The bulleted list appears in the style you selected.

● In this example, the bulleted list uses square bullets.

Can I stop a bulleted list for one line of text and continue it on the following line?
Yes. If you omit the <LI> and </LI> tags for a line of text within the list, a Web browser reads the line as regular text. For example:

```
<UL>
<LI>Dogs</LI>
<LI>Cats</LI>
and the ever-popular
<LI>Potbellied pigs</LI>
</UL>
```

Create a Nested List

You can use a nested list to add a list within a list to your Web page. Nested lists allow you to display listed text at different levels within the list hierarchy, such as when you are displaying products arranged in categories and subcategories. Web browsers use indentation to show where list items exist in the hierarchy. You can use both numbered and bulleted lists within an existing list. To create plain numbered and bulleted lists, see the sections earlier in this chapter.

Create a Nested List

1 Click where you want to insert a nested list, or add a new line within the existing list and type <OL> for a numbered list or <UL> for an unordered list.

Note: To create a numbered list, see the section "Create a Numbered List." To create a bulleted list, see the section "Create a Bulleted List."

2 Type the new list text, including the <LI> and </LI> tags, using the same technique you used to create the original list.

3 Type </OL> or </UL> at the end of the nested list.

● The text appears as a nested list on the Web page.

Browsers usually set off nested lists with different bullet styles. In this example, a nested list gets an open circle.

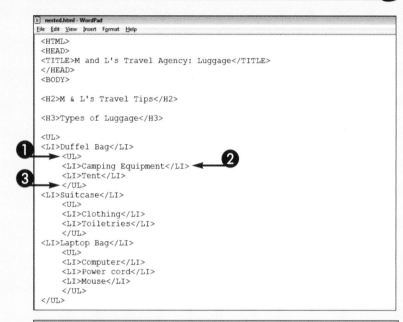

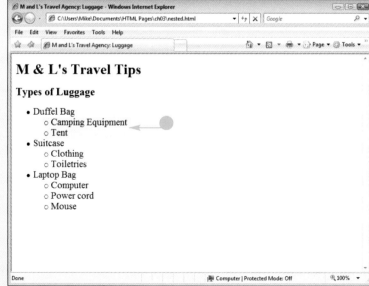

Create a Definition List

You can use a definition list in your document to set text apart in the format of a glossary or dictionary. Items in a definition list come in pairs, with the first element being the term to be defined and the second being the definition.

You use the <DL> tag to delimit your definition list, the <DT> tag to define your terms, and the <DD> tag to add your definitions. When displayed, definitions are typically indented relative to the terms.

Create a Definition List

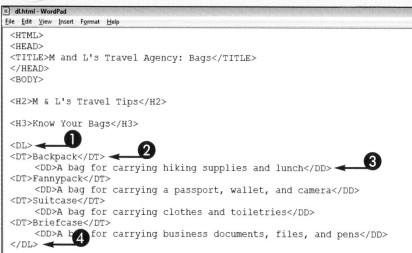

① Type <DL> above the text you want to set as a definition list.

② Type <DT> in front of each term and </DT> after each term.

③ Type <DD> in front of each definition and </DD> after each definition.

④ Type </DL> after the definition list text.

● The text appears as a definition list on the Web page.

Insert Special Characters

You can use HTML code to insert special characters into your Web page text. Special characters are characters that do not usually appear on your keyboard.

The codes used to insert special characters are called *entities*. Entities consist of number or name codes preceded by an ampersand and ending with a semicolon, such as `&frac12;` for the fraction ½ or `&para;` for a paragraph symbol.

Insert Special Characters

① Click where you want to insert a special character.

② Type the number or name code for the character, with an ampersand (&) before the code and a semicolon (;) following the code.

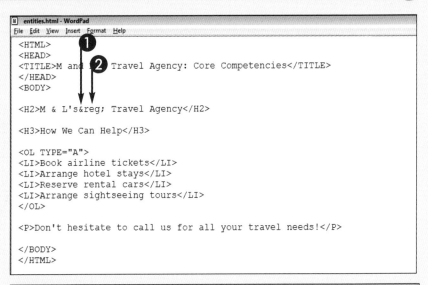

● The Web browser displays the designated character in the text.

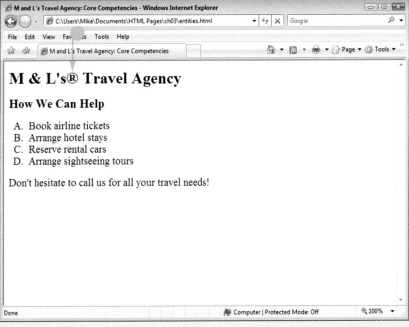

Special Characters

To properly insert many special characters into your Web page text, you need to know their entity codes. The following table lists the common special characters you can insert. For more on inserting these special characters, see the section "Insert Special Characters."

Description	Special Character	Code
copyright	©	&copy;
registered trademark	®	&reg;
trademark	™	&trade;
paragraph mark	¶	&para;
nonbreaking space		
quotation mark	"	&quot;
left angle quote	«	&laquo;
right angle quote	»	&raquo;
ampersand	&	&amp;
inverted exclamation	¡	&iexcl;
inverted question mark	¿	&iquest;
broken vertical bar	¦	&brvbar;
section	§	&sect;
not	¬	&not;
acute accent	´	&acute;
cedilla	¸	&cedil;
bullet	•	&bull;
capital N, tilde	Ñ	&NTilde;
small n, tilde	ñ	&ntilde;
capital A, tilde	Ã	&Atilde;
small a, tilde	ã	&atilde;
capital A, grave accent	À	&Agrave;
small a, grave accent	à	&agrave;
capital O, slash	Ø	&Oslash;

Description	Special Character	Code
small o, slash	ø	&oslash;
em dash	—	&mdash;
en dash	–	&ndash;
micro	m	&micro;
macron	¯	&macr;
superscript one	^{1}	&sup1;
superscript two	^{2}	&sup2;
superscript three	^{3}	&sup3;
one-half fraction	½	&frac12;
one-fourth fraction	¼	&frac14;
three-fourths fraction	¾	&frac34;
degree	°	&deg;
multiply	×	&times;
divide	÷	&divide;
plus or minus	±	&plusmn;
less than	<	&lt;
greater than	>	&gt;
dagger	†	&dagger;
double dagger	‡	&Dagger;
cent	¢	&cent;
pound sterling	£	&pound;
euro	€	&euro;
yen	¥	&yen;
general currency	¤	&curren;

Chapter 4

Formatting Text

You can apply formatting tags to control the appearance of text on your Web page. For example, you can apply additional tags to normal paragraph text to make the text bold or italic. By adding the <FONT> tag along with special attributes, you can change the size and color of words on your page. You can also adjust page margins and the background color to make your text content look its best.

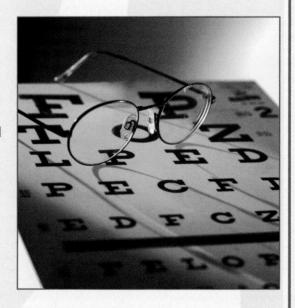

Make Text Bold

You can add bold formatting to your text to give it more emphasis or make your page more visually appealing. For example, you might make a company name bold in a paragraph or add bold formatting to a list of items. You add bold text to a page by surrounding the text with `<B>` and `</B>` tags. In most browsers, the `<STRONG>` tag has the same effect as the `<B>` tag.

Make Text Bold

1 Type `<B>` in front of the text you want to make bold.

2 Type `</B>` at the end of the text.

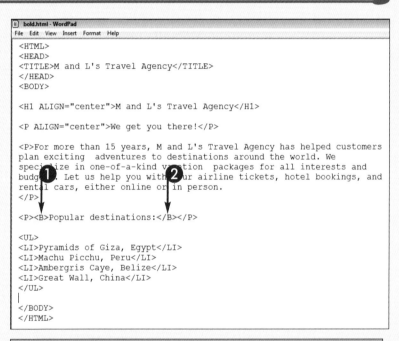

● When displayed in a Web browser, the text appears as bold.

Note: To create bold text using the `font-style` property in CSS, see Chapter 10.

Italicize Text

You can italicize your text to give it more emphasis or make your page more visually appealing. Common uses for italicized text include highlighting a new term or setting apart the title of a literary work. You add italicized text to a page by surrounding the text with `<I>` and `</I>` tags. In most browsers, the `<EM>` tag has the same effect as the `<I>` tag.

Italicize Text

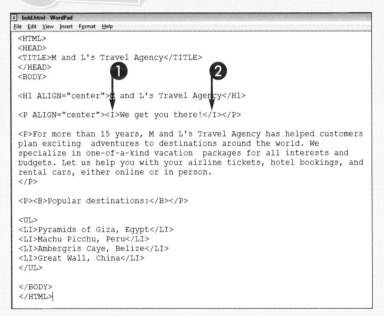

① Type `<I>` in front of the text you want to italicize.

② Type `</I>` at the end of the text.

● When displayed in a Web browser, the text appears in italics.

Note: *To italicize text using the* `font-style` *property in CSS, see Chapter 10.*

53

Add Underlining to Text

You can underline your text for added emphasis. For example, you might underline a term or an important name. You underline text in a page by surrounding the text with `<U>` and `</U>` tags.

Use caution when applying underlining to Web pages because some users may mistake the underlined text for a hyperlink. See Chapter 6 to learn more about using links in Web pages.

Add Underlining to Text

1 Type `<U>` in front of the text you want to underline.

2 Type `</U>` at the end of the text.

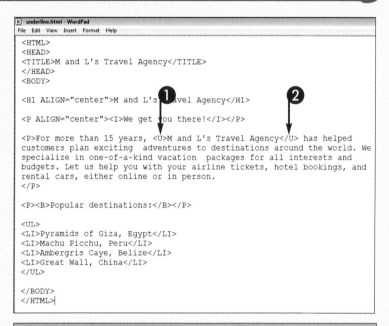

● The text appears underlined on the Web page.

Note: *To underline text using the* `text-decoration` *property in CSS, see Chapter 10.*

Change Fonts

You can change the appearance of your text using the font tags <FONT> and </FONT>, along with the FACE attribute. You can use the attribute to specify a font by name.

Not all Web browsers can display all fonts. You should assign common fonts typically found on most computers, such as Times New Roman and Arial. If possible, you should also list more than one font name in the FACE attribute in case the first font is not available on the viewer's computer.

Change Fonts

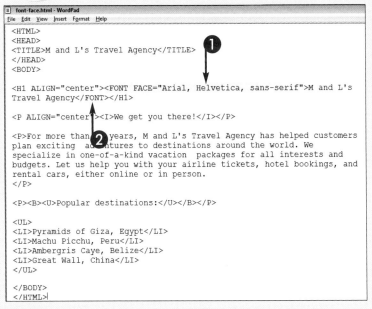

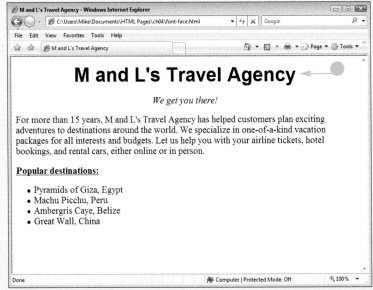

❶ Type <FONT FACE="?"> in front of the text you want to change. Replace ? with one or more font names or families, separated with commas.

If the first font you list is not available on the user's computer, the second font is used.

Commonly supported font families are serif, sans serif, and monospace.

❷ Type </FONT> at the end of the text.

● The text appears in the new font on the Web page.

Note: To change the font using the font-family property in CSS, see Chapter 10.

Change Font Size

You can change the font size of your Web page text using the `SIZE` attribute inside the `<FONT>` tag. You can specify seven font sizes in HTML. Font Size 1 creates the smallest text, whereas Font Size 7 creates the largest. You can add multiple `<FONT>` tags to paragraph text to make different words different sizes in the same paragraph.

Although the `SIZE` attribute lets you set the text size for a section of text, the `<BASEFONT>` tag lets you set the font size for the entire page.

Change Font Size

CHANGE A SECTION OF TEXT

1 Type `<FONT SIZE="?">` before the text you want to change, replacing *?* with a number from 1 to 7.

2 Type `</FONT>` at the end of the text.

3 Type additional `<FONT>` tags and `SIZE` attributes for any other text that you want to size.

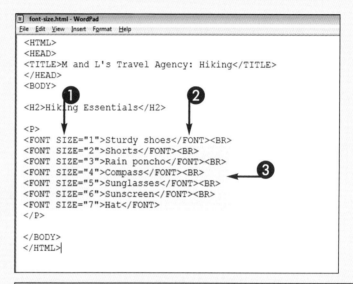

● The text appears at the designated font size on the Web page.

This figure shows samples of all seven font size levels.

Note: *To change the font size using the* `font-size` *property in CSS, see Chapter 10.*

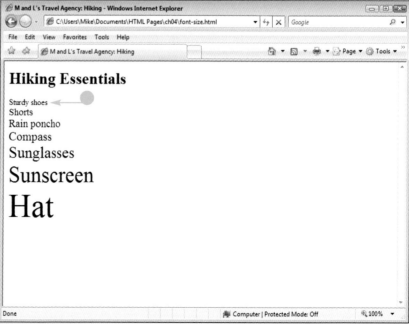

```
<TITLE>M and L's Travel Agency: Hiking</TITLE>
</HEAD>
<BODY>
<BASEFONT SIZE="5">

<H2>Hiking Essentials</H2>

<P>
Sturdy shoes<BR>
Shorts<BR>
Rain poncho<BR>
```
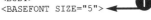

Hiking Essentials

Sturdy shoes
Shorts
Rain poncho
Compass
Sunglasses
Sunscreen
Hat

CHANGE ALL THE TEXT

1 Type <BASEFONT SIZE="?"> at the top of your Web page text, replacing ? with a size you want from 1 to 7.

Note: *The <BASEFONT> tag is supported by Internet Explorer but not by other browsers such as Firefox and Safari.*

● All the text appears at the new size in the Web browser.

Note: *The <BASEFONT> tag does not affect the size of any headings (<H1>) within your Web page text.*

Simplify It

What size will my text appear in my page if I size it using the SIZE attribute?
The exact size of the text depends on what browser you use, although most modern browsers display at the same sizes. This table shows at what sizes Internet Explorer 7 and Firefox 3 display text.

You can also size text using relative font sizing. If you type a plus (+) or minus (−) sign before a size number, the browser displays text at a size relative to the surrounding text. For example, if you type <FONT SIZE="+2">, the browser displays the text two sizes larger than the surrounding text. If you type <FONT SIZE="-2">, the browser displays the text two sizes smaller than the surrounding text.

SIZE Attribute	Font Size
1	7 points
2	10 points
3	12 points
4	14 points
5	18 points
6	24 points
7	36 points

Change the Text Color

You can enhance your text by adding color. The COLOR attribute works with the <FONT> tag to change text on a page from the default black to a color. You can specify the color using a hexadecimal value or, for certain common colors, the color's name.

Legibility is always a concern when it comes to applying color attributes to text. Be sure to choose a color that is easy to read on your Web page. Use caution when applying colored text to a colored background. Always test your page to make sure the colors do not clash and your text remains legible.

CHANGE A SECTION OF TEXT

① Type `<FONT COLOR="?">` in front of the text you want to change, replacing *?* with the name or hexadecimal value of the desired color.

This example shows the color name for red.

② Type `</FONT>` at the end of the text.

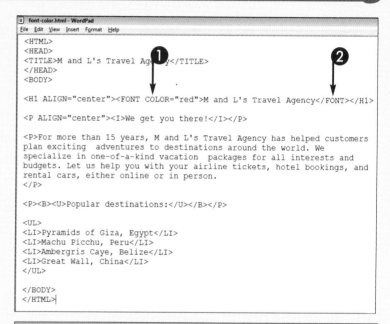

● The text appears in the designated color on the Web page.

Note: *To change the font color using the* `color` *property in CSS, see Chapter 10.*

```
<TITLE>M and L's Travel Agency</TITLE>
</HEAD>
<BODY TEXT="#008000">
```

```
<H1 ALIGN="center"><FONT COLOR="red">M and L's Travel Agency</FONT></H1>

<P ALIGN="center"><I>We get you there!</I></P>

<P>For more than 15 years, M and L's Travel Agency has helped customers
plan exciting  adventures to destinations around the world. We
specialize in one-of-a-kind vacation  packages for all interests and
budgets. Let us help you with your airline tickets, hotel bookings, and
rental cars, either online or in person.
</P>
```

M and L's Travel Agency

We get you there!

For more than 15 years, M and L's Travel Agency has helped customers plan exciting adventures to destinations around the world. We specialize in one-of-a-kind vacation packages for all interests and budgets. Let us help you with your airline tickets, hotel bookings, and rental cars, either online or in person.

Popular destinations:

- Pyramids of Giza, Egypt
- Machu Picchu, Peru
- Ambergris Caye, Belize
- Great Wall, China

CHANGE ALL THE TEXT

1 Within the <BODY> tag, type TEXT="?", replacing *?* with the name or hexadecimal value of the desired color.

This example uses a hexadecimal value instead of a color name. Always precede a hexadecimal value with a # sign.

● All the text appears in the new color in the Web browser.

● Text that you have colored using the FONT tag remains that color.

Note: *The* TEXT *attribute does not affect the color of links. To learn more about links, see Chapter 6.*

What colors can I set for my Web page text?
HTML coding sets colors using six-digit hexadecimal values preceded by a number sign (#), as shown in the following table. Browsers can also understand the color names listed below.

Color	Hexadecimal Value	Color	Hexadecimal Value
Aqua	#00FFFF	Navy	#000080
Black	#000000	Olive	#808000
Blue	#0000FF	Purple	#800080
Fuchsia	#FF00FF	Red	#FF0000
Gray	#808080	Silver	#C0C0C0
Green	#008000	Teal	#008080
Lime	#00FF00	White	#FFFFFF
Maroon	#800000	Yellow	#FFFF00

Adjust Margins

You can adjust the margins of your Web page to change the amount of space that appears at the top, bottom, left edge, or right edge. By default, the page margins are set at 10 pixels for the right and left margins and 15 pixels for the top and bottom margins. You may want to add space in your margins to improve the legibility of your content. You can also decrease the space to 0 pixels so your images are placed flush with the edges of the browser window.

Adjust Margins

1 Within the `<BODY>` tag, type `MARGIN="?"`.

Replace *MARGIN* with the margin attribute you want to change: `LEFTMARGIN`, `RIGHTMARGIN`, `TOPMARGIN`, `BOTTOMMARGIN`, `MARGINWIDTH`, or `MARGINHEIGHT`.

Replace *?* with the amount of indentation you want, measured in pixels.

You can set the margin for one side of the page or all four sides, all within the `<BODY>` tag.

● The Web browser displays your page with the specified margins.

Note: *To learn how to change the alignment of text on a page, see Chapter 3.*

Note: *To adjust margins using style sheets, see Chapter 11.*

Set a Background Page Color

You can add color to the background of the page using the BGCOLOR attribute in the <BODY> tag. The default background color is white. It is a good idea to choose a background color that does not obscure your text. You can specify the color using a hexadecimal value or, for certain common colors, the color's name. To add more complex, multicolor designs to your page background, you can add a background image. See Chapter 5 for details.

Set a Background Page Color

① Within the <BODY> tag, type BGCOLOR="?", replacing ? with a color name or hexadecimal value.

Note: *For a table of 16 color codes you can apply, see the section "Change the Text Color."*

The page appears in the Web browser with a background color assigned.

Note: *To change the background using style sheets, see Chapter 10.*

Add a Horizontal Rule

You can add a solid line, or horizontal rule, across your page to separate blocks of information. By default, most browsers display a horizontal rule as a thin gray line. Horizontal rules must occupy a line by themselves and cannot appear within a paragraph.

You can define the thickness and length of a horizontal line using the `SIZE` and `WIDTH` attributes.

ADD A SIMPLE LINE

1 Type `<HR>` where you want to insert a horizontal rule.

● The browser displays the line across the page.

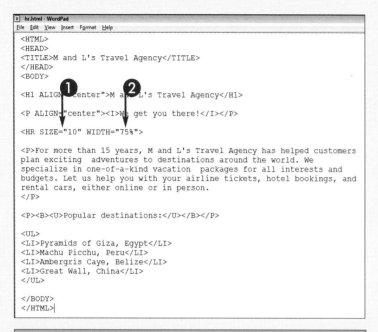

```
<HTML>
<HEAD>
<TITLE>M and L's Travel Agency</TITLE>
</HEAD>
<BODY>

<H1 ALIGN="center">M and L's Travel Agency</H1>

<P ALIGN="center"><I>We get you there!</I></P>

<HR SIZE="10" WIDTH="75%">

<P>For more than 15 years, M and L's Travel Agency has helped customers
plan exciting  adventures to destinations around the world. We
specialize in one-of-a-kind vacation  packages for all interests and
budgets. Let us help you with your airline tickets, hotel bookings, and
rental cars, either online or in person.
</P>

<P><B><U>Popular destinations:</U></B></P>

<UL>
<LI>Pyramids of Giza, Egypt</LI>
<LI>Machu Picchu, Peru</LI>
<LI>Ambergris Caye, Belize</LI>
<LI>Great Wall, China</LI>
</UL>

</BODY>
</HTML>
```

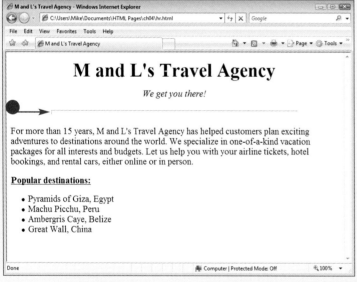

SET A LINE THICKNESS AND WIDTH

1 Within the <HR> tag, type SIZE="?", replacing ? with the thickness you want to assign, measured in pixels.

2 Within the <HR> tag, type WIDTH="?%", replacing ? with the percentage of the page you want the rule to extend across.

You can also type a numeric value to set the width of the rule in pixels.

● The browser displays the line across the page.

How do I make my line appear more solid?
By default, the browser displays horizontal rules with shading, giving the lines a three-dimensional effect. To remove the shading, add the NOSHADE attribute to your <HR> tag so that it reads <HR NOSHADE>.

Can I add color to a horizontal line?
Yes. You can insert the COLOR attribute and assign a color value to a line. For example, if you type <HR COLOR="#0000FF">, the browser displays the line as blue. See the section "Change the Text Color" for more about HTML colors.

Chapter 5

Adding Images

Are you ready to add images to your Web page? Images include photographs, logos, clip art, backgrounds, clickable buttons, and more. You can add images to your Web page using the <IMG> tag and then adjust the alignment, size, and padding of the images with tag attributes. You can also use HTML code to determine how nearby text wraps around your images. Understanding how to place images on a Web page is important because photos and illustrations can be key to adding visual appeal.

Understanding Web Page Images

You can use images in a variety of ways on your Web pages. Images include everything from graphics and clip art to photographs and other visual objects. Images can illustrate text, show a product, provide background decoration, or act as navigational buttons for a Web site. Most of the images used on the Web today are of one of three file formats: JPEG, GIF, and PNG. Knowing when to use each file format, and how to minimize the file size when you save an image, can help you create pages that look great and download fast.

Image File Formats

Although numerous file types are used for computer images, JPEG and GIF are the two most popular types used on the Web. Both formats are cross-platform and offer file compression. PNG is a newer arrival in the image file format world and is gaining popularity among Web developers. The current versions of all of today's popular Web browsers can display JPEG, GIF, and PNG images. All three formats offer file-size compression, which make images download quickly from a Web server to your computer.

JPEG

JPEG, which stands for *Joint Photographic Experts Group*, supports 24-bit color, allowing for millions of colors. The JPEG format is commonly used with complex images, such as photos or graphics that use millions of colors and feature lots of detail. JPEG is not a good choice for solid-color artwork because it results in a larger overall file size, which translates to longer download times. JPEG images usually use a .jpg file name extension.

GIF

GIF, which stands for *Graphics Interchange Format*, supports up to 256 colors. The GIF format is more commonly used for simple images, such as logos and graphics containing basic shapes and lines. If your image or graphic contains few colors and not a lot of detail, GIF is a good file format choice. A single GIF file can also store multiple images and display them as an animation. GIF images use a .gif file name extension.

PNG

The PNG (*Portable Network Graphics*) format offers rich color support and advanced compression schemes, so it is a good choice for a variety of image types. Like JPEG, PNG supports 24-bit color but can also be saved with fewer colors, similar to GIF. Because PNG is a relatively new file format, use it if your intended audience most likely uses up-to-date browsers. PNG images use a .png file name extension.

Downloading Considerations

Browsers must download an image before users can view it on the Web page. Large images can take a long time to display, especially if Internet connection speeds are slow. For this reason, consider the overall file size of an image when deciding whether or not to add it to a Web page. If you fill your page with several large pictures, the download time for the page to fully display will be excessive.

Optimize Images

Most image-editing programs allow you to adjust the quality of an image to control its file size. You can also control file size by shrinking or cropping an image. For best results, make sure your image file size does not exceed 60K. If you use larger image files, users with slow connections may not be willing to wait for the pictures to download. With GIFs and some PNGs, you can decrease the number of colors in an image to reduce the file size. Affordable image editors include Adobe Photoshop Elements and Corel Paint Shop Pro. Paint, which comes free with Windows, also offers image-optimization features.

Alternative Text

Some Web users may turn off the browser's image-display setting to help speed up the downloading of Web pages. Also, some visually impaired users view the Web using screen readers that do not display images at all. To accommodate such users, be sure to include alternative text (●) describing the images on your page. Alternative text can appear in place of the image and allows users to understand how the image relates to the rest of the page. Learn how to add alternative text in the section "Add Alternative Text."

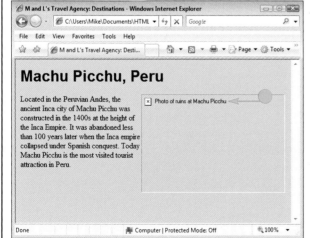

Insert an Image

You can add images to your Web page to add visual interest or illustrate a topic. For example, you can add a photograph of a product or a company logo to a business's Web page. HTML coding lets you display images as *inline* elements, which means they appear within the body of the page along with text.

You can use image files from a digital camera or scanner, or you can create illustrations with a graphics program. If you are not the original author of the image, you need permission to use the image before placing it on a Web site.

INSERT A PHOTOGRAPH

1 Type `<IMG SRC="?">` where you want to insert a photographic image, replacing *?* with the relative path to the file you want to insert.

In this example, because the image was saved in the same folder as the HTML file, you reference it with just the file name.

● The Web browser displays the image on the page.

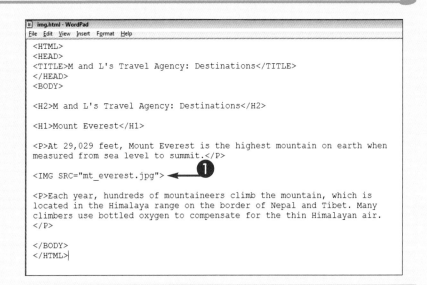

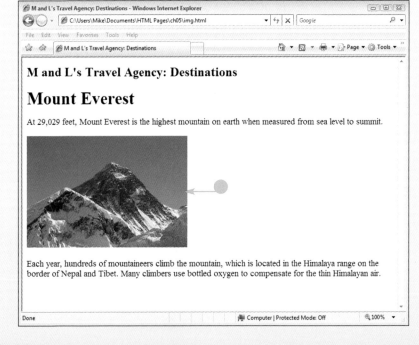

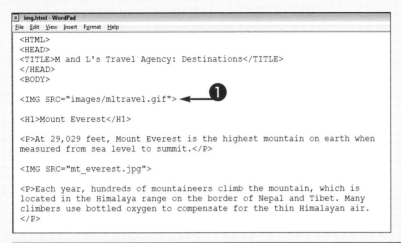

INSERT A GRAPHIC FILE

① Type `<IMG SRC="?">` where you want to insert a graphic, replacing *?* with the relative path to the file you want to insert.

In this example, because the graphic was saved in an `images` subdirectory relative to the HTML file, you reference it with the subdirectory name followed by a forward slash (/) and then the file name.

● The Web browser displays the graphic on the page.

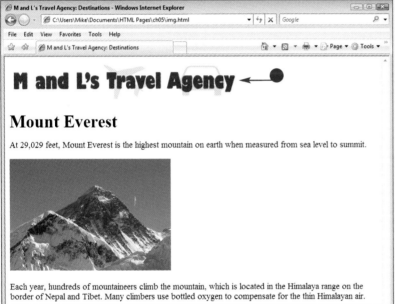

How can I download an image from a Web page?
Internet Explorer, Firefox, and most other Web browsers allow you to copy an image from a Web site by right-clicking the image and selecting a save command. If you save an image in the same folder as your HTML files, you can then use the image on your pages using the previous steps. Make sure you have permission from the image owner before using the image on your Web site.

How can I insert an image in my eBay auction?
Many auction sites, such as eBay, allow you to include certain HTML code in your listing descriptions. If you have your auction item's image file hosted on a Web server, you can use an HTML `<IMG>` tag to insert the image into your auction description. Using HTML to insert an image yourself is an alternative to using eBay's photo-hosting feature. See Chapter 13 for more about moving content to a Web server.

Specify an Image Size

If your image appears too big or too small on a Web page, you can use HTML coding to change the size with image attributes. You can set the width and height of an image in pixels or as a percentage of the overall window size. This can enable you to combine your images nicely with the text and other content around them. Make sure to carefully test your page when resizing images using HTML because too much stretching or shrinking can cause a loss of image quality.

Specify an Image Size

1 Click inside the <IMG> tag and type WIDTH="?", replacing *?* with the width measurement you want to set.

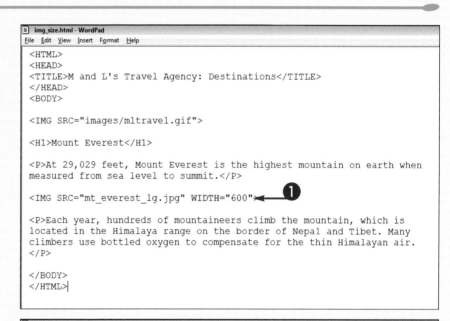

2 Type a space.

3 Type HEIGHT="?", replacing *?* with the height measurement you want to set.

```
<H1>Mount Everest</H1>

<P>At 29,029 feet, Mount Everest is the highest mountain on earth when
measured from sea level to summit.</P>

<IMG SRC="mt_everest_lg.jpg" WIDTH="60%" HEIGHT="70%">

<P>Each year, hundreds of mountaineers climb the mountain, which is
located in the Himalaya range on the border of Nepal and Tibet. Many
climbers use bottled oxygen to compensate for the thin Himalayan air.
</P>

</BODY>
</HTML>
```

M and L's Travel Agency

Mount Everest

At 29,029 feet, Mount Everest is the highest mountain on earth when measured from sea level to summit.

Each year, hundreds of mountaineers climb the mountain, which is located in the Himalaya range on the

● You can also set the attribute value as a percentage. This tells the browser to display the image at a percentage of the browser window size.

When giving a percentage value, be sure to follow it with a percent sign (%).

● The Web browser displays the image at the specified size on the page.

Note: *If you specify only one dimension, whether the width or the height, for your image, a browser sizes the other dimension proportionally based on the original size.*

What size should I set for a Web page image?
The best size for an image depends on how you want to use it on the Web page. The vast majority of Web users access pages with their monitors set at least 800 pixels in width and 600 pixels in height. At these settings, browsers can usually display images 750 pixels in width and 400 pixels in height without requiring the user to scroll. Making your images smaller can allow users to see more than one image at a time, depending on the layout.

Is it better to resize an image in an editing program or using HTML coding?
Resizing images using HTML can reduce the quality of your images, especially if you use HTML to enlarge them. Also, shrinking an image using HTML does not actually reduce its file size, which means the image does not download any faster. For these reasons, it is better to resize images using an image editor if you have one. This allows you to maintain an image's quality and optimize its file size.

Add Alternative Text

For users who have images turned off in their browsers, you can add alternative text that identifies the images on your page. Alternative text, sometimes called *placeholder text*, can describe what appears in an image and is an important addition to your Web page markup.

Most search engines, because they process text but not images, use alternative text to better understand the content of your page. This can help improve the placement of your Web site in search results.

Add Alternative Text

1 Click inside the <IMG> tag and type ALT="?", replacing *?* with alternative text describing the image.

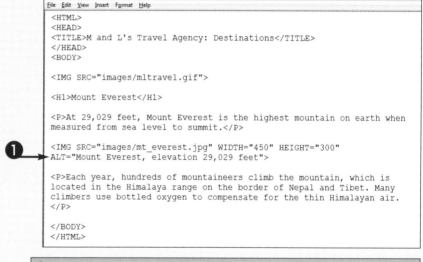

● If the user's browser has images turned off, or if the image cannot be found on the Web server, the browser displays the alternative text in lieu of the image.

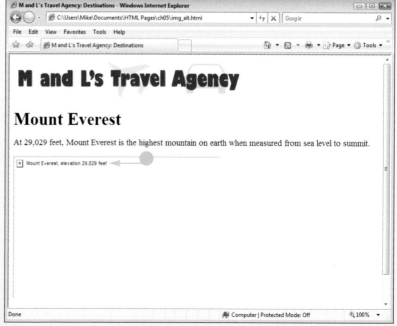

Create an Image Label

You can add a label that appears whenever the user positions the mouse pointer over a particular image on a Web page. You can use labels to offer detailed information about the image.

Labels work differently from alternative text. Alternative text appears on the page itself when images are turned off. A label appears in a pop-up box when the user positions the mouse over the image. You add a label by including a `TITLE` attribute in the `<IMG>` tag.

Create an Image Label

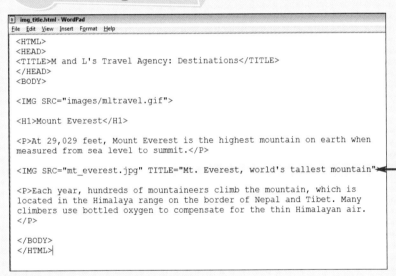

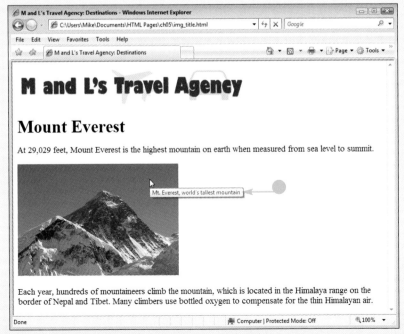

1 Within the `<IMG>` tag, type `TITLE="?"`, replacing *?* with the image label you want to appear.

● The label appears when you position the mouse pointer over the image in the browser window.

Note: *Label text can also help search engines determine the type of image content on your page.*

Align an Image Horizontally

You can use the `left` and `right` alignment attributes to control the horizontal positioning of an image on a page. The alignment attributes also control how text wraps around the image. When you align an image to the right, text after it wraps around the left, and vice versa for left alignment.

You can center-align an image using the `<DIV>` tag. See "Center an Image" for details. You can also align an image vertically on a page. See the section "Align an Image Vertically" to learn more.

Align an Image Horizontally

1 Click inside the `<IMG>` image tag and type `ALIGN="?"`, replacing *?* with the alignment you want to apply, either `left` or `right`.

The Web browser aligns the image as specified.

● In this example, the image is aligned to the right.

Note: *To center-align an image, see the section "Center an Image."*

Note: *For greater control over image alignment, consider placing your images in tables. Learn more about using tables in Chapter 7.*

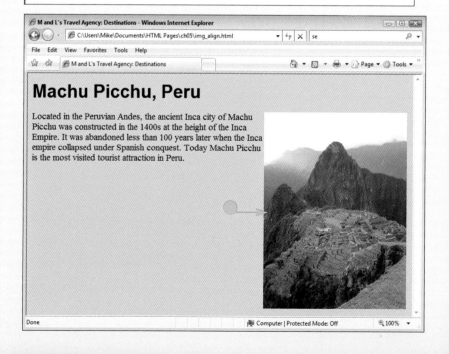

Align an Image Vertically

You can use the alignment attributes to control the vertical positioning of an image on a page relative to text that follows it. The alignment attributes are `top`, `middle`, **and** `bottom`. This can be useful when adding short caption text to an image.

You can also align an image horizontally on a page. See the section "Align an Image Horizontally" to learn more.

Align an Image Vertically

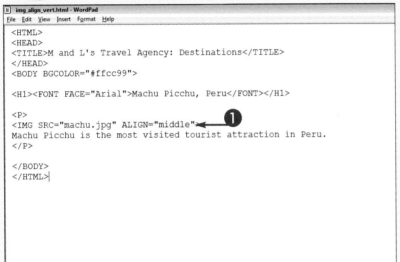

① Click inside the `<IMG>` image tag and type `ALIGN="?"`, replacing *?* with the alignment you want to apply, `middle`, `top`, or `bottom` (`bottom` is the default).

If the image shares the same line as text, the alignment attribute controls the position of the image relative to the text.

The Web browser aligns the image as specified.

● In this example, the image is middle-aligned with existing text.

Note: *For greater control over image alignment, consider placing your images in tables. Learn more about using tables in Chapter 7.*

Center an Image

You can center your image on the page using a `<DIV>` tag and the `ALIGN` attribute. Centering an image can give it more emphasis and help it stand out from the text or other page elements. You can center an image at the top of a Web page to give the page a fancy or colorful title. You can also align an image horizontally or vertically on the page. See the other sections in this chapter for details.

Center an Image

1 Click before the `<IMG>` tag and type `<DIV>`.

2 Click inside the `<DIV>` tag and type `ALIGN="center"`.

3 Click after the closing bracket of the `<IMG>` tag and type `</DIV>`.

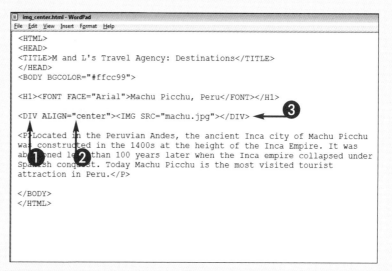

● The image appears centered on the Web page.

Stop Text Wrap

You can stop text wrapping around your images using the line break tag along with the `CLEAR` attribute. This causes the text or other content following the line break tag to begin at the bottom of the image. You can cause text to wrap around your image in the first place by aligning the image using the `ALIGN` attribute. See "Align an Image Horizontally" for details.

Stop Text Wrap

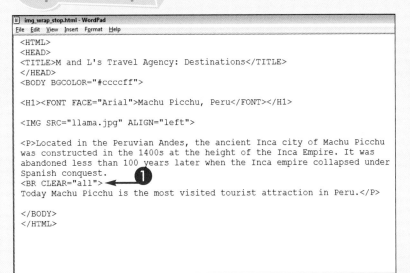

```
img_wrap_stop.html - WordPad
File  Edit  View  Insert  Format  Help

<HTML>
<HEAD>
<TITLE>M and L's Travel Agency: Destinations</TITLE>
</HEAD>
<BODY BGCOLOR="#ccccff">

<H1><FONT FACE="Arial">Machu Picchu, Peru</FONT></H1>

<IMG SRC="llama.jpg" ALIGN="left">

<P>Located in the Peruvian Andes, the ancient Inca city of Machu Picchu
was constructed in the 1400s at the height of the Inca Empire. It was
abandoned less than 100 years later when the Inca empire collapsed under
Spanish conquest.
<BR CLEAR="all">     1
Today Machu Picchu is the most visited tourist attraction in Peru.</P>

</BODY>
</HTML>
```

1 Click where you want to end the text wrap and type `<BR CLEAR="?">`, replacing *?* with the margin you want to clear, `left`, `right`, or `all`.

The text wrapping ends at the selected point on the page.

● In this example, the next paragraph starts on a different line from the image.

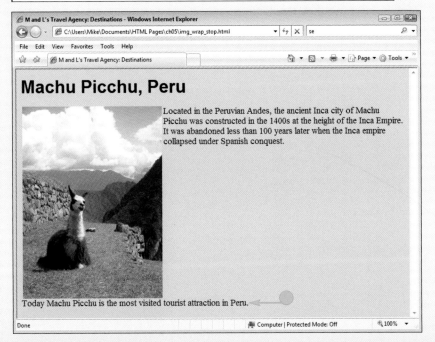

Machu Picchu, Peru

Located in the Peruvian Andes, the ancient Inca city of Machu Picchu was constructed in the 1400s at the height of the Inca Empire. It was abandoned less than 100 years later when the Inca empire collapsed under Spanish conquest.

Today Machu Picchu is the most visited tourist attraction in Peru.

Add Space around an Image

Most Web browsers display only a small amount of space between images and text. You can increase the amount of space, also called *padding*, to make the page more visually appealing and easier to read. You can control padding on the left and right sides of an image

with the `HSPACE` attribute. You can control the padding above and below an image with the `VSPACE` attribute. Padding can add whitespace between the image and its caption.

The values used with the attributes specify the padding in pixels.

❶ Click inside the `<IMG>` tag and type `HSPACE="?"` or `VSPACE="?"`, replacing *?* with the amount of space you want to insert.

You can add one or both attributes to an image.

If you add both attributes, separate them with a space in the HTML coding.

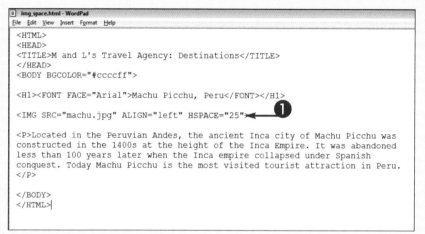

● The Web browser displays the image with the specified amount of space around it.

`HSPACE` and `VSPACE` add space to two sides at a time. To add space to just one side, for example the bottom of an image, use style sheets. See Chapter 11 for details.

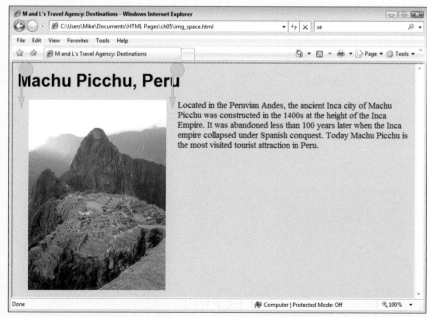

Add a Background Image

You can turn an image into a background for your Web page by setting an attribute in the <BODY> tag. When selecting an image for a background, try to factor in how your text will appear against the image. You may need to change the color of the text to make it legible. See Chapter 4 for details about changing the text color.

If you use a large image file, it fills the entire background. If you use a smaller image, the browser tiles the image across and down the page to fill the background with a repeating pattern. *Seamless* background images have opposite edges that align with one another. This can make a tiling background look like a single image.

Add a Background Image

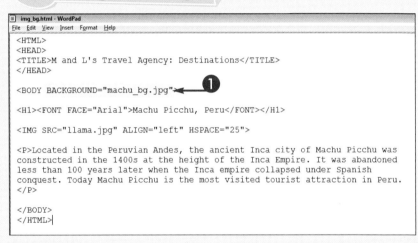

① Click inside the <BODY> tag and type BACKGROUND="?", replacing ? with the path to the image file you want to use.

In this example, because the image was saved in the same folder as the HTML file, you reference it with just the file name.

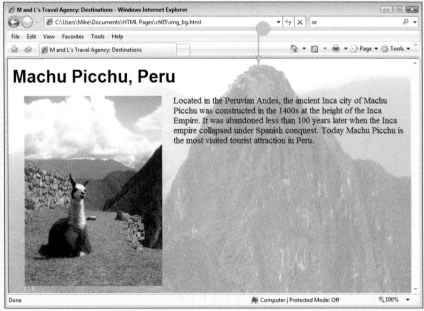

● The Web browser displays the image as the page background.

Note: *To learn how to change the text color, see Chapter 4.*

Chapter 6

Adding Links

Are you ready to start adding links to your Web pages? This chapter shows you how to create links in your HTML documents to allow users to jump to other Web sites or to other pages within your own site. You learn how to add e-mail links and control the appearance of links. You also get an introduction to URLs, which are the Web addresses that define the destinations of your links. Links are created using <A> tags in combination with the HREF attribute.

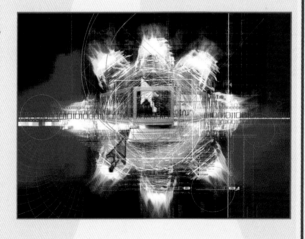

Understanding Links

Hyperlinks, or *links* for short, are what make Web pages different from other computer documents. Any publicly accessible Web page can be connected to another by creating a link. Links enable users to navigate from one topic to the next on a Web site, and from one Web site to another. The user clicks the link and the browser opens the destination page. You create links with the <A> tag and HREF attribute.

Types of Links

Links can be text or images. Text links typically appear as underlined, differently colored words on a page. Any image on a Web page can also be turned into a link. For example, graphical site maps and navigation buttons that appear at the top or side of a page can be turned into links to make it easy for users to access other pages on the same Web site. When a user positions the mouse pointer over a link, the pointer takes the shape of a pointing hand, indicating the presence of an active, clickable link (●).

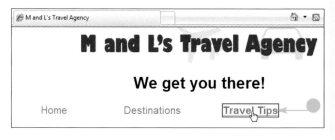

Link Destinations

You can use links on your Web page to direct users to other pages on the Internet. For example, you might include a link on your company Web page to a local city directory detailing activities and hotels in the area. If your Web site consists of more than one page, you can include links to other pages on the site. For example, your main page may provide links to pages about your business, products, and ordering information as well as to a map of your location. You can also provide links to different areas on the same page. This can be useful if a page is particularly long. It allows users to jump right to the information they want to view without having to scroll.

Absolute and Relative Links

You can use two types of links in your HTML documents: absolute and relative. *Absolute links* use a complete Web address, or *URL*, to point to a specific page on a specific Web server:

```
<A HREF="http://www.example.
com/page.html">Click here</A>
```

Relative links use shorthand to reference a page and do not specify the server. You generally use relative links to reference documents on the same Web site:

```
<A HREF="page.html">Click
here</A>
```

Understanding URLs

Every page on the Web has a unique address called a URL. Short for *Uniform Resource Locator*, a URL identifies the domain name of the Web server and the directory path to the file on that server. Absolute links specify a complete Web page URL, whereas relative links use shorthand to specify pages relative to the page containing the link.

HTTP Prefix

All URLs for Web pages include the standard HTTP (Hypertext Transfer Protocol) prefix, as in http://www. example.com. Although most browsers automatically insert the `http://` prefix for you when you type an address such as www.example.com, you must include the prefix when referencing URLs in your HTML. There may be times when you use a prefix other than HTTP in your URLs. If you are linking to a document that resides on a file transfer site, you may use the FTP prefix (`ftp://`). If you want to create a link that opens an e-mail program, allowing a user to send an e-mail message, you may use the MAILTO prefix (`mailto:`). There is also an encrypted version of the HTTP prefix, `https://`, which you may use when linking to secure areas of Web sites, such as those involving payment transactions.

Domain Name

Following the prefix in a URL is the domain name of the Web server where the page is stored. Typically, domain names correspond to the company or organization hosting your Web page files. Hosts can include commercial companies, educational institutions, and government agencies. In the URL http://www.example. com, "example.com" is the name of the domain, with "www." specifying a Web server at that domain. Occasionally you may use a numeric IP (Internet Protocol) address such as 208.215.179.146 in your URL instead of a domain name.

http://www.example.com/products/info/widget.html

Directory Path

Following the domain name in a URL is information about the directories in which the page is stored on the server. You use slashes (/) to separate the domain name, directories, and file name. Directory information does not exist in a URL if the HTML document for the page is stored in a Web directory's main, or *root*, directory.

File Name

For basic Web pages, the URL ends with the name of the HTML file. This information tells the Web server what document to retrieve and return to the Web browser. You may see additional information at the end of URLs for pages that are generated dynamically, such as those on sites that use technologies such as PHP or Java. When you reference a Web site's home page, you often omit the path and file name from a URL, such as in http://www.example.com. In such cases, the server returns a default page for the site, usually titled index.html, located in the Web server's root directory.

Link to Another Page

You can create a link in your HTML document that, when clicked, takes the visitor to another page on the Web. You can link to a page on your own Web site or to a page elsewhere on the Web. You create a link using the <A> tag with an HREF attribute. You surround the content that you are turning into a link with an opening and closing <A> tag.

To create a link, you must first know the URL of the page to which you want to link, such as http://www.wiley.com/index.html.

Link to Another Page

INSERT A TEXT LINK

1 Type the text you want to use as a link.

2 Type <A HREF="?"> in front of the text, replacing ? with the URL of the page to which you want to link.

3 Type </A> at the end of the link text.

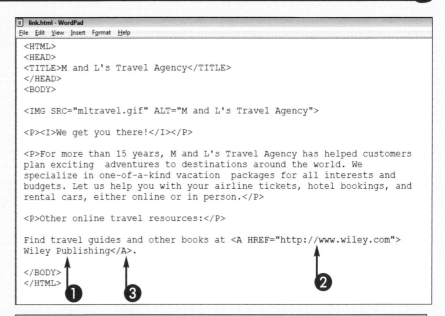

- The Web browser displays the text as an underlined link.

- The mouse pointer (⇱), when positioned over the link, takes the shape of a hand pointer (🖑), indicating a link.

- The URL for the link appears in the status bar.

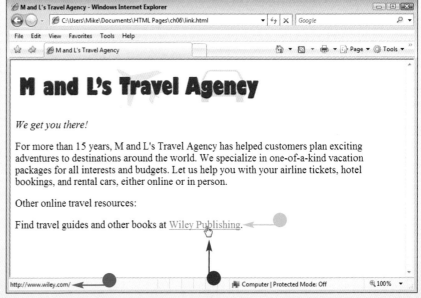

```
<IMG SRC="mltravel.gif" ALT="M and L's Travel Agency">

<P><I>We get you there!</I></P>

<P>For more than 15 years, M and L's Travel Agency has helped customers
plan exciting  adventures to destinations around the world. We
specialize in one-of-a-kind vacation  packages for all interests and
budgets. Let us help you with your airline tickets, hotel bookings, and
rental cars, either online or in person.</P>

<P>Click the llama for more information:</P>

<A HREF="http://www.wiley.com"><IMG SRC="llama_sm.jpg"></A>        ③

</BODY>
</HTML>
       ②                           ①
```

M and L's Travel Agency

We get you there!

For more than 15 years, M and L's Travel Agency has helped customers plan exciting adventures to destinations around the world. We specialize in one-of-a-kind vacation packages for all interests and budgets. Let us help you with your airline tickets, hotel bookings, and rental cars, either online or in person.

Click the llama for more information:

http://www.wiley.com/ ◄   🖳 Computer | Protected Mode: Off   🔍 100% ▼

INSERT AN IMAGE LINK

① Add the image you want to use as a link using the `<IMG>` tag.

Note: *To learn how to add images to a page, see Chapter 5.*

② Type `<A HREF="?">` in front of the image code, replacing *?* with the URL of the page to which you want to link.

③ Type `</A>` after the image code.

● The Web browser displays the image as a link.

● The mouse pointer (⇡), when positioned over the link, takes the shape of a hand pointer (☝), indicating a link.

● The URL for the link appears in the status bar.

Simplify It

How do I link to another page on my Web site?
You can link to another page on your site using a relative link. In a relative link, you specify the location of the destination page relative to the page that contains the link without specifying the domain name of the server. If the destination page is located in the same directory as the containing page, you can simply specify the file name, as in `<A HREF="photos.html">`. If the destination page is in a subdirectory relative to the containing page, you need to specify that subdirectory as well, as in `<A HREF="media/photos.html">`.

My link image includes a border. How do I remove the border?
When you turn an image into a link, a browser automatically places a border around the image. To remove the border, type `BORDER="0"` in the `<IMG>` tag, as in `<A HREF=http://www.example.com><IMG SRC="vacation.jpg" BORDER="0"></A>`.

Open a New Window with a Link

You can add instructions to an HTML link that tell the browser to open the link page in a new browser window. You may add this instruction if you want to keep a window to your own site open so the user can easily return to your page.

You use a target attribute within the link anchor element (<A>) to open links in new windows. To make all the links on your page open in new windows, you can use the BASE element. To learn more about how links and URLs work, see the sections at the beginning of this chapter.

Open a New Window with a Link

LINK TO A NEW WINDOW

1 Click within the <A> tag for the link you want to edit and type TARGET="?", replacing *?* with a name for the new window.

Other links on your Web page can reference the same target name to open pages in the same new window.

If you want the link to open in a new, unnamed window, type "_blank".

● When the link is clicked, a new browser window opens.

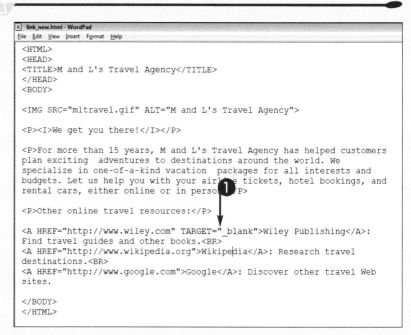

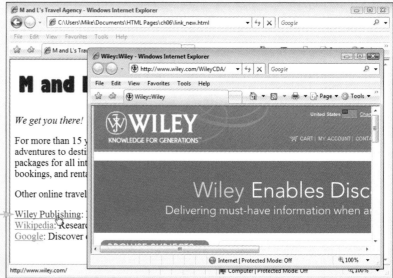

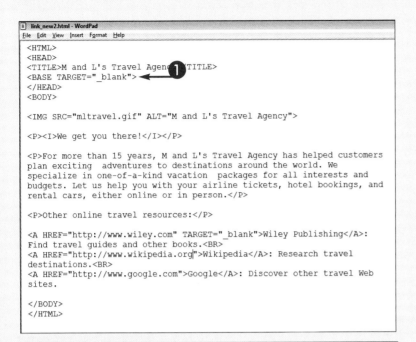

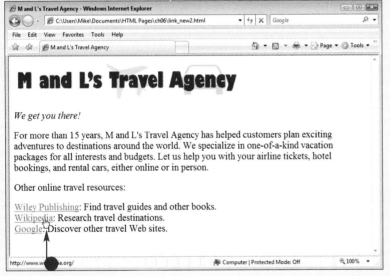

MAKE ALL LINKS OPEN NEW WINDOWS

1 Click between the `<HEAD>` and `</HEAD>` tags and type `<BASE TARGET="?">`, replacing *?* with a name for the new window, such as `main`.

If you want the link to open in a new, unnamed window, type `"_blank"`.

● When a user clicks any of the links on the page, a new browser window opens.

Can I make multiple links on a page open in the same window?
Yes. Just use the same `TARGET` value for the links, for example `TARGET="new1"`. The first time a user clicks one of the links, a `"new1"` window opens. Subsequent link clicks open pages in the same window.

Should I open new windows for every link?
Probably not. If a new window opens every time a link is clicked on your pages, users may quickly become overwhelmed by the number of open windows. You may want to open new windows only when links lead to a page outside the current Web site. This way, the current Web site remains open on the user's computer.

Link to an Area on the Same Page

You can add links to your page that take the user to another place on the same page. This is particularly useful for longer documents. For example, you can add links that take the user to different headings in your document. This saves the user from having to scroll.

To link to places on the same page, you must assign names to the areas to which you want to link. You can do this with the anchor tag (`<A>`) and the `NAME` attribute. Such assigned names are sometimes called *named anchors*.

Link to an Area on the Same Page

NAME AN AREA

① Click in front of the section of text to which you want to create a link and type `<A NAME="?">`, replacing *?* with a unique name for the area.

It is best to keep your names short and simple, using only letters and numbers in the names.

② Type `</A>` at the end of the section.

CREATE A LINK TO THE AREA

① In front of the text or image you want to turn into a link, type `<A HREF="#?">`, replacing *?* with a name of the section to which you want to link.

Note: *Be sure to include the pound sign (#) when linking to other areas of a page.*

② Type `</A>` after the link text.

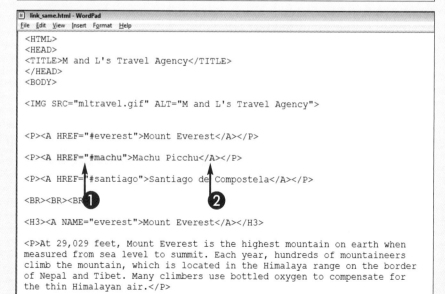

```
link_same.html - WordPad
File  Edit  View  Insert  Format  Help

<H3><A NAME="everest">Mount Everest</A></H3>

<P>At 29,029 feet, Mount Everest is the highest mountain on earth when
measured from sea level to summit. Each year, hundreds of mountaineers
climb the mountain, which is located in the Himalaya range on the border
of Nepal and Tibet. Many climbers use bottled oxygen to compensate for
the thin Himalayan air.</P>

<BR><BR><BR>

<H3><A NAME="machu">Machu Picchu</A></H3>

<P>Located in the Peruvian Andes, the ancient Inca city of Machu Picchu
was constructed in the 1400s at the height of the Inca Empire. It was
abandoned less than 100 years later when the Inca empire collapsed under
Spanish conquest. Today Machu Picchu is the most visited tourist
attraction in Peru.</P>

<BR><BR><BR>
```

```
link_same.html - WordPad
File  Edit  View  Insert  Format  Help
<HTML>
<HEAD>
<TITLE>M and L's Travel Agency</TITLE>
</HEAD>
<BODY>

<IMG SRC="mltravel.gif" ALT="M and L's Travel Agency">

<P><A HREF="#everest">Mount Everest</A></P>

<P><A HREF="#machu">Machu Picchu</A></P>

<P><A HREF="#santiago">Santiago de Compostela</A></P>

<BR><BR><BR>

<H3><A NAME="everest">Mount Everest</A></H3>

<P>At 29,029 feet, Mount Everest is the highest mountain on earth when
measured from sea level to summit. Each year, hundreds of mountaineers
climb the mountain, which is located in the Himalaya range on the border
of Nepal and Tibet. Many climbers use bottled oxygen to compensate for
the thin Himalayan air.</P>
```

M and L's Travel Agency

Mount Everest

Machu Picchu ← ③

Santiago de Compostela

Mount Everest

At 29,029 feet, Mount Everest is the highest mountain on earth when measured from sea level to summit. Each year, hundreds of mountaineers climb the mountain, which is located in the Himalaya range on the border of Nepal and Tibet. Many climbers use bottled oxygen to compensate for the thin Himalayan air.

Machu Picchu

Machu Picchu ←

Located in the Peruvian Andes, the ancient Inca city of Machu Picchu was constructed in the 1400s at the height of the Inca Empire. It was abandoned less than 100 years later when the Inca empire collapsed under Spanish conquest. Today Machu Picchu is the most visited tourist attraction in Peru.

Santiago de Compostela

Located in the Galicia region of northwest Spain, Santiago de Compostela marks the end of the famous medieval pilgrimage route, the Way of St. James. Each year, tens of thousands of Christian pilgrims spend weeks or months traveling by foot, bicycle and even donkey along the route from the south of France. They finish at Santiago's cathedral where, legend has it, the remains of St. James are buried.

Note: To use an image as a link, see the section "Link to Another Page" to learn more.

③ Click the link.

● The browser scrolls to the designated section of the page.

Can I place a link at the bottom of my page that returns the user to the top of the page?
Yes. It is a good idea to add a link to the bottom of a long page to help the user navigate to the top again without having to scroll. To create such a link, create a named anchor at the top of the page following the steps shown in this section, and then insert a link that references that named anchor. Good text to use for such a link is "Return to Top" or "Back to Top."

How do I link to a specific location on another page on my Web site?
You can use the same technique shown in this section to link to a section on another page. First, name the area on the other page using the <A NAME= "?"> tag and attribute, and then create a link to the page, adding a # and then the name to the relative link, such as <A HREF="page.html# section1">.

Link to Another File Type

You can add links to non-HTML resources, such as Word document files, spreadsheet files, image files, compressed files, and more. To make such files Web-accessible, you must store them in the same locations on the Web server as your HTML files. Then you can reference them with a URL just as you do an HTML page.

Thanks to special plug-ins, some Web browsers can open certain non-HTML files. For a file that it cannot open, a browser may prompt users to save the file on their computers. For more about plug-ins, see Chapter 12.

Link to Another File Type

1 Type the text for the link.

It is good form to include a description on the page that identifies what type of file the link opens.

```
link_other.html - WordPad
File  Edit  View  Insert  Format  Help
<HTML>
<HEAD>
<TITLE>M and L's Travel Agency</TITLE>
</HEAD>
<BODY>

<IMG SRC="mltravel.gif" ALT="M and L's Travel Agency">

<P><I>We get you there!</I></P>

<P>For more than 15 years, M and L's Travel Agency has helped customers
plan exciting  adventures to destinations around the world. We
specialize in one-of-a-kind vacation  packages for all interests and
budgets. Let us help you with your airline tickets, hotel bookings, and
rental cars, either online or in person.</P>

<IMG SRC="lake.jpg" ALIGN="left" >
<IMG SRC="sedona.jpg" ALIGN="left">

<BR CLEAR="all"><BR><BR>

<P>Download a set of images from top adventure destinations! The set has
been saved as a single .zip file.</P>
```

2 Type `<A HREF="?">`, replacing ? with the relative path and name of the file.

3 Type `</A>` at the end of the link text.

```
link_other.html - WordPad
File  Edit  View  Insert  Format  Help
<HTML>
<HEAD>
<TITLE>M and L's Travel Agency</TITLE>
</HEAD>
<BODY>

<IMG SRC="mltravel.gif" ALT="M and L's Travel Agency">

<P><I>We get you there!</I></P>

<P>For more than 15 years, M and L's Travel Agency has helped customers
plan exciting  adventures to destinations around the world. We
specialize in one-of-a-kind vacation  packages for all interests and
budgets. Let us help you with your airline tickets, hotel bookings, and
rental cars, either online or in person.</P>

<IMG SRC="lake.jpg" ALIGN="left" >
<IMG SRC="sedona.jpg" ALIGN="left">

<BR CLEAR="all"><BR><BR>

<P>Download a <A HREF="topimages.zip">set of images</A> from top
adventure destinations! The set has been saved as a single .zip file.
</P>
```

M and L's Travel Agency

We get you there!

For more than 15 years, M and L's Travel Agency has helped customers plan exciting adventures to destinations around the world. We specialize in one-of-a-kind vacation packages for all interests and budgets. Let us help you with your airline tickets, hotel bookings, and rental cars, either online or in person.

Download a set of images from top adventure destinations! The set has been saved as a single .zip file.

M and L's Travel Agency

We get you there!

For more than 15 years, M and L's Travel Agency has helped customers plan exciting adventures to destinations around the world. We specialize in one-of-a-kind vacation packages for all interests and budgets. Let us help you with your airline tickets, hotel bookings, and rental cars, either online or in person.

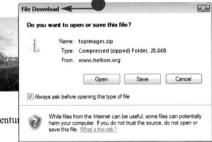

Download a set of images from top adventu... .zip file.

● The link appears on the Web page.

When the link is clicked, the browser may display the file in the browser window.

Note: To open the file in a new window, see the section "Open a New Window with a Link."

● If the browser cannot open the file, a File Download dialog box may appear that allows the user to download the file to his or her computer.

Simplify It

Can I include links to plain text files?
Yes, and most browsers can open and display such files. Because browsers do not read plain text files as HTML files, browsers display the text unformatted and without inline images or other features. This can be useful if you want to deliver raw text data that viewers can easily save in their browser.

What happens if the user cannot download or open the file?
If the user encounters problems accessing a non-HTML file, his or her browser or computer may display an error message. To help with possible problems that might occur, be sure to include information about the file format and size on the Web page; also include links to any useful tools that can help the user work with the file. For example, if the link is to a PDF file, include a link to the Adobe Web site where the user can download the Adobe Reader program, which can read PDFs.

Link to an E-mail Address

You can create a link in your Web page that allows users to send an e-mail message. In most browsers, clicking an e-mail link opens a new message in the default e-mail client program. The user can fill out a subject and message and then send the information to the address specified in the link. Adding e-mail links is a good way to solicit feedback and questions from your Web site visitors. An alternative way to allow users to send you information is with a form. See Chapter 8 for details about forms.

Link to an E-mail Address

1 Type the text you want to use as an e-mail link.

It is standard practice to use the e-mail address as the text link.

```
link_mail.html - WordPad
File  Edit  View  Insert  Format  Help
<HTML>
<HEAD>
<TITLE>M and L's Travel Agency</TITLE>
</HEAD>
<BODY>

<IMG SRC="mltravel.gif" ALT="M and L's Travel Agency">

<P>For more than 15 years, M and L's Travel Agency has helped customers
plan exciting  adventures to destinations around the world. We
specialize in one-of-a-kind vacation  packages for all interests and
budgets. Let us help you with your airline tickets, hotel bookings, and
rental cars, either online or in person.</P>

<IMG SRC="lake.jpg" ALIGN="left" >
<IMG SRC="sedona.jpg" ALIGN="left">
<IMG SRC="canyon.jpg" ALIGN="left">

<BR CLEAR="all"><BR><BR>

<P>Contact us at:
info@mandltravel.com</P>
```

2 In front of the link text, type `<A HREF="mailto:?">`, replacing ? with the e-mail address you want to use.

3 Type `</A>` at the end of the link text.

```
link_mail.html - WordPad
File  Edit  View  Insert  Format  Help
<HTML>
<HEAD>
<TITLE>M and L's Travel Agency</TITLE>
</HEAD>
<BODY>

<IMG SRC="mltravel.gif" ALT="M and L's Travel Agency">

<P>For more than 15 years, M and L's Travel Agency has helped customers
plan exciting  adventures to destinations around the world. We
specialize in one-of-a-kind vacation  packages for all interests and
budgets. Let us help you with your airline tickets, hotel bookings, and
rental cars, either online or in person.</P>

<IMG SRC="lake.jpg" ALIGN="left" >
<IMG SRC="sedona.jpg" ALIGN="left">
<IMG SRC="canyon.jpg" ALIGN="left">

<BR CLEAR="all"><BR><BR>

<P>Contact us at:
<A HREF="mailto:info@mandltravel.com">info@mandltravel.com</A></P>
```

M and L's Travel Agency

For more than 15 years, M and L's Travel Agency has helped customers plan exciting adventures to destinations around the world. We specialize in one-of-a-kind vacation packages for all interests and budgets. Let us help you with your airline tickets, hotel bookings, and rental cars, either online or in person.

Contact us at: info@mandltravel.com

● The link appears in the Web browser.

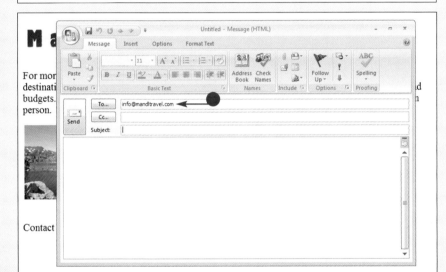

● When the link is clicked, the user's e-mail editor opens with the To field prefilled with the e-mail address.

Simplify It

Can I specify a subject for an e-mail message?
Yes. You can use the ?subject parameter within the link tag to include a subject line with the e-mail message. When the user clicks the link and the e-mail client opens, the subject area is prefilled. You can use this technique to help recognize e-mail generated from your Web site. For example:

```
<A HREF="MAILTO:webmaster@
example.com ?subject=
comments">E-mail a comment</>
```

Is it safe to use my e-mail address in a link?
You should use caution when placing a personal e-mail address on a Web page. E-mail addresses on Web pages are notorious magnets for unsolicited e-mail because such addresses can be harvested automatically by spamming tools that crawl the Web. For this reason, you may want to create a separate e-mail account just for your Web-generated e-mail messages. See your Internet service provider for more information.

Change Link Colors

You can control the color of links on a page. Links can appear as different colors depending on whether they have or have not been clicked before. You can also define the color that a link turns when a user clicks it.

You assign link colors in the `<BODY>` tag. Use the `LINK` attribute to assign a color to unclicked links. Use the `ALINK` attribute, which stands for active link, to specify the color that appears when a link is being clicked. Use the `VLINK` attribute, which stands for visited link, to change the color of previously clicked links.

Change Link Colors

1 Click within the `<BODY>` tag and type `LINK="?"`, replacing *?* with the color value you want to apply to the unselected links on your page.

Note: *To learn more about HTML color, see Chapter 4.*

2 Type an empty space.

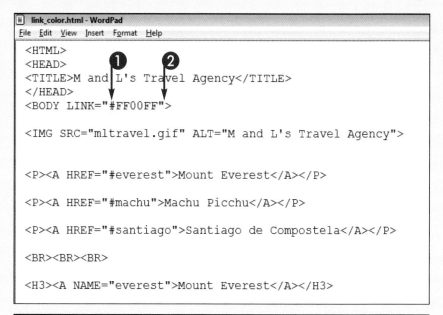

3 Type `ALINK="?"`, replacing *?* with the color value you want to apply to active links on your page.

4 Type an empty space.

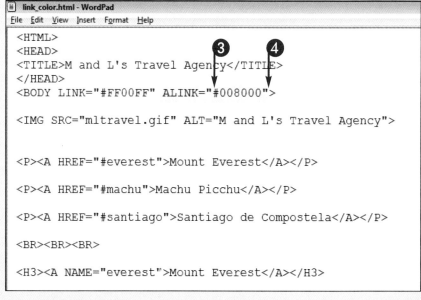

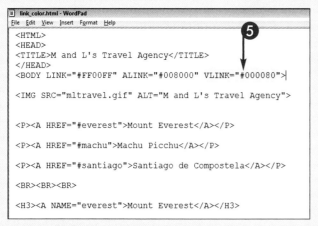

```
<HTML>
<HEAD>
<TITLE>M and L's Travel Agency</TITLE>
</HEAD>
<BODY LINK="#FF00FF" ALINK="#008000" VLINK="#000080">

<IMG SRC="mltravel.gif" ALT="M and L's Travel Agency">


<P><A HREF="#everest">Mount Everest</A></P>

<P><A HREF="#machu">Machu Picchu</A></P>

<P><A HREF="#santiago">Santiago de Compostela</A></P>

<BR><BR><BR>

<H3><A NAME="everest">Mount Everest</A></H3>
```

5 Type VLINK=" ? ", replacing *?* with the color value you want to apply to the previously selected links on your page.

● The browser displays the links in the colors you chose.

Note: *To learn how to change link colors using CSS, see Chapter 10.*

Can I type color names rather than hexadecimal values?

Yes. You can use any of the 16 Web-safe colors by name rather than by hexadecimal value to change link colors. For example, you can type:

```
<BODY LINK="teal" VLINK="gray"
ALINK="red">
```

and achieve the same effect as typing:

```
<BODY LINK="#008080" VLINK="#808080"
ALINK="#FF0000">
```

For a list of color names and their hexadecimal values, see Chapter 4.

How do I remove underlines from my text links?

You can remove the underlining that browsers apply to links using Cascading Style Sheets, or CSS. CSS gives you greater formatting controls for your Web page text. To learn more about CSS, see Chapter 10.

Chapter 7

Working with Tables

Are you looking for a way to organize data on your Web page into rows and columns? Or to divide your page into sections for placing headers, footers, and navigation links? This chapter shows you how to use HTML tables to do all of this. You create tables using an outer <TABLE> tag and various other tags within it. A <TR> tag defines a row in a table, and <TD> tags define

data cells within the row. In addition to organizing data with tables, you can add color or background images behind the data in tables.

Understanding Table Structure

HTML tables enable you to effectively present large amounts of data in rows and columns. Tables can include text, images, and multimedia. For example, you can use tables to display a company's sales results or a grid of photos in an online photo gallery. You can also use tables to organize the overall structure of a Web page. For example, you can create a two-column table that organizes a list of navigational links in one column and the main text and image content in another.

Table Structure

Every table is basically a rectangle containing rows and columns. The places where the columns and rows intersect are called *cells*. Each cell can hold Web page content. Using HTML attributes, you can set the size of an entire table as well as the size of particular cells. You can also turn borders of a table and its cells on or off, depending on whether you want to draw attention to the table's structure.

Cell Spanning

Cells can span two or more columns or rows to form bigger containers for data. For example, a table may include a title cell at the top that spans multiple columns across the table (●), or one that extends downward across several rows. When you span cells in a table, interior cell walls disappear to create larger cells.

Traditional Tables

You can use a traditional table, like the table shown here, on a Web page to present data in a tabular format. For example, you might insert a table to hold a list of products and prices or to display a class roster. You can set a fixed width and height for the table to make it fit in with the rest of the page content.

Temperature Extremes in Mexico

City	Temperature (°C)	
	Low	High
Acapulco	11	40.5
Ciudad Victoria	-6.1	46
Guadalajara	-5.5	39.6
La Paz	-0.6	43.1
Mexicali	-8	52
Mexico City	-4.4	33.9
Monterrey City	-8.5	46.5

Presentation Tables

You can use a presentation-style table to showcase the content on the page in interesting ways. Instead of defining an exact size, you can specify a table size using percentages. Whenever the user resizes his or her browser window, the table resizes as well. This allows for a more "liquid" layout. This type of table is good for page layouts as well as data tables. See "Create Newspaper-Style Columns" for an example of a presentation table.

M and L's Travel Agency

Popular Travel Adventures

At 29,029 feet, **Mount Everest** is the highest mountain on earth when measured from sea level to summit. Each year, hundreds of mountaineers climb the mountain, which is located in the Himalaya range on the border of Nepal and Tibet. Many climbers use bottled oxygen to compensate for the thin Himalayan air.

Located in the Peruvian Andes, the ancient Inca city of **Machu Picchu** was constructed in the 1400s at the height of the Inca Empire. It was abandoned less than 100 years later when the Inca empire collapsed under Spanish conquest. Today Machu Picchu is the most visited tourist attraction in Peru.

Located in the Galicia region of northwest Spain, **Santiago de Compostela** marks the end of the famous medieval pilgrimage route, the Way of St. James. Each year, tens of thousands of Christian pilgrims spend weeks or months traveling by foot, bicycle and even donkey along the route from the south of France. They finish at Santiago's cathedral where, legend has it, the remains of St. James are buried.

Table Elements

The building blocks of HTML tables are the <TABLE>, <TR>, and <TD> tags. The <TABLE> element defines the table itself. The <TR> tag defines a table row. The <TD> tag defines the table data, or cell content, within each row. In addition to these codes, you can assign table headers, adjust the alignment of data, and add background colors and images.

Table Borders

You can control the width of the borders in your table using a BORDER attribute. To turn off borders, you can set the BORDER value to 0, or leave the attribute unset because no borders is the default in most browsers. Visible borders can be useful for traditional data tables to show where cells begin and end (●). For presentation tables, you can turn borders off so as not to call attention to the underlying page structure (●).

Table Backgrounds

Table backgrounds can help delineate table cell structure just like borders. You can use a different color in table heading cells to set off those cells from the data cells. In presentation tables, background colors can set off headers, navigation, and footer sections of a page from the main content. You can also add background images to a table just as you can to an entire Web page.

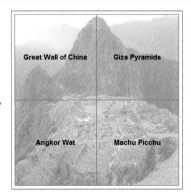

Great Wall of China · Giza Pyramids

Angkor Wat · Machu Picchu

Add a Table

You can insert a table onto your page to organize data or control the page layout. HTML tables are made up of cells arranged into rows and columns. You can assign different page elements to different cells to control the positioning of those elements on the page.

Cells can hold text, images, and other Web page content. You define the placement of a table on a page with the <TABLE> tag. Inside the <TABLE> tag, you can define rows with the <TR> tag and data cells within those rows with <TD> tags.

Add a Table

① Type <TABLE> where you want to insert a table.

② Type <TR> to start the first row in the table.

To make it easier to distinguish between rows, type each row tag on a new line.

③ Type <TD> for the first cell you want to create.

④ Type the cell data.

Note: If you want your first row to include bold column labels, you can use the <TH> tag instead of <TD>. See the section "Add Column Labels" to learn more.

⑤ Type </TD> to complete the cell.

⑥ Repeat steps **3** to **5** to add cells.

To make it easier to distinguish between cells, you can place each cell on a new line in your HTML document.

⑦ Type </TR> at the end of the first row.

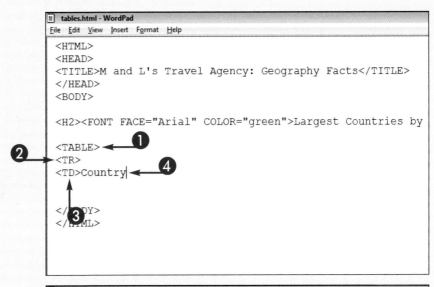

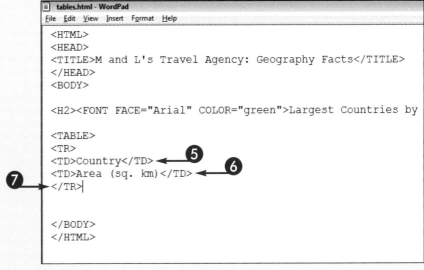

```
<H2><FONT FACE="Arial" COLOR="green">Largest Countries by

<TABLE>
<TR>
<TD>Country</TD>
<TD>Area (sq. km)</TD>
</TR>
<TR>
<TD>Russia</TD>
<TD>17,075,400</TD>
</TR>
<TR>
<TD>Canada</TD>
<TD>9,976,140</TD>
</TR>
<TR>
<TD>United States</TD>
<TD>9,629,091</TD>
</TR>
</TABLE>
```

⑧ Continue adding rows and cell data as needed.

⑨ Type </TABLE> at the end of the table data.

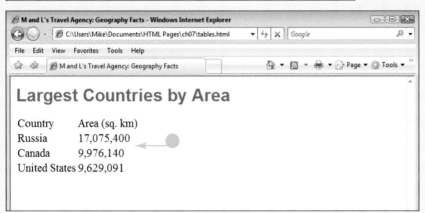

The Web browser displays the data in a tabular format.

● In this example, the table cells need some padding and spacing or borders.

Note: See the sections "Assign a Table Border" and "Adjust Cell Padding and Spacing" to learn more.

How do I set a size for a table?
You can set the dimensions of a table as exact pixel values or as percentages of the browser window using the <TABLE> tag's WIDTH and HEIGHT attributes. If you want to set a fixed size and have the entire table width visible in browsers, set the width at 750 pixels or less because most users surf the Web with their monitors set to at least 800 pixels in width. For more information, see the section "Adjust the Table Size."

What is the best way to build a table?
Before you start coding your table, draw it out on paper to organize the cell contents, designate column headers and rows, and determine its general layout and size. When you are ready to begin coding, start by typing the tags to define the table structure, putting numbers in the cells as placeholders. You can check the structure in a Web browser to see how it looks and then return to your editor and start filling in the real cell data.

Assign a Table Border

Table borders make your cells easier to distinguish and give the table a visible structure on a page. A border is simply a line that appears around the table as well as around each cell within the table. By default, a table does not have a border unless you specify one. You can use the BORDER attribute to turn table borders on or off.

When you set a border thickness, it applies only to the outer edge of the table, not to the cells within the table. Border thickness is measured in pixels. Borders appear gray unless you specify a color. See the section "Adjust Cell Padding and Spacing" to learn how to control interior borders.

Assign a Table Border

1 In the `<TABLE>` tag, type `BORDER="?"`, replacing ? with the value for the border thickness you want to set.

Note: See the section "Add a Table" to learn how to create a basic table.

```
tables-borders.html - WordPad
File  Edit  View  Insert  Format  Help

<H2><FONT FACE="Arial" COLOR="green">Largest Countries by

<TABLE BORDER="5">
<TR>
<TD>Rank</TD>
<TD>Country</TD>
<TD>Area (sq. km)</TD>
</TR>
<TR>
<TD>1</TD>
<TD>Russia</TD>
<TD>17,075,400</TD>
</TR>
<TR>
<TD>2</TD>
<TD>Canada</TD>
<TD>9,976,140</TD>
</TR>
```

2 To set a border color, type `BORDERCOLOR="?"` in the `<TABLE>` tag, replacing ? with the color value you want to apply.

```
tables-borders.html - WordPad
File  Edit  View  Insert  Format  Help

<H2><FONT FACE="Arial" COLOR="green">Largest Countries by

<TABLE BORDER="5" BORDERCOLOR="red">
<TR>
<TD>Rank</TD>
<TD>Country</TD>
<TD>Area (sq. km)</TD>
</TR>
<TR>
<TD>1</TD>
<TD>Russia</TD>
<TD>17,075,400</TD>
</TR>
<TR>
<TD>2</TD>
<TD>Canada</TD>
<TD>9,976,140</TD>
</TR>
```

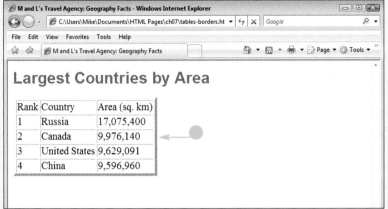

● In this example, the browser displays a table with a default gray border.

● In this example, the browser displays the same table with a colored border.

Can I specify a border with a style sheet?
Yes. In your style sheet, type TABLE or TD. Then type {BORDER: VALUES}, replacing *VALUES* with a border size (in pixels), border style, and border color, separating the values with spaces. For example, to create a 1-pixel, solid-red border, type {BORDER: 1px solid red}. See Chapter 10 to learn more about applying borders with style sheets.

Do I need to add borders if I am using a table as a layout for my Web page?
No. It is usually not a good idea to use the BORDER attribute for presentation tables. With a presentation table, you want the table structure to define different sections of the page invisibly. If you assign a border, a browser adds a border to every section, which can distract from your page content.

Adjust Cell Padding and Spacing

You can use padding to add space between the border and the contents of a cell. Padding can make table content more legible. You can use spacing to increase the border size or distance between cells. Increasing the spacing can add emphasis to the borders when you have borders turned on. Padding and spacing size is measured in pixels. If you leave padding and spacing attributes out, most browsers add 1 pixel of padding and 2 pixels of spacing by default.

SET CELL PADDING

1 In the `<TABLE>` tag, type `CELLPADDING="?"`, replacing *?* with the pixel value you want to assign.

● In this example, a table border is turned on to show the padding more clearly.

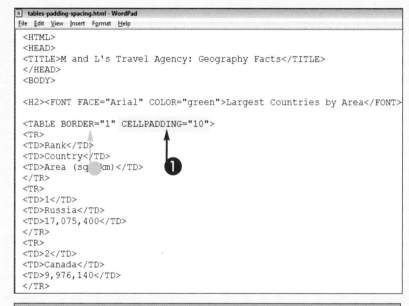

● The Web browser displays the designated amount of space between the cell contents and the cell borders.

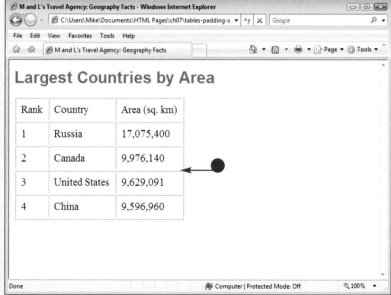

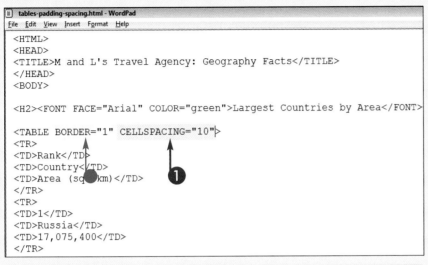

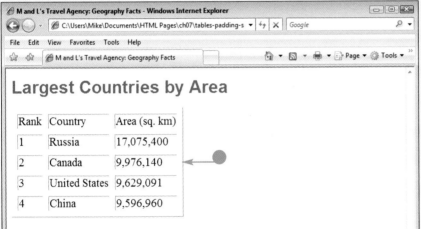

SET CELL SPACING

1 In the `<TABLE>` tag, type `CELLSPACING="?"`, replacing *?* with the pixel value you want to assign.

● In this example, a table border is turned on to clearly show the spacing.

● The Web browser displays the designated amount of space for the cell borders.

What happens if I set the spacing and padding values to 0?
If you set the CELLSPACING and CELLPADDING values to 0, the browser removes any spacing or padding between the cells. You may use this technique to make images in adjacent cells appear as a single image. You can set the BORDER attribute to 0 as well to remove the border between cells. Most browsers also remove the border if you leave the BORDER attribute unspecified.

How do I control the padding on just one side of a cell?
The CELLPADDING attribute applies padding to all sides of cells equally. To control padding on just one side of a cell, you can apply a style rule to a `<TD>` tag using style sheets. For example, you can apply 10 pixels of padding to the top of a table cell using the `padding-top` property. See Chapter 11 for information on controlling padding with style sheets.

Adjust Cell Width and Height

You can control a cell's width using the WIDTH attribute and its height using the HEIGHT attribute. This enables you to allocate more space to columns or rows that have more content. If you do not set a specific width or height, the content of the cell determines the cell's size.

You can specify dimensions using a pixel value or using a percentage relative to the width or height of the overall table. You can also specify the height and width of the overall table. See the section "Adjust the Table Size" for details.

Adjust Cell Width and Height

SET CELL WIDTH

1 In the <TD> tag, type WIDTH="?", replacing ? with the value or percentage you want to set for the cell.

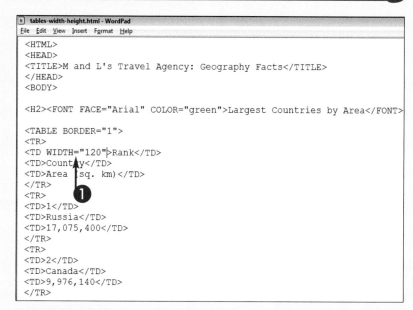

● The Web browser displays a set width for the cell, as well as for all the other cells in the same column.

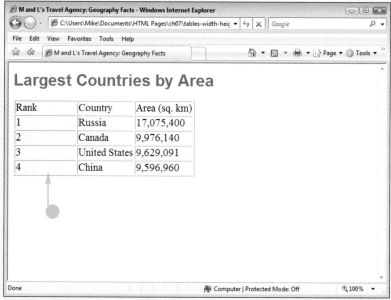

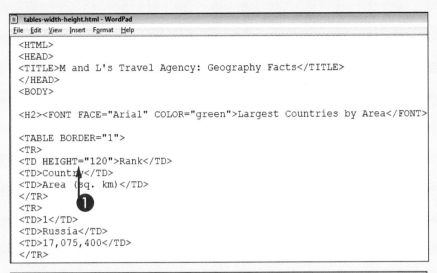

SET CELL HEIGHT

1 In the `<TD>` tag, type `HEIGHT="?"`, replacing *?* with the pixel value or percentage you want to set for the cell.

Note: *See the section "Adjust the Table Size" to set the height of the entire table.*

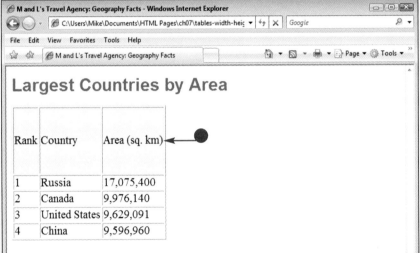

● The Web browser displays a set height for the cell, as well as for all the other cells in the same row.

If I want to precisely control the dimensions in my table, do I need to set a width and height for all the cells?
If you have a table with more than one cell, no. Setting a width of one cell also sets the width for all the cells above or below, and setting the height of a cell also sets the height for all the cells to the left or right. Because of this, you only need to set the width or height once for each row or column.

Can I set the width for a single cell and not have it affect the other cells?
When you change the width of a cell, all the cells in the same column adjust to the same width. If you want one cell to span one or more columns, you can use another set of codes to control the individual cell width. See the section "Extend Cells across Columns and Rows" to learn more.

Add Column Labels

If you are building a table to populate with data, you can add descriptive labels, also called *headers*, to the top of each column using the `<TH>` tag. For example, if your table lists products and prices, your column headers might include labels such as Product Number, Product Name, and Price. You can also add headers to the cells on the sides to label the rows of a table. Column headers appear in bold type and are centered within each cell.

① Type `<TH>` after the `<TR>` tag for the row you want to use as your column labels.

Note: *See the section "Add a Table" to learn how to create a basic table.*

② Type label text for the first column.

③ Type `</TH>` at the end of the label.

④ Repeat steps **1** to **3** to add as many column labels as you need, ending the row with the `</TR>` tag.

● The Web browser displays the labels as column headers in the table.

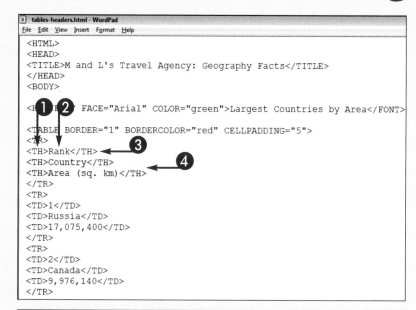

Add a Background Color to Cells

You can add color to individual cells in your table or to certain rows and columns. You can use background color to draw attention to the cell contents or to distinguish header cells from data cells.

When applying a background color, be careful not to choose a color that makes the table data difficult to read. See Chapter 4 to learn more about setting color values in HTML. You can apply a background color to an entire table by adding a BGCOLOR attribute to the <TABLE> tag.

Add a Background Color to Cells

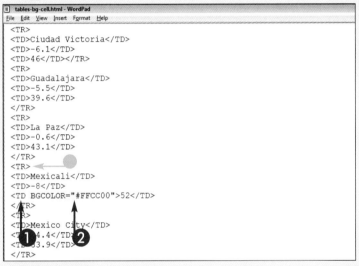

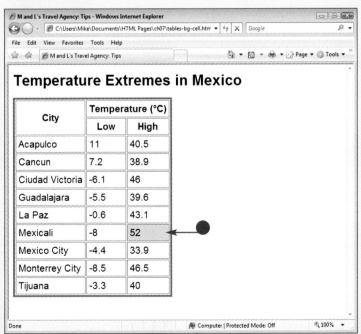

① Click the tag for the cell or row to which you want to add a background color.

② Type BGCOLOR="?", replacing ? with the color value you want to assign.

Note: See Chapter 4 to learn more about assigning color values.

● To add color to a row, you can add the color attribute to the <TR> tag.

The Web browser displays the background color in the cell, row, or column.

● In this example, a color is added to a single cell.

Insert a Background Image

You can add a background image to appear behind your entire table. Background images can give your table a more interesting design by complementing the data that appears in the table cells.

When using an image as a background, be careful the design and colors do not clash with the table data or make it illegible. You may need to change the text color to make the text stand out from the underlying background image or lighten the image in an image editor. See Chapter 4 to learn how to assign color to text.

Insert a Background Image

① Click in the <TABLE> tag and type BACKGROUND="?", replacing *?* with the name and path to the image file you want to use.

Note: *See Chapter 5 to learn how to add and work with images.*

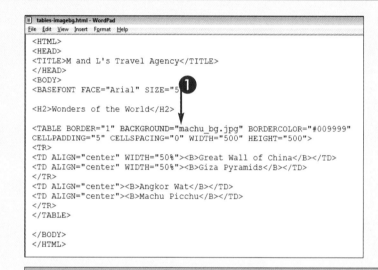

● The Web browser displays the table with the specified background image.

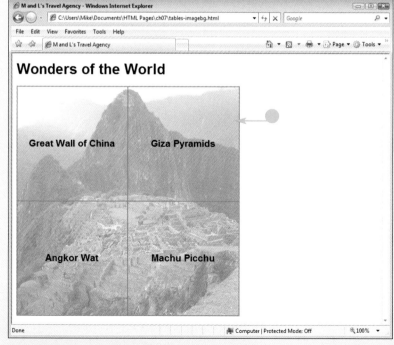

Create Newspaper-Style Columns

You can use the table format to present columns of text on your Web page, much like a newspaper. For example, you may want to organize your text into two or three columns. Paragraphs of text are contained within each column. This is an example of using a table for presentation purposes — that is, to lay out sections of content on the page. You can use the vertical alignment attribute to make each column align at the top of the table.

Create Newspaper-Style Columns

① Within the `<TR>` and `</TR>` tags, type `<TD VALIGN="top">` to start the first column of text.

Note: *See the section "Add a Table" to learn how to create a basic table.*

● You can optionally specify a `WIDTH` attribute to constrain a column's width.

② Type your column text.

③ Type `</TD>` at the end of the text.

④ Repeat steps **1** to **3** to add more columns and text.

The Web browser displays the text as columns on the page.

Adjust the Table Size

You can control the exact size of a table using the `WIDTH` and `HEIGHT` attributes in the `<TABLE>` tag. You can specify a table size in pixels or set the size as a percentage of the browser window.

When setting a width in pixels, limit the value to 750 pixels or less to ensure the table fits on the screen. If you prefer a more flexible table, set the size as a percentage. This allows the table to be resized if the browser window is resized.

Adjust the Table Size

SET A TABLE SIZE IN PIXELS

1 In the `<TABLE>` tag, type `WIDTH="?"`, replacing *?* with the pixel value you want to assign.

2 Type a space.

3 Type `HEIGHT="?"`, replacing *?* with the pixel value you want to assign.

Note: *The* `HEIGHT` *attribute is not as well supported as the* `WIDTH` *attribute and may not display properly in all browsers.*

● The Web browser displays the table at the specified size.

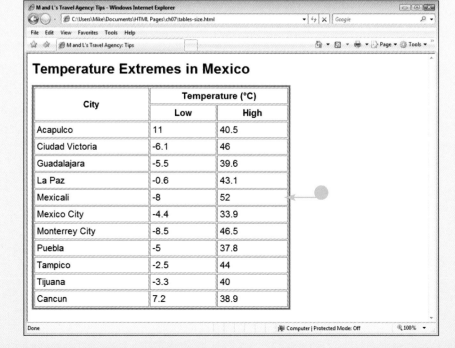

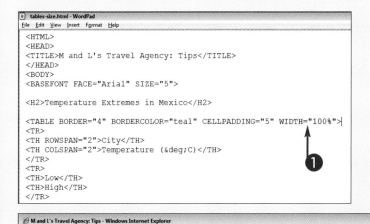

```
<HTML>
<HEAD>
<TITLE>M and L's Travel Agency: Tips</TITLE>
</HEAD>
<BODY>
<BASEFONT FACE="Arial" SIZE="5">

<H2>Temperature Extremes in Mexico</H2>

<TABLE BORDER="4" BORDERCOLOR="teal" CELLPADDING="5" WIDTH="100%">
<TR>
<TH ROWSPAN="2">City</TH>
<TH COLSPAN="2">Temperature (&deg;C)</TH>
</TR>
<TR>
<TH>Low</TH>
<TH>High</TH>
</TR>
```

SET A TABLE SIZE AS A PERCENTAGE

1 In the `<TABLE>` tag, type `WIDTH="?"`, replacing *?* with the percentage value you want to assign.

You can add a height setting if your table needs one by typing `HEIGHT="?"` in the `<TABLE>` tag.

Note: *The* `HEIGHT` *attribute is not as well supported as the* `WIDTH` *attribute and may not display properly in all browsers.*

● The Web browser displays the table at the specified size.

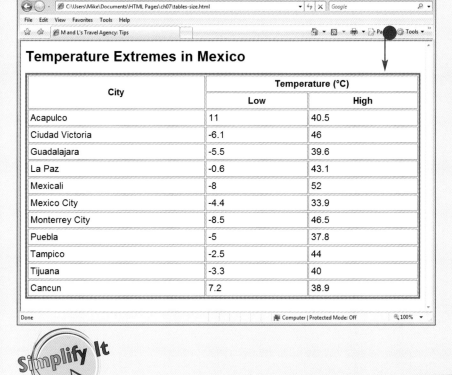

Temperature Extremes in Mexico

City	Temperature (°C)	
	Low	High
Acapulco	11	40.5
Ciudad Victoria	-6.1	46
Guadalajara	-5.5	39.6
La Paz	-0.6	43.1
Mexicali	-8	52
Mexico City	-4.4	33.9
Monterrey City	-8.5	46.5
Puebla	-5	37.8
Tampico	-2.5	44
Tijuana	-3.3	40
Cancun	7.2	38.9

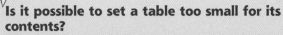

Simplify It

Is it possible to set a table too small for its contents?
No. If you accidentally set a size too small for the contents, the browser ignores the measurements and tries to make the table fit as best it can. On the other hand, if you set a table too wide, users can be forced to scroll to see parts of the table. For best results, do not make your table wider than 750 pixels.

To what size does a browser set my table if I do not specify an exact width?
If you do not set a width using the `WIDTH` attribute, the browser sizes the table based on the cell contents. When text is in the table, the browser expands a table far enough to fit its largest contents, but not past the right edge of the browser window. If a table contains large images, it may have to extend beyond the browser's viewing area to accommodate the images.

Change Cell Alignment

You can control the alignment of data within your table cells using the `ALIGN` and `VALIGN` attributes. The `ALIGN` attribute controls horizontal alignment: left, center, and right. By default, all table data you enter into cells is left-aligned. The `VALIGN` attribute controls vertical alignment: top, middle, and bottom. By default, the table data is vertically aligned to appear in the middle of each cell.

You can add alignment attributes to a single cell, a row, or all the data in the table. To learn how to position a table on the page, see the section "Change Table Alignment."

Change Cell Alignment

SET HORIZONTAL ALIGNMENT

① Click inside the tag for the cell, row, or table you want to align.

② Type `ALIGN="?"`, replacing *?* with the horizontal alignment attribute: `left`, `center`, or `right`.

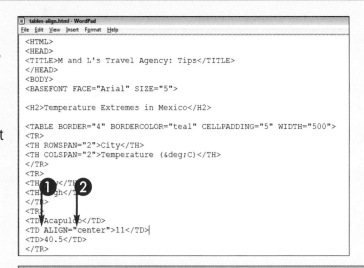

The Web browser displays the table with the specified alignment.

● In this example, the contents of a single cell are centered.

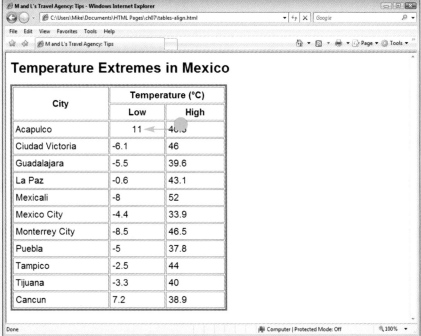

```
<HTML>
<HEAD>
<TITLE>M and L's Travel Agency: Tips</TITLE>
</HEAD>
<BODY>
<BASEFONT FACE="Arial" SIZE="5">

<H2>Temperature Extremes in Mexico</H2>

<TABLE BORDER="1" BORDERCOLOR="teal" CELLPADDING="5" WIDTH="500">
<TR>
<TH ROWSPAN="2" VALIGN="bottom">City</TH>
<TH COLSPAN="2">Temperature (&deg;C)</TH>
</TR>
<TR>
<TH>Low</TH>
<TH>High</TH>
</TR>
```

SET VERTICAL ALIGNMENT

1 Click inside the tag for the cell or row you want to align.

2 Type VALIGN="?", replacing *?* with the horizontal alignment attribute: top, middle, or bottom.

The Web browser displays the table with the specified alignment.

● In this example, a single column heading is bottom-aligned.

Temperature Extremes in Mexico

City	Temperature (°C)	
	Low	High
Acapulco	11	40.5
Ciudad Victoria	-6.1	46
Guadalajara	-5.5	39.6
La Paz	-0.6	43.1
Mexicali	-8	52
Mexico City	-4.4	33.9
Monterrey City	-8.5	46.5
Puebla	-5	37.8
Tampico	-2.5	44
Tijuana	-3.3	40
Cancun	7.2	38.9

Simplify It

How do I justify data in a table cell?
Justification sets both left and right alignment and stretches the text to span the area between the cell borders. Although there is an ALIGN value for justification, justify, not all Web browsers currently support the setting.

The empty cells in my bordered table look broken. What can I do about this?
If you put no data or blank spaces inside a <TD> or <TH> tag, some browsers do not display the border for that cell. This can make the table look broken. You can fix this by adding a , or *non-breaking space,* to the empty tag. This forces the browser to display a border for the empty cell. For more about   and other special characters, see Chapter 3.

Extend Cells across Columns and Rows

You can create a larger cell in your table by extending the cell across two or more columns or rows. The ability to span cells, also called *merging cells*, allows you to create unique cell structures within your table. For example, you might include a large cell across the top of a table to hold a heading or an image. For presentation tables, you might include a long cell down the side of a table to create an area for navigation.

Extend Cells across Columns and Rows

EXTEND CELLS ACROSS COLUMNS

1 Click inside the tag for the cell you want to extend across columns.

2 Type COLSPAN="?", replacing *?* with the number of columns you want to span.

The Web browser displays the cell spanning the designated number of columns.

● In this example, a heading column spans the top of the table.

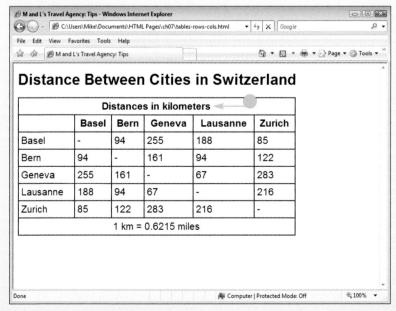

```
tables-rows-cols.html - WordPad
File  Edit  View  Insert  Format  Help
<HTML>
<HEAD>
<TITLE>M and L's Travel Agency: Tips</TITLE>
</HEAD>
<BODY>
<BASEFONT FACE="Arial" SIZE="5">

<H2>Distance Between Cities in Switzerland</H2>

<TABLE BORDER="1" BORDERCOLOR="maroon" CELLSPACING="0" CELLPADDING="5"
WIDTH="600">
  <TR>
    <TH COLSPAN="6">Distances in kilometers</TH>
  </TR>
  <TR>
    <TH> </TH>
    <TH>Basel</TH>
    <TH>Bern</TH>
    <TH>Geneva</TH>
    <TH>Lausanne</TH>
    <TH>Zurich</TH>
  </TR>
  <TR>
    <TD>Basel</TD>
    <TD>-</TD>
    <TD>94</TD>
```

Distance Between Cities in Switzerland

Distances in kilometers					
	Basel	Bern	Geneva	Lausanne	Zurich
Basel	-	94	255	188	85
Bern	94	-	161	94	122
Geneva	255	161	-	67	283
Lausanne	188	94	67	-	216
Zurich	85	122	283	216	-
1 km = 0.6215 miles					

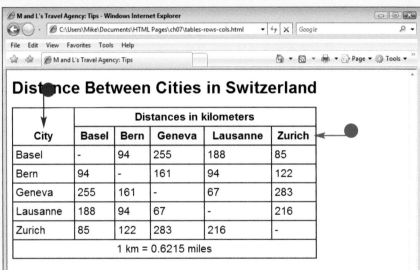

EXTEND CELLS ACROSS ROWS

① Click inside the tag for the cell you want to extend across rows.

② Type ROWSPAN="?", replacing ? with the number of rows you want to span.

If you are using the HTML from the previous example, also remove the blank data cell in the city row.

The Web browser displays the cell spanning the designated number of rows.

● In this example, a heading spans two rows at the top of the table.

● In this example, a heading also spans five columns. You can combine column and row spanning to create complex table designs.

Simplify It

Can I extend a cell across columns and rows at the same time?
Yes. If you add the COLSPAN and ROWSPAN attributes to the same row or header tag, you can make a cell span across and down in the table. Just remember to remove cells in the columns and rows that you want the current cell to span.

How can I set off a row that spans the top of my table?
You can create a title cell for a table by creating a top cell that spans all the cells beneath it. To set that cell off from the others, you can add a background color. See the section "Add a Background Color to Cells" for more information. You can also make that cell a header cell by using the <TH> tag. See the section "Add Column Labels" for details.

Change Table Alignment

You can control the positioning of a table on your Web page using the `ALIGN` attribute. You can use this attribute to center a table or align it on the left or right side of the page. The `ALIGN` attribute also determines the way in which text wraps around your table element. For example, if you align the table to the right, text wraps around the left side of the table.

Change Table Alignment

1 Click in the `<TABLE>` tag and type `ALIGN="?"`, replacing *?* with the alignment you want to apply: `left`, `right`, or `center`.

Note: *Text does not wrap around a centered table, but it does wrap around those that are left- or right-aligned.*

To stop text from wrapping, type `<BR CLEAR="?">` before the text, replacing *?* with the alignment value you want to clear.

The Web browser displays the table with wrapping text.

● In this example, the table is right-aligned, with text wrapping around the left side.

```
tables-align-table.html - WordPad
File  Edit  View  Insert  Format  Help
<HTML>
<HEAD>
<TITLE>M and L's Travel Agency</TITLE>
</HEAD>
<BODY BGCOLOR="CCFFCC">
<BASEFONT FACE="Arial" SIZE="3">

<H2>Distance Between Cities in Switzerland</H2>

<TABLE ALIGN="right" BORDER="1" CELLPADDING="5" CELLSPACING="0"
BORDERCOLOR="#339933" WIDTH="600">
  <TR>
    <TH ROWSPAN="2" VALIGN="bottom">City</TH>
    <TH COLSPAN="5">Distances in kilometers</TH>
  </TR>
  <TR>
    <TD>Basel</TD>
    <TD>Bern</TD>
    <TD>Geneva</TD>
    <TD>Lausanne</TD>
    <TD>Zurich</TD>
  </TR>
  <TR>
    <td class="bl">Basel</TD>
    <TD>-</TD>
    <TD>94</TD>
```

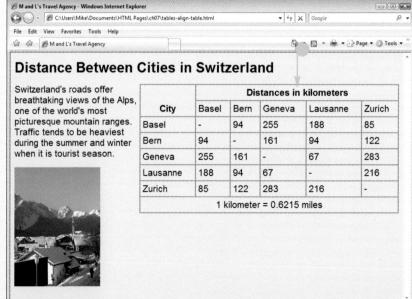

M and L's Travel Agency - Windows Internet Explorer

C:\Users\Mike\Documents\HTML Pages\ch07\tables-align-table.html

File Edit View Favorites Tools Help

M and L's Travel Agency — Page ▾ Tools ▾

Distance Between Cities in Switzerland

Switzerland's roads offer breathtaking views of the Alps, one of the world's most picturesque mountain ranges. Traffic tends to be heaviest during the summer and winter when it is tourist season.

City	Distances in kilometers				
	Basel	Bern	Geneva	Lausanne	Zurich
Basel	-	94	255	188	85
Bern	94	-	161	94	122
Geneva	255	161	-	67	283
Lausanne	188	94	67	-	216
Zurich	85	122	283	216	-
1 kilometer = 0.6215 miles					

Done — Computer | Protected Mode: Off — 100%

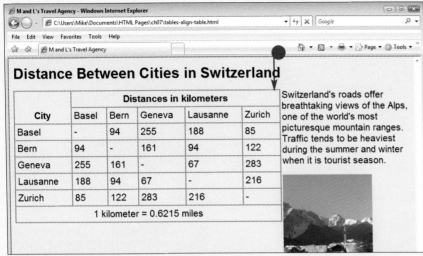

● In this example, the
left-aligned, with t
wrapping around the right
side.

Note: *If you do not specify an
alignment value, tables are left-
aligned and do not have text
wrapping.*

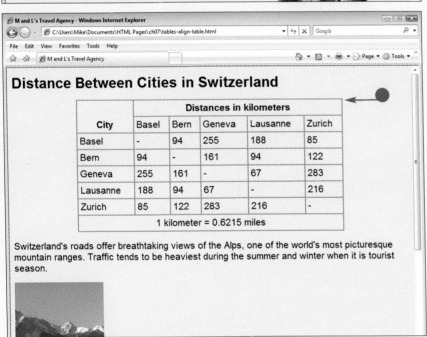

● In this example, the table is
center-aligned, and no text
wrapping occurs.

How do I control line breaks in a cell?
To create a line break in a cell, you can use the <BR> tag or the <P> tag. These are the same text formatting tags used for regular page text. See Chapters 3 and 4 to learn more about line breaks and other text formatting.

How can I indent a table from the left or right side?
You can indent a table using a style sheet rule. Apply MARGIN-LEFT to indent a left-aligned table or MARGIN-RIGHT to indent a right-aligned table. See Chapters 9, 10, and 11 to learn more about style sheets.

Chapter 8

Creating Forms

Looking for a way to allow your Web site visitors to communicate with you? This chapter shows you how to build forms that gather information from users and send it to Web servers for processing. You can build forms that allow users to send feedback about a site or buy products by submitting credit card information. To create a form, you can use a variety of input fields, including text fields, check boxes, drop-down menus, and radio buttons. The sections in this chapter describe how to add these fields and when to use them.

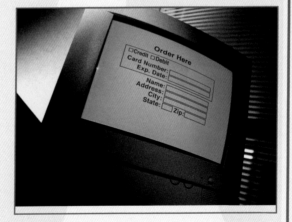

Understanding Forms

You can use forms to collect information from the people who visit your Web site. For example, you might enable visitors to send you feedback, post comments on articles, or purchase goods or services from your business. You collect information by creating an HTML form on your page. When the user submits the form information, the information is sent back to the Web server where it is processed. Forms are an important way to make a site interactive instead of just a collection of static pages with text and images.

Forms and Scripts

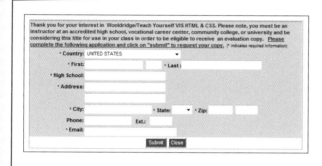

In an HTML form, input elements such as text fields, menus, and check boxes collect data from a Web site user. After a user fills in the data, he or she clicks a button to submit the form, and the browser sends the data back to the Web server. The Web server typically handles the data by processing it with a program known as a CGI script. For example, you can write CGI scripts to parse the data and send back a custom Web page in response or store the data in a database. You can examine the database to see what information users have submitted.

Implementing CGI Scripts

You can write your own CGI scripts if you know a programming language such as Perl, PHP, or Java, or you can adapt one of the many free CGI scripts available on the Web. Sites like the CGI Resource Index (http://cgi.resourceindex.com), Matt's Script Archive (www.scriptarchive.com), and HotScripts.com (www.hotscripts.com) are good places to start. Many Web hosts also make CGI scripts accessible to their customers. The place where CGI scripts are stored on a Web server is usually called a CGI-bin directory (the directory may be called something else, depending on the server).

HTML for Forms

Web page forms have three important parts: a <FORM> tag, form input elements, and a Submit button. When designing and building a form, you write HTML to define the different objects that allow users to type or select information. These objects can include text fields, radio buttons, check boxes, and more. All forms should include a Submit button for sending the data to a Web server for processing. The <FORM> tag usually specifies the script that processes the form information on the Web server.

Types of Forms

You can create different types of forms to enable different types of interaction. For example, you can create a search form that allows users to search your Web site for information by submitting keywords. You can add data-collection forms to gather information from users, such as names, postal addresses, and e-mail addresses. Your form can allow users to comment on and rate the articles posted on your Web site. You can also use forms to help customers add items to an online shopping cart and make a purchase on your site.

Confirmation

After the form data is processed, a script typically sends a confirmation HTML page back to the browser window noting whether or not the form data was sent successfully. You might also code your script so that it sends a confirmation message by e-mail. It is always good practice when collecting form data to provide visitors with a confirmation or assurance that some sort of action will be taken based on their submission.

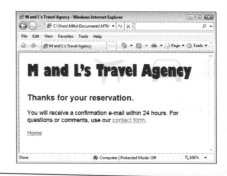

Sending Data to Databases

Another use for CGI scripts is to send form data to a database. Database systems are designed to store and manage large amounts of information. CGI scripts can translate form data from the Web server into a format readable by a database. If you plan to use your form data in conjunction with a database, you need to learn more about how databases work with the Web. Popular database systems include Microsoft SQL Server, Oracle, and MySQL.

Sending Data to an E-mail Address

If you do not want to use a CGI script, you can use a command directly in your <FORM> tag that tells a browser to send form data to an e-mail address. When a user submits the form, the browser inserts a list of field names and values in an e-mail message, which the user can then send. This option is useful only if the form is simple; more complex forms require scripts or databases to process and make sense of the information. To learn more about sending form data via e-mail, see the section "Send Form Data to an E-mail Address."

Types of Form Elements

Forms are made up of a variety of input elements. Some elements, such as text boxes, give users a way to add information in a free-form manner. Others, such as radio buttons, constrain what the user can submit. You can mix different types of input elements in a single form. At the end of a form is usually a Submit button that allows the user to send the entered information back to the Web server. A script then processes the information on the Web server.

Text Boxes

Text boxes are input fields designed specifically for users to type data into, such as typing a name or comment. A text box can be a single line to collect a limited amount of characters, such as a phone number or postal code. Text boxes can also be large, multiline fields that allow for submitting paragraphs of input. In single-line text boxes, you can control the maximum number of characters a user can type.

Radio Buttons

Radio buttons are the small, circular buttons found on forms. Like check boxes, radio buttons are used to present several choices to the user. Unlike with check boxes, however, users may select only one radio button in a set, similar to how the buttons on old automobile radios work. For example, if you include a feedback form on your page that rates your Web site, you might include radio buttons for the values Excellent, Good, Average, and Poor. The user can select only one of the four options.

Check Boxes

Check boxes enable a user to select one or more options from a list. For example, if you want to collect information about a user's familiarity with computers, you can place a set of check boxes next to a list of computer applications. When designing a form, you have the option of presenting check boxes as already checked.

Menu

A menu enables you to present a large set of choices in a form. In a drop-down menu, a user clicks a box to open a list of options from which he or she can select only one. For example, users often choose from a drop-down menu when selecting their state or country in an address form.

List

Lists are another way to present a set of choices to the user. Unlike menus, lists take up multiple lines of space on your page. They also can allow users to select more than one option by ctrl-clicking. You move through the list of items using scroll buttons located on the side of the list.

Submit Button

Users need a way to send their data to the Web server. They can do this using a Submit button, which usually appears at the end of the form input elements. Data is collected only after the user clicks this button.

Reset Button

You can add a Reset button to your HTML form that allows the user to reset all the input fields and start over. This button usually appears at the end of the form, next to the Submit button.

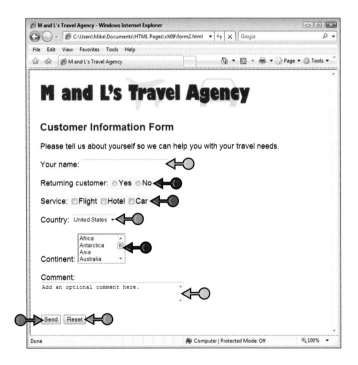

Create a Form

You can use a form to gather information from the people who visit your Web site. To create a form, you use the <FORM> tag to point to the CGI script that will process the form, define the form elements, and display a Submit button to send the data to the script.

Most forms use a CGI script to instruct the Web server to process the collected information. Consult your Web host to find out the location of a directory where you can store your script on the server. You can also forgo a CGI script and send the form data to an e-mail address. See the section "Send Form Data to an E-mail Address" to learn more.

Create a Form

① Click where you want to insert a form and type <FORM METHOD="?", replacing ? with post or get.

The type of method to use can depend on the information you are collecting or the script that processes the form data.

If you are including a file upload element in your form, use the post method.

② Type a space and ACTION="?">, replacing ? with the name and location of the CGI script you want to use to process the form data.

Note: *You may need to contact your Web host to determine the name and path of the CGI script.*

③ Type </FORM>.

You can now add input elements to your form between the <FORM> and </FORM> tags.

Note: *See the remaining sections in this chapter to learn more about adding input elements.*

```
form-create.html - WordPad
File  Edit  View  Insert  Format  Help

<HTML>
<HEAD>
<TITLE>M and L's Travel Agency</TITLE>
</HEAD>
<BODY BGCOLOR="#FFFFCC" LEFTMARGIN="25">
<BASEFONT FACE="Arial" SIZE="4">

<IMG SRC="mltravel_yellow.gif" ALT="M and L's Travel Agency">

<H2><FONT COLOR="#000066">Customer Information Form</FONT></H2>

<P>Please tell us about yourself so we can help you with your travel
</P>

<FORM METHOD="post" ACTION="cgi-bin/customer.cgi">           ②


</BODY>                     ①
</HTML>
```

```
form-create.html - WordPad
File  Edit  View  Insert  Format  Help

<HTML>
<HEAD>
<TITLE>M and L's Travel Agency</TITLE>
</HEAD>
<BODY BGCOLOR="#FFFFCC" LEFTMARGIN="25">
<BASEFONT FACE="Arial" SIZE="4">

<IMG SRC="mltravel_yellow.gif" ALT="M and L's Travel Agency">

<H2><FONT COLOR="#000066">Customer Information Form</FONT></H2>

<P>Please tell us about yourself so we can help you with your travel
</P>

<FORM METHOD="post" ACTION="cgi-bin/customer.cgi">
                            ③
</FORM>|

</BODY>
</HTML>
```

Send Form Data to an E-mail Address

You can instruct the browser to send form data to an e-mail address. When the user clicks the Submit button for the form, a new e-mail message opens in the default e-mail client. Data from the form is inserted into the e-mail message as name/value pairs, for example `month=May`.

You might use this type of form if your Web server does not support CGI scripts. Note that e-mail-based forms may not work for all users because the forms require that the browser is correctly configured to use an e-mail client and that the e-mail client supports this feature.

Send Form Data to an E-mail Address

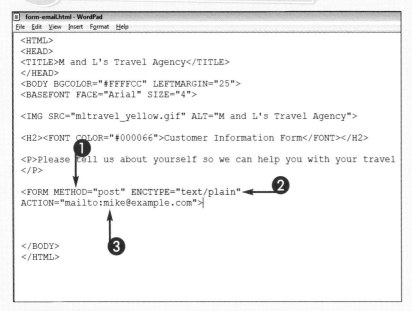

form-email.html - WordPad
File   Edit   View   Insert   Format   Help

```
<HTML>
<HEAD>
<TITLE>M and L's Travel Agency</TITLE>
</HEAD>
<BODY BGCOLOR="#FFFFCC" LEFTMARGIN="25">
<BASEFONT FACE="Arial" SIZE="4">

<IMG SRC="mltravel_yellow.gif" ALT="M and L's Travel Agency">

<H2><FONT COLOR="#000066">Customer Information Form</FONT></H2>

<P>Please tell us about yourself so we can help you with your travel
</P>

<FORM METHOD="post" ENCTYPE="text/plain"
ACTION="mailto:mike@example.com">



</BODY>
</HTML>
```

form-email.html - WordPad
File   Edit   View   Insert   Format   Help

```
<HTML>
<HEAD>
<TITLE>M and L's Travel Agency</TITLE>
</HEAD>
<BODY BGCOLOR="#FFFFCC" LEFTMARGIN="25">
<BASEFONT FACE="Arial" SIZE="4">

<IMG SRC="mltravel_yellow.gif" ALT="M and L's Travel Agency">

<H2><FONT COLOR="#000066">Customer Information Form</FONT></H2>

<P>Please tell us about yourself so we can help you with your travel
</P>

<FORM METHOD="post" ENCTYPE="text/plain"
ACTION="mailto:mike@example.com">

</FORM>

</BODY>
</HTML>
```

1 Click where you want to insert a form and type `<FORM METHOD="post"`.

2 Type a space and `ENCTYPE="text/plain"`.

3 Type a space and `ACTION="mailto:?">`, replacing *?* with the e-mail address to which you want to send the form data.

4 Type `</FORM>`.

You can now add input elements to your form between the `<FORM>` and `</FORM>` tags.

Note: *See the remaining sections in this chapter to learn more about adding input elements.*

Add a Text Box

You can add a text box to your form to allow users to type a single-line reply or response. When creating a text box, you must identify the input field with a unique name. You can also control the text box size and the maximum number of characters a user can type in the field.

By default, browsers display the text box field at a width of 20 characters. You can make the text box wider using the SIZE attribute. You can control the number of characters allowed in a text box by specifying a value with the MAXLENGTH attribute.

Add a Text Box

1 Between the <FORM> and </FORM> tags, add a new line for the text box.

2 Type <INPUT TYPE= "text".

3 Type a space and NAME="?", replacing ? with a unique identifier for the text box.

```
form-text.html - WordPad
File  Edit  View  Insert  Format  Help
<HTML>
<HEAD>
<TITLE>M and L's Travel Agency</TITLE>
</HEAD>
<BODY BGCOLOR="#FFFFCC" LEFTMARGIN="25">
<BASEFONT FACE="Arial" SIZE="4">

<IMG SRC="mltravel_yellow.gif" ALT="M and L's Travel Agency">

<H2><FONT COLOR="#000066">Customer Information Form</FONT></H2>

<P>Please tell us about yourself so we can help you with your travel
</P>

<FORM METHOD="POST" ACTION="cgi-bin/customer.cgi">

Your name:

<INPUT TYPE="text" NAME="customername"

</FORM>

</BODY>
</HTML>
```

4 Type a space and SIZE="?", replacing ? with a width in characters.

5 To define a maximum number of characters for the field, type MAXLENGTH="?">, replacing ? with the maximum number of characters allowed.

Note: *Do not forget to type a closing bracket (>) at the end of your input element tag.*

```
form-text.html - WordPad
File  Edit  View  Insert  Format  Help
<HTML>
<HEAD>
<TITLE>M and L's Travel Agency</TITLE>
</HEAD>
<BODY BGCOLOR="#FFFFCC" LEFTMARGIN="25">
<BASEFONT FACE="Arial" SIZE="4">

<IMG SRC="mltravel_yellow.gif" ALT="M and L's Travel Agency">

<H2><FONT COLOR="#000066">Customer Information Form</FONT></H2>

<P>Please tell us about yourself so we can help you with your travel
</P>

<FORM METHOD="POST" ACTION="cgi-bin/customer.cgi">

Your name:

<INPUT TYPE="text" NAME="customername" SIZE="50" MAXLENGTH="45">

</FORM>

</BODY>
</HTML>
```

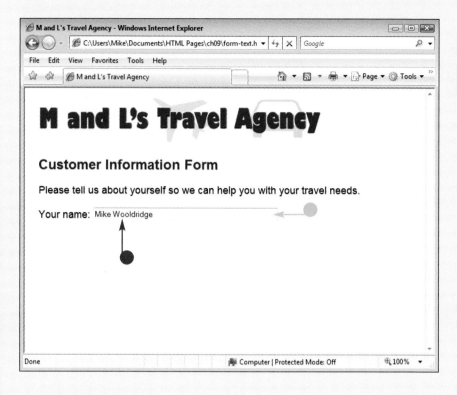

- The Web browser displays the text box in the form.

- The user can click inside the text box and type the required information.

Can I add a default value to a text box?
Yes. A default value is text that appears in the text box when the user views the form. You can use default values to display instructions about the type of data required, give users an example of the data you are looking for, or show a popular choice or response. To specify a default, you can add the VALUE attribute to the <INPUT> tag. For example:

```
<FORM METHOD="post" ACTION="/
cgi-bin/feedback.pl">

<INPUT TYPE="text" NAME=
"e-mail" VALUE="Enter your
e-mail address">

</FORM>
```

How do I create a password text box?
Password text boxes are similar to regular text boxes with one difference. Instead of displaying the characters that are typed, the input field displays the data as asterisks (*) or bullets (•). This prevents others from seeing the password text. To create a text box for password entry, you specify the password type in the <INPUT> tag. Your code might look like this:

```
<FORM METHOD="post" ACTION="/
cgi-bin/feedback.pl">

<INPUT TYPE="password"
NAME="secret" SIZE="45">

</FORM>
```

Add a Large Text Area

If your form requires a large text-entry box, you can create a large text area that holds multiple lines of text. For example, if you create a feedback form, you can use a large text area to allow users to type paragraphs of text.

When defining a text area, you can control the size of the text box and how text wraps within the field. Text area size is measured in rows and columns, with the measurement based on the number of characters that can be displayed.

Add a Large Text Area

① Between the <FORM> and </FORM> tags, add a new line for the large text box.

② Type <TEXTAREA.

③ Type a space and NAME="?", replacing ? with a unique name for the text area.

Note: You can use the <BR> or <P> tag to separate input elements onto different lines in your form.

④ Type a space and ROWS="?", replacing ? with the number of rows you want to specify to determine the height of the text area.

⑤ Type a space and COLS="?", replacing ? with a number of character columns to determine the width of the text area.

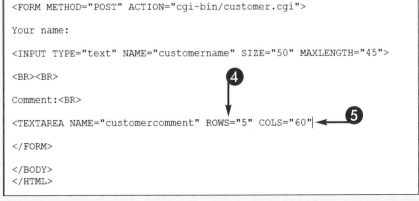

130

```
<FORM METHOD="POST" ACTION="cgi-bin/customer.cgi">

Your name:

<INPUT TYPE="text" NAME="customername" SIZE="50" MAXLENGTH="45">

<BR><BR>

Comment:<BR>

<TEXTAREA NAME="customercomment" ROWS="5" COLS="60" WRAP="hard">
Add your comment here.
</TEXTAREA>

</FORM>
```

6 Type a space and WRAP="?">, replacing *?* with a text wrap control.

soft wraps text within the text area but does not wrap text in the form results.

hard wraps text within both the text area and the form results.

off turns off text wrapping, forcing users to create new lines of text as they type.

7 Type </TEXTAREA>.

● You can add a default message between the <TEXTAREA> and </TEXTAREA> tags.

● The Web browser displays the text box in the form.

● The user can click inside the text box and type information.

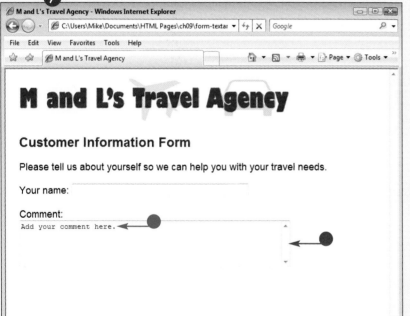

What happens if the user types more than can be viewed in the text area?
If the user types more text than is visible in the text area, scroll bars become active at the side of the text box. Scroll bars allow the user to scroll and view the text. The text area automatically holds as much text as the user needs to type, up to 32,700 characters.

Is there a way to keep users from typing text into a large text area?
Yes. You can use the READONLY attribute if you want to display default text in a text area and do not want users to move or edit the text. For example, you might use a large text area to explain something about your form or offer detailed instructions. You can place the READONLY attribute within the <TEXTAREA> tag.

Add Check Boxes

You can add check boxes to your form to allow users to select from one or more options. You might use check boxes to find out what types of services a user is interested in. When a user selects a check box and submits the form, the browser sends information associated with the check box to the Web server as a name/value pair, for example `flight=yes`. Check box values are often set to "yes" or "true" to denote that boxes were selected, but they can have other values as well.

Add Check Boxes

① Between the `<FORM>` and `</FORM>` tags, type `<INPUT TYPE= "checkbox"`.

② Type a space and `NAME="?"`, replacing *?* with a unique name for the check box.

③ Type a space and `VALUE="?">`, replacing *?* with a value to be assigned if the check box is checked.

Note: *The check box value does not appear on the form.*

④ Type the text you want to appear beside the check box.

⑤ Repeat steps **1** to **4** to create more check boxes for a group of check box options.

Note: *You can optionally use `<BR>` or `<P>` tags to separate input elements onto different lines in your form.*

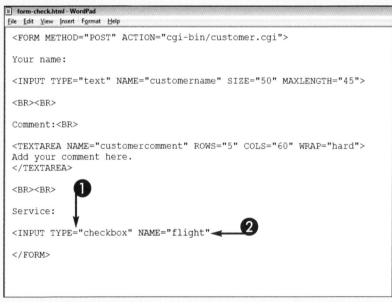

```
form-check.html - WordPad
File  Edit  View  Insert  Format  Help

<FORM METHOD="POST" ACTION="cgi-bin/customer.cgi">

Your name:

<INPUT TYPE="text" NAME="customername" SIZE="50" MAXLENGTH="45">

<BR><BR>

Comment:<BR>

<TEXTAREA NAME="customercomment" ROWS="5" COLS="60" WRAP="hard">
Add your comment here.
</TEXTAREA>

<BR><BR>

Service:

<INPUT TYPE="checkbox" NAME="flight"

</FORM>
```

```
form-check.html - WordPad
File  Edit  View  Insert  Format  Help

<FORM METHOD="POST" ACTION="cgi-bin/customer.cgi">

Your name:

<INPUT TYPE="text" NAME="customername" SIZE="50" MAXLENGTH="45">

<BR><BR>

Comment:<BR>

<TEXTAREA NAME="customercomment" ROWS="5" COLS="60" WRAP="hard">
Add your comment here.
</TEXTAREA>

<BR><BR>

Service:

<INPUT TYPE="checkbox" NAME="flight" VALUE="yes">Flight
<INPUT TYPE="checkbox" NAME="hotel" VALUE="yes">Hotel
<INPUT TYPE="checkbox" NAME="car" VALUE="yes">Car

</FORM>
```

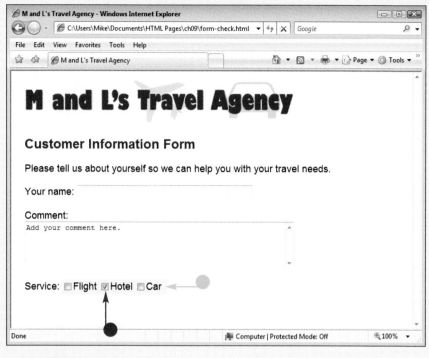

● The Web browser displays the check boxes in the form.

● The user can click the box to insert a check mark.

How do I automatically show the check box as selected?	How do I get the check boxes onto separate lines?
You can use the CHECKED attribute to show a check box as selected by default when the user views that page. You add the CHECKED attribute to the <INPUT> tag:	You can use the <P> or tag. Your code might look like this:

```
<FORM METHOD="post" ACTION="/
cgi-bin/questionnaire.pl">

<INPUT TYPE="checkbox"
NAME="newsletter" VALUE="yes"
CHECKED>

</FORM>
```

```
<FORM METHOD="post" ACTION="/
cgi-bin/questionnaire.pl">

<P>What type of movie do you
like the best?</P>

<INPUT TYPE="checkbox"
NAME="drama" VALUE="true">

<BR><INPUT TYPE="checkbox"
NAME="comedy" VALUE="true">

<BR><INPUT TYPE="checkbox"
NAME="action" VALUE="true">

</FORM>
```

Add Radio Buttons

You can use radio buttons if you want to allow users to choose only one item from a group. The user clicks a button to activate the selection. You might use radio buttons to enable users to answer yes-or-no questions in a form. When a user selects a radio button and submits the form, the browser sends information associated with the selected radio button to the Web server as a name/value pair, for example `returning=yes`.

Add Radio Buttons

① Between the <FORM> and </FORM> tags, type <INPUT TYPE="radio".

② Type a space and NAME="?", replacing ? with a unique name for the radio button group.

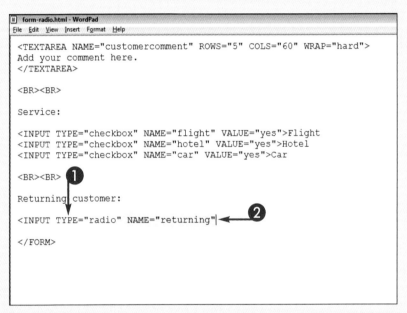

```
form-radio.html - WordPad
File  Edit  View  Insert  Format  Help

<TEXTAREA NAME="customercomment" ROWS="5" COLS="60" WRAP="hard">
Add your comment here.
</TEXTAREA>

<BR><BR>

Service:

<INPUT TYPE="checkbox" NAME="flight" VALUE="yes">Flight
<INPUT TYPE="checkbox" NAME="hotel" VALUE="yes">Hotel
<INPUT TYPE="checkbox" NAME="car" VALUE="yes">Car

<BR><BR>

Returning customer:

<INPUT TYPE="radio" NAME="returning"

</FORM>
```

③ Type a space and VALUE="?">, replacing ? with a value describing the radio button.

Note: *The radio button value does not appear on the form.*

```
form-radio.html - WordPad
File  Edit  View  Insert  Format  Help

<TEXTAREA NAME="customercomment" ROWS="5" COLS="60" WRAP="hard">
Add your comment here.
</TEXTAREA>

<BR><BR>

Service:

<INPUT TYPE="checkbox" NAME="flight" VALUE="yes">Flight
<INPUT TYPE="checkbox" NAME="hotel" VALUE="yes">Hotel
<INPUT TYPE="checkbox" NAME="car" VALUE="yes">Car

<BR><BR>

Returning customer:

<INPUT TYPE="radio" NAME="returning" VALUE="yes">

</FORM>
```

```
Service:

<INPUT TYPE="checkbox" NAME="flight" VALUE="yes">Flight
<INPUT TYPE="checkbox" NAME="hotel" VALUE="yes">Hotel
<INPUT TYPE="checkbox" NAME="car" VALUE="yes">Car

<BR><BR>

Returning customer:

<INPUT TYPE="radio" NAME="returning" VALUE="yes">Yes        4
<INPUT TYPE="radio" NAME="returning" VALUE="no">No          5
|
</FORM>
```

M and L's Travel Agency

Customer Information Form

Please tell us about yourself so we can help you with your travel needs.

Your name:

Comment:
Add your comment here.

Service: ☐Flight ☐Hotel ☐Car

Returning customer: ○ Yes ○ No

④ Type the text you want to appear beside the radio button.

⑤ Repeat steps **1** to **4** to add more radio buttons to the group, using the same name for all the buttons in a set.

Note: You can optionally use <BR> or <P> tags to separate input elements onto different lines in your form.

● The Web browser displays the radio buttons on the form.

● The user can click the radio button to select that option.

What happens if I give radio buttons in a set different names?
When radio buttons have different NAME attributes, the browser treats them as parts of different radio button sets. This means the user is able to turn more than one of them on at a time by clicking. Make sure all the radio buttons in a set have the same NAME attribute to avoid this.

Can I show a particular radio button as selected by default?
Yes. You can use the CHECKED attribute to show one radio button in the group as selected by default. The CHECKED attribute is inserted after the VALUE attribute in your HTML code. Your code might look like this:

```
<FORM METHOD="post" ACTION="/
cgi-bin/questionnaire.pl">

<INPUT TYPE="radio"
NAME="agerange" VALUE="40-50"
CHECKED>

</FORM>
```

Add a Menu

You can add a menu to a form to give users a list of choices. Menus allow you to display choices as a drop-down list that appears when the user clicks the list. By storing a long list of choices as a drop-down list, you can free up space for other input items in the form. When a user selects a menu item and submits the form, the browser sends information associated with the menu and the selected item to the Web server as a name/value pair, for example `continent=africa`.

① Between the `<FORM>` and `</FORM>` tags, type `<SELECT NAME="?"`, replacing ? with a unique name for the menu.

② Type a space and `SIZE="?">`, replacing ? with the height, measured in character lines, for the menu input.

If you want to display a drop-down menu, set the height to 1.

③ Start a new line and type `<OPTION VALUE="?">`, replacing ? with a descriptive word for the menu item.

④ Type the text you want to appear in the menu list.

⑤ Repeat steps **3** and **4** to add more menu items to the list.

⑥ To make one menu item appear as selected in the list, type `SELECTED` after the VALUE attribute.

⑦ Type `</SELECT>`.

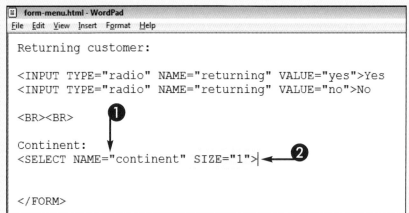

```
form-menu.html - WordPad
File  Edit  View  Insert  Format  Help

Returning customer:

<INPUT TYPE="radio" NAME="returning" VALUE="yes">Yes
<INPUT TYPE="radio" NAME="returning" VALUE="no">No

<BR><BR>

Continent:
<SELECT NAME="continent" SIZE="1">

</FORM>
```

```
form-menu.html - WordPad
File  Edit  View  Insert  Format  Help

Returning customer:

<INPUT TYPE="radio" NAME="returning" VALUE="yes">Yes
<INPUT TYPE="radio" NAME="returning" VALUE="no">No

<BR><BR>

Continent:
<SELECT NAME="continent" SIZE="1">
<OPTION VALUE="africa">Africa
<OPTION VALUE="antarctica">Antarctica
<OPTION VALUE="asia">Asia
<OPTION VALUE="australia">Australia
<OPTION VALUE="europe">Europe
<OPTION VALUE="northamerica" SELECTED>North America
<OPTION VALUE="southamerica">South America
</SELECT>

</FORM>
```

The Web browser displays the menu on the form.

● The user can click here to display the drop-down list.

● The user can click a list item to make a selection.

How do I display a menu of items on my form as a scrollable list?

Type the number of menu entries to display at a time as the SIZE attribute value. This makes the menu appear as a rectangular box that displays the items as a list. If the number of menu items is more than the display size, users can scroll to view the entire list. If the menu size is 1, a drop-down menu is displayed.

How can I create a submenu?

Use the <OPTGROUP> tag and the LABEL attribute (note that not all browsers support the <OPTGROUP> tag):

```
<P>What is your favorite flower?</P>
<SELECT NAME="favoriteflower">
<OPTGROUP LABEL="Perennial">
<OPTION VALUE="Daisy">Daisy
<OPTION VALUE="Rose">Rose
</OPTGROUP>
<OPTGROUP LABEL="Annual">
<OPTION VALUE="Petunia">Petunia
<OPTION VALUE="Pansy">Pansy
</OPTGROUP>
</SELECT>
```

Add a Submit Button

You can add a Submit button to your form so users can send you the data they enter into the form. It is common practice to add the Submit button to the bottom of the form, below the text boxes, check boxes, radio buttons, and other elements. You can choose any label you want for the button. It is a good idea to choose a label that conveys to users that they need to click the button to submit their data. If you do not include a label, most browsers display "Submit Query" on the button.

Add a Submit Button

1 Between the `<FORM>` and `</FORM>` tags, type `<INPUT TYPE="submit"`.

2 Type a space and type `VALUE="?">`, replacing *?* with the text you want to appear on the button.

● The browser displays the button on the form.

When the user clicks the button, the form data is sent to the value of the `ACTION` attribute specified in the `<FORM>` tag.

Note: For more about the `<FORM>` tag, see "Create a Form."

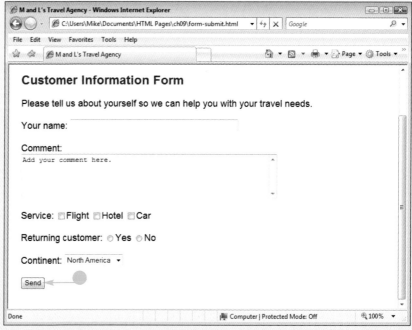

Add a Reset Button

You can add a Reset button to your form to allow users to clear the data they have entered. For example, the user may want to type different information, or change his or her mind about submitting the information. A Reset button lets users erase all the information they typed into the various input fields. It is standard practice to put the Reset button at the bottom of the form, next to the Submit button.

Add a Reset Button

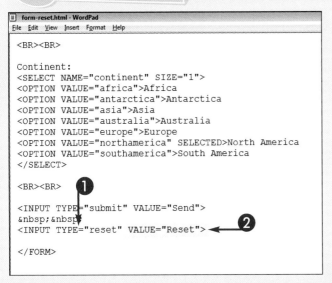

```
form-reset.html - WordPad
File  Edit  View  Insert  Format  Help

<BR><BR>

Continent:
<SELECT NAME="continent" SIZE="1">
<OPTION VALUE="africa">Africa
<OPTION VALUE="antarctica">Antarctica
<OPTION VALUE="asia">Asia
<OPTION VALUE="australia">Australia
<OPTION VALUE="europe">Europe
<OPTION VALUE="northamerica" SELECTED>North America
<OPTION VALUE="southamerica">South America
</SELECT>

<BR><BR>

<INPUT TYPE="submit" VALUE="Send">
  
<INPUT TYPE="reset" VALUE="Reset">

</FORM>
```

M and L's Travel Agency - Windows Internet Explorer

C:\Users\Mike\Documents\HTML Pages\ch09\form-reset.html   Google

File Edit View Favorites Tools Help

M and L's Travel Agency   Page ▾ Tools ▾

Customer Information Form

Please tell us about yourself so we can help you with your travel needs.

Your name:

Comment:
Add your comment here.

Service: ☐ Flight ☐Hotel ☐Car

Returning customer: ○ Yes ○ No

Continent: North America ▾

[Send] [Reset]

Done   Computer | Protected Mode: Off   100%

① Between the <FORM> and </FORM> tags, type <INPUT TYPE="reset".

② Type a space and VALUE="?">, replacing ? with the text label you want to appear on the button.

If you do not include a label, most browsers display *Reset* on the button.

● The browser displays the button on the form.

When the user clicks the button, the form is reset to its original settings.

Chapter 9

Creating Style Sheets

Looking for an easy way to apply complex styles to your Web page content? This chapter shows you how to use Cascading Style Sheets, or CSS, to assign formatting to your HTML documents and across your Web site. You can create style sheet rules within your Web page or in an external file. You can apply styles from an external file by linking the file to your HTML document. Style sheets can be used to modify the existing styles of HTML tags. You can also create rules known as *classes* that are independent of HTML tags.

Understanding Style Sheets

You can use CSS to exercise precise control over the appearance of your HTML documents. Style sheets can help you maintain a consistent look and feel throughout your Web site. By relegating formatting controls to a separate CSS document, you can free your HTML documents of repetitive coding and concentrate on the content that makes up your pages. Like HTML documents, CSS documents are simple text files. You can use style sheets to control the appearance and positioning of text, images, tables, input fields, and more on your Web pages.

Defining Style Sheets

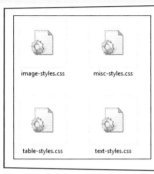

A style sheet is usually a text file that is separate from your HTML document. Style sheets can also be internal, residing within your HTML code. A style sheet holds formatting codes that control your Web page's appearance. You can use style sheets to change the look of any Web page element, such as paragraphs, lists, backgrounds, and more. Any time you want to apply the formatting from an external style sheet to an HTML document, you attach the style sheet to the page using a LINK tag. Style sheet files have a .css file extension.

Controlling Multiple Pages

You can link every page in your Web site to a single style sheet. Any changes you make to the style sheet formatting are reflected in every HTML document linking to the sheet. By storing all the formatting information in one place, you can easily update the appearance of your site's pages all at once. This can be a real timesaver if your site consists of lots of pages.

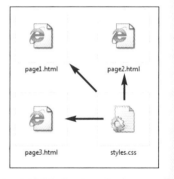

Style Sheet Syntax

```
<HTML>
<HEAD>
<TITLE>Great Destinations</TITLE>

<STYLE>
BODY { font-family: "Arial";
       background: #CCFFCC }
H2   { color: gray }
P    { border: solid #333399 1px;
       padding: 20px }
</STYLE>

</HEAD>
<BODY>
```

Style sheets are made up of rules, and each rule has two distinct parts: a selector and a declaration. The selector specifies the element to which you want to apply a style rule, and the declaration specifies the formatting for the selector. For example, in the style rule H2 {color: silver}, the selector is H2 and {color: silver; } is the declaration (●). When applied to a page, this rule makes all level 2 headings appear in silver.

Style Sheet Declarations

A declaration consists of one or more property-value pairs such as `fontsize: 12px;` or `position: absolute;`. Each property and value is separated by a colon; multiple property-value pairs in a declaration are separated by semicolons. Putting each property-value pair on a separate line when writing your rules is good form. Similar to HTML, you can add extra spaces and line breaks to your style sheet code to make your code more readable. Learn more about writing style rules in Chapters 10 and 11.

Style Classes

If you want to apply formatting only to a particular instance of a tag, you can use a class attribute inside that tag. You can assign a distinct name to a class and add a style rule that applies only to that class. For example, perhaps you want to add special formatting to one paragraph but not others. You define the style rule on your style sheet and then refer to the class name in that paragraph tag.

```
<HEAD>
<TITLE>Destinations</TITLE>
<LINK REL="stylesheet" TYPE="txt/css"
HREF="styles.css">
<STYLE TYPE="text/css">
BODY { font-family: Arial; color: #CC0000 }
</STYLE>
</HEAD>
<BODY>

<H2>Machu Picchu, Peru</H2>
<P>Located in the Peruvian Andes, the ancient
Inca city of Machu Picchu was constructed in
the 1400s at the height of the Inca Empire.</P>
```

Inheritance

Tags you add inside other tags inherit the outer tag's formatting, unless you specify otherwise. For example, if you define a style for the <BODY> tag (●), any heading or paragraph tags you nest within the <BODY> tag inherit the same formatting (●). HTML inheritance makes it easy to keep the formatting consistent as you add new items within an element.

Internal and External Style Sheets

You can connect an HTML document to an internal style sheet or an external style sheet. Internal style sheets exist within an HTML page, between the <HEAD> and </HEAD> tags, whereas external style sheets are separate files (●). External style sheets are useful because you can link them to more than one HTML document. You might use an internal style sheet if your site consists of a single page.

```
<HTML>
<HEAD>
<STYLE>
<LINK REL="stylesheet" TYPE="text/css"
HREF="styles.css">
<LINK REL="stylesheet" TYPE="text/css"
HREF="style-font.css">
<LINK REL="stylesheet" TYPE="text/css"
HREF="styles-tables.css">
</STYLE>
</HEAD>
<BODY>
```

Create an Internal Style Sheet

You can create an internal style sheet that resides within the `<HEAD>` tag of your HTML document. The styles of an internal style sheet are delineated by `<STYLE>` and `</STYLE>` tags and apply only to the HTML in that document. Internal style sheets are handy if your Web site consists of a single page because you can change both style rules and HTML in the same file. If you want to apply the same styles to multiple Web pages, consider putting the styles in an external style sheet. See the section "Create an External Style Sheet" for details.

Create an Internal Style Sheet

① Within the `<HEAD>` and `</HEAD>` tags, add a new line and type `<STYLE TYPE="text/css">`.

② Add a new line and type the element tag for which you want to create a style rule.

In this example, a new style rule is created for the H2 element.

You can add extra spaces for legibility.

```
css-internal.html - WordPad
File  Edit  View  Insert  Format  Help
<HTML>
<HEAD>
<TITLE>M and L's Travel Agency: Destinations</TITLE>
<STYLE TYPE="text/css">          ◄── ①
H2 |
</HEAD>
<BODY BGCOLOR="tan">

②  <FONT FACE="Arial">Machu Picchu, Peru</FONT></H2>

<IMG SRC="machu.jpg" ALIGN="left">
<IMG SRC="llama.jpg" ALIGN="right">

<P>Located in the Peruvian Andes, the ancient Inca city of Machu
constructed in the 1400s at the height of the Inca Empire. It was
less than 100 years later when the Inca empire collapsed under Sp
conquest. Today Machu Picchu is the most visited tourist attracti
</P>

</BODY>
</HTML>
```

③ Type `{`.

④ Type the properties and values for the rule.

If you intend to add more than one property-value pair to a declaration, be sure to separate the pairs with semicolons.

⑤ Type `}` to end the rule.

Note: *To learn more about writing style rules, see Chapters 10 and 11.*

```
css-internal.html - WordPad
File  Edit  View  Insert  Format  Help
<HTML>
<HEAD>
<TITLE>M and L's Travel Agency: Destinations</TITLE>
<STYLE TYPE="text/css">
H2 { font-family: Arial; font-style: italic }  ◄── ⑤
</HEAD>  ③                 ④
<BODY BGCOLOR="tan">

<H2>③<FONT FACE="Arial">④chu Picchu, Peru</FONT></H2>

<IMG SRC="machu.jpg" ALIGN="left">
<IMG SRC="llama.jpg" ALIGN="right">

<P>Located in the Peruvian Andes, the ancient Inca city of Machu
constructed in the 1400s at the height of the Inca Empire. It was
less than 100 years later when the Inca empire collapsed under Sp
conquest. Today Machu Picchu is the most visited tourist attracti
</P>

</BODY>
</HTML>
```

```
css-internal.html - WordPad
File   Edit   View   Insert   Format   Help

<HTML>
<HEAD>
<TITLE>M and L's Travel Agency: Destinations</TITLE>
<STYLE TYPE="text/css">
H2 { font-family: Arial; font-style: italic }
H3 { font-family: Verdana; color: #CC0000 }      6
P { color: blue }
</STYLE>                              7
</HEAD>
<BODY BGCOLOR="tan">

<H2><FONT FACE="Arial">Machu Picchu, Peru</FONT></H2>

<IMG SRC="machu.jpg" ALIGN="left">
<IMG SRC="llama.jpg" ALIGN="right">

<P>Located in the Peruvian Andes, the ancient Inca city of Machu
constructed in the 1400s at the height of the Inca Empire. It was
less than 100 years later when the Inca empire collapsed under Sp
conquest. Today Machu Picchu is the most visited tourist attracti
</P>

</BODY>
</HTML>
```

⑥ Repeat steps **2** to **5** to continue adding style rules to your internal style sheet.

⑦ Add a new line and type </STYLE>.

You can save your page and test it in a browser to see the style sheet results.

Note: *To learn more about viewing HTML documents in a browser, see Chapter 2.*

Simplify It

Do all browsers recognize style sheets?
Some older browsers do not support style sheets, so they ignore the <STYLE> tags. However, the content inside the <STYLE> tags is not ignored in these browsers, so any coding you type between the <STYLE> tags can appear on the page. You can prevent an older browser from displaying style tag coding by typing HTML comment code (<!-- and -->) before and after the style rules. For more about HTML comments, see Chapter 3:

```
<STYLE TYPE="text/css">
<!--
HR {color: red}
P {margin-left: 20px}
-->
</STYLE>
```

Can I link another Web page to my internal style sheet?
No. A page cannot access another page's internal style sheet. If you want multiple Web pages to take advantage of a set of style rules, you must define those rules in an external style sheet and link the pages to the sheet. An internal style sheet is useful only if you want to apply those styles to a single HTML document. See the section "Create an External Style Sheet" to learn more.

Create an External Style Sheet

You can use an external style sheet to define formatting and layout instructions and then apply those instructions to your HTML documents. Style sheets can include rules for customizing text, tables, form elements, and more. You can save the style sheet as a text file and assign the .css file extension to identify the file as a Cascading Style Sheet. For easy access, you can save the file in the same folder as your HTML files. If you have multiple style sheets and want to keep them separate, you can save them in a subdirectory.

For more on style sheets and how they work, see the section "Understanding Style Sheets."

Create an External Style Sheet

① Create a new document in your text editor.

Note: *To create and save HTML documents, see Chapter 2.*

② To create a style rule, type the element tag for which you want to define formatting properties.

This example creates a style rule for level 2 headings.

③ Type a space.

④ Type {.

⑤ Type one or more property-value pairs.

Separate each property and value with a colon. Separate multiple pairs with semicolons. You can add extra spaces for legibility.

In this example, the rule includes setting a font and a font style.

Note: *To learn more about writing style rules, see Chapters 10 and 11.*

⑥ Type } to end the rule.

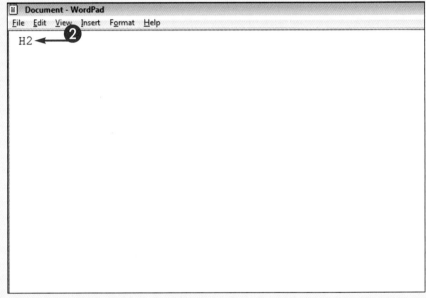

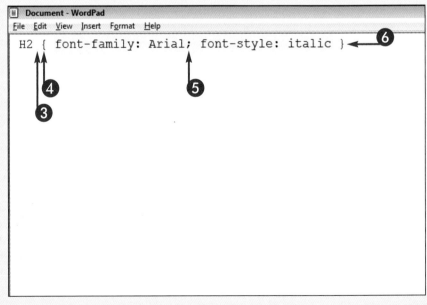

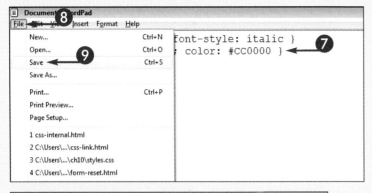

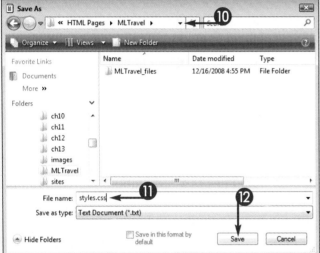

7 Repeat steps **2** to **6** to continue adding rules to your style sheet.

8 Click **File**.

9 Click **Save**.

The Save As dialog box appears.

10 Navigate to the folder that contains your HTML pages.

11 Type a unique file name for your style sheet and a **.css** extension.

12 Click **Save**.

Your text editor saves the new style sheet.

Note: *To learn how to apply a style sheet to an HTML document, see the section "Link to a Style Sheet."*

How do I add comments to my styles?
You can add comments to your style sheets to describe and identify your style rules. Style sheet comments begin with / * and end with * /. For example, you might add a comment explaining the rationale for applying a style rule:

```
P {color: red} /* Apply to
error descriptions */
```

Web browsers do not interpret comment information in style sheets.

Can I override the normal styles of an HTML tag with CSS?
Yes. You may use CSS to change how HTML tags normally appear, even making some tags behave like others. For example, you can change the style of a heading tag so that it looks just like regular paragraph text, or vice versa. See Chapter 10 for some of the many types of styles you can apply to tags with CSS.

Link to a Style Sheet

You can link to an external style sheet to assign a set of formatting rules to your HTML document. You use the <LINK> tag to specify the file name and location of the style sheet. You can link multiple documents to the same style sheet to give all the pages in your site a consistent look and feel. You can also assign multiple style sheets to a single document by adding more than one <LINK> tag. To learn how to create a style sheet, see the section "Create an External Style Sheet."

Link to a Style Sheet

① Open the HTML document you want to link to a style sheet.

② Click within the <HEAD> and </HEAD> tags and add a new line.

③ Type <LINK REL= "stylesheet" TYPE= "text/css".

```
css-link.html - WordPad
File  Edit  View  Insert  Format  Help

<HTML>
<HEAD>
<TITLE>M and L's Travel Agency: Destinations</TITLE>   ③
<LINK REL="stylesheet" TYPE="text/css"|   ←
</HEAD>                                    ②
<BODY BGCOLOR="tan">

<H1><FONT FACE="Arial">Machu Picchu, Peru</FONT></H1>

<IMG SRC="machu.jpg" ALIGN="left">
<IMG SRC="llama.jpg" ALIGN="right">

<P>Located in the Peruvian Andes, the ancient Inca city of Machu
constructed in the 1400s at the height of the Inca Empire. It was
less than 100 years later when the Inca empire collapsed under Sp
conquest. Today Machu Picchu is the most visited tourist attracti
</P>

</BODY>
</HTML>
```

④ Type a blank space and HREF="?">, replacing ? with the name of the style sheet file.

If the style sheet is located in a subdirectory, precede the file name with the subdirectory name and a slash, for example css/styles.css.

The style sheet is now linked with the page.

You can test your page in a browser to see the style sheet results.

```
css-link.html - WordPad
File  Edit  View  Insert  Format  Help

<HTML>
<HEAD>
<TITLE>M and L's Travel Agency: Destinations</TITLE>              ④
<LINK REL="stylesheet" TYPE="text/css" HREF="styles.css">|   ←
</HEAD>
<BODY BGCOLOR="tan">

<H1><FONT FACE="Arial">Machu Picchu, Peru</FONT></H1>

<IMG SRC="machu.jpg" ALIGN="left">
<IMG SRC="llama.jpg" ALIGN="right">

<P>Located in the Peruvian Andes, the ancient Inca city of Machu
constructed in the 1400s at the height of the Inca Empire. It was
less than 100 years later when the Inca empire collapsed under Sp
conquest. Today Machu Picchu is the most visited tourist attracti
</P>

</BODY>
</HTML>
```

Apply a Style Locally

You can apply a style to a single instance of a tag in your document using an HTML attribute. The `STYLE` attribute allows you to apply a style rule to a tag without having to define the rule separately in an internal or external style sheet.

A style applied locally overrides any styles found on external or internal style sheets for the same tag. Applying styles locally works best for one-time changes. You should use internal or external style sheets for styles you plan to apply more than once.

Apply a Style Locally

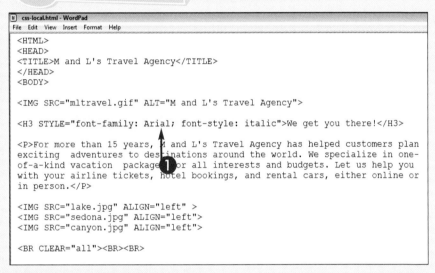

① Click in the tag for the element you want to change and type `STYLE="?"`, replacing *?* with the properties and values you want to assign.

Separate multiple property-value pairs with semicolons.

Note: *To learn more about writing style rules, see Chapters 10 and 11.*

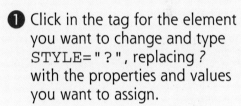

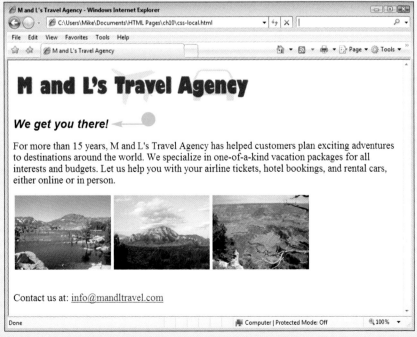

② Open the HTML document in a Web browser.

Note: *To learn about viewing an HTML document in a Web browser, see Chapter 2.*

● The Web browser applies the style to the tag content.

Apply a Style Class

You can create a CSS class to apply a style rule to specific instances of HTML tags in a page. For example, if you want the introductory paragraphs formatted differently from all the other paragraphs, you can create a class specifically for the introductory paragraphs. After you create the class and assign it using the CLASS attribute, the browser applies the formatting to all the affected paragraphs.

You can set up a class in an internal or external style sheet. To learn more about creating style sheets, see the sections "Create an Internal Style Sheet" and "Create an External Style Sheet."

Apply a Style Class

DEFINE A CLASS

1 In your external or internal style sheet, type the tag for which you want to create a class.

2 Type a period.

3 Type a name for the class.

```
styles.css - WordPad
File  Edit  View  Insert  Format  Help

H3 { font-family: Arial }
P { width: 600px; font-size: 12px }
P.special
```

4 Type {.

5 Type one or more property-value pairs for the class.

Separate multiple pairs with semicolons.

Note: To learn more about writing style rules, see Chapters 10 and 11.

6 Type } to end the style rule.

Your class is now defined.

If you are editing an external style sheet, save the sheet.

```
styles.css - WordPad
File  Edit  View  Insert  Format  Help

H3 { font-family: Arial }
P { width: 600px; font-size: 12px }
P.special { color: #660000 }
```

```
<H3><A NAME="everest">Mount Everest</A></H3>

<P>At 29,029 feet, Mount Everest is the highest mountain on earth when
measured from sea level to summit. Each year, hundreds of mountaineers climb
the mountain, which is located in the Himalaya range on the border of Nepal
and Tibet. Many climbers use bottled oxygen to compensate for the thin
Himalayan air.</P>

<BR>

<H3><A NAME="machu">Machu Picchu</A></H3>

<P CLASS="special">Located in the Peruvian Andes, the ancient Inca city of
Machu Picchu was constructed in the 1400s at the height of the Inca Empire.
It was abandoned less than 100 years later when the Inca empire collapsed
under Spanish conquest. Today Machu Picchu is the most visited tourist
attraction ❷ Peru.</P>
```

M and L's Travel Agency

Mount Everest

At 29,029 feet, Mount Everest is the highest mountain on earth when measured from sea level to summit. Each year, hundreds of mountaineers climb the mountain, which is located in the Himalaya range on the border of Nepal and Tibet. Many climbers use bottled oxygen to compensate for the thin Himalayan air.

Machu Picchu

Located in the Peruvian Andes, the ancient Inca city of Machu Picchu was constructed in the 1400s at the height of the Inca Empire. It was abandoned less than 100 years later when the Inca empire collapsed under Spanish conquest. Today Machu Picchu is the most visited tourist attraction in Peru.

ASSIGN A CLASS

❶ Open the HTML document and click in the tag to which you want to assign a class.

❷ Type CLASS="?", replacing *?* with the class name.

You can assign multiple classes by separating class names with a space.

❸ Open the HTML document in a Web browser.

Note: *To learn about viewing an HTML document in a Web browser, see Chapter 2.*

● The Web browser applies the styles associated with the class to the tag content.

Simplify It

What is a generic class?
You can use a generic class to format more than one type of tag. For example, you might use a generic class to format both paragraphs and level 3 headings in a document. When defining a generic class, simply type a period followed by the class name, such as `.myclass`. Do not type an HTML tag before the period. When applying the class, use the class name, such as `<P CLASS="myclass">` or `<H3 CLASS="myclass">`.

What is a style sheet ID?
A style sheet ID is similar to a style sheet class. You use it to define a set of style sheet rules and then apply those rules to an element on your page. It is different than a class in that you should use an ID when applying a set of style rules to one place on your pages. For example, you might use an ID to format the title text on your home page. If a style is applied in multiple places, you should use a class. To create an ID, precede its name with a number sign (#):

```
#myid1 {font-size: 36px}
```

To apply the ID in your HTML, use the `ID` attribute.

Apply Styles with DIV and SPAN Tags

You can apply styles to different sections of your Web page using the <DIV> and <SPAN> tags. The tags serve as empty containers with which you can apply styles. <DIV> is a block-level tag, which means it adds blank lines above and below the content it surrounds, similar to the paragraph tag. <SPAN> is an inline tag, meaning it can be used to add styles to text within a paragraph.

You associate a class with <DIV> or <SPAN> content using the CLASS attribute. For more information about creating classes, see the section "Apply a Style Class."

Apply Styles with DIV and SPAN Tags

SET UP THE CLASSES

1 In your style sheet, type DIV.?, replacing ? with the class name you want to assign for the DIV style.

In this example, styles are applied using an internal style sheet.

2 Type {.

3 Type the property-value pairs for the DIV style, separating multiple pairs with semicolons.

Note: To learn more about writing style rules, see Chapters 10 and 11.

4 Type }.

5 Type SPAN.?, replacing ? with the class name you want to assign for the SPAN style.

6 Type {.

7 Type the property-value pairs for the SPAN style, separating multiple pairs with semicolons.

8 Type }.

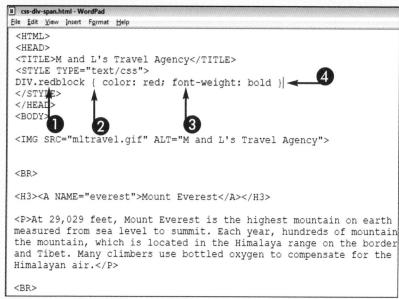

```
css-div-span.html - WordPad
File  Edit  View  Insert  Format  Help
<HTML>
<HEAD>
<TITLE>M and L's Travel Agency</TITLE>
<STYLE TYPE="text/css">
DIV.redblock { color: red; font-weight: bold }
</STYLE>
</HEAD>
<BODY>

<IMG SRC="mltravel.gif" ALT="M and L's Travel Agency">


<BR>

<H3><A NAME="everest">Mount Everest</A></H3>

<P>At 29,029 feet, Mount Everest is the highest mountain on earth
measured from sea level to summit. Each year, hundreds of mountain
the mountain, which is located in the Himalaya range on the border
and Tibet. Many climbers use bottled oxygen to compensate for the
Himalayan air.</P>

<BR>
```

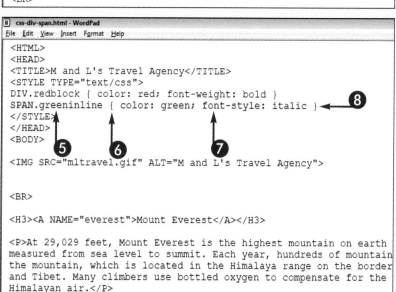

```
css-div-span.html - WordPad
File  Edit  View  Insert  Format  Help
<HTML>
<HEAD>
<TITLE>M and L's Travel Agency</TITLE>
<STYLE TYPE="text/css">
DIV.redblock { color: red; font-weight: bold }
SPAN.greeninline { color: green; font-style: italic }
</STYLE>
</HEAD>
<BODY>

<IMG SRC="mltravel.gif" ALT="M and L's Travel Agency">


<BR>

<H3><A NAME="everest">Mount Everest</A></H3>

<P>At 29,029 feet, Mount Everest is the highest mountain on earth
measured from sea level to summit. Each year, hundreds of mountain
the mountain, which is located in the Himalaya range on the border
and Tibet. Many climbers use bottled oxygen to compensate for the
Himalayan air.</P>
```

```
<P>At 29,029 feet, Mount Everest is the highest mountain on earth when
measured from sea level to summit. Each year, hundreds of mountaineers climb
the mountain, which is located in the Himalaya range on the border of Nepal
and Tibet. Many climbers use bottled oxygen to compensate for the thin
Himalayan air.</P>

<BR>

<H3><A NAME="machu">Machu Picchu</A></H3>

<DIV CLASS="redblock">Located in the <SPAN CLASS="greeninline">Peruvian Andes
</SPAN>, the ancient Inca city of Machu Picchu was constructed in the 1400s
at the height of the Inca Empire. It was abandoned less than 100 years later
when the Inca empire collapsed under Spanish conquest. Today Machu Picchu is
the most visited tourist attraction in Peru.</DIV>

<BR>

<H3><A NAME="santiago">Santiago de Compostela</A></H3>
```

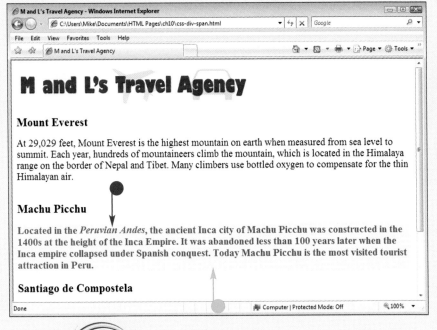

APPLY THE TAGS

1 In front of the text block to which you want to apply a style, type `<DIV CLASS="?">`, replacing *?* with the `DIV` class name.

2 Type `</DIV>` at the end of the text block.

3 In front of the inline text to which you want to apply a style, type `<SPAN CLASS="?">`, replacing *?* with the `SPAN` class name.

4 Type `</SPAN>` at the end of the section.

5 Save the document.

6 Open the HTML document in a Web browser.

Note: To learn about viewing an HTML document in a Web browser, see Chapter 2.

● The browser applies the `DIV` style to the block of text.

● The browser applies the `SPAN` style to the inline text.

Simplify It

Do style property-value pairs need to be on a single line?
No. Similar to HTML, you can add line breaks and spaces within your CSS without changing the effects of your rules. It can be a good idea to put each property-value pair on a separate line to make viewing and editing your rules easier. You can also use tabs to make CSS properties and values line up with one another.

How do class styles affect styles that have already been applied to a tag?
When you apply a class to a tag, the class-based rules override any conflicting rules already assigned to the tag. For example, if you turn the paragraph text for a page red with the style `P {color:red; }` and then apply the class `P.bluetext {color:blue; }` to a paragraph, the text in that paragraph appears blue instead of red.

Chapter 10

Formatting Text with Style Sheets

Ready to start formatting your Web page with style sheets? This chapter shows you how to apply formatting to your HTML elements using style sheet properties. You can emphasize words on your page by making the words bold, italic, capitalized, or a different size. By adding color, either to text or as a background, you can make elements on your page stand out or match your Web site's theme. You can also use style sheet rules to change the style and color of links.

ALGERIAN CONDENSED LET: THE QUICK BROWN FOX JUMPED OVER THE LAZY DOG.
Arriba Arriba LET: The quick brown fox jumped over the lazy dog.
Avant Garde Mono ITCTT: The quick brown fox jumped over the lazy dog.
PortagoITC TT: THE QUICK BROWN FOX JUMPED OVER THE LAZY DOG.
Blackmoor LET: The quick brown fox jumped over the lazy dog.
BancoITC TT-Heavy: The quick brown fox jumped over the lazy dog.
BraganzaSCITC TT: THE QUICK BROWN FOX JUMPED OVER THE LAZY DOG.
BraganzaITC TT: The quick brown fox jumped over the lazy dog.
Bodoni SvtyTwo SC ITC TT: THE QUICK BROWN FOX JUMPED OVER THE LAZY DOG.
Cabaret LET: The quick brown fox jumped over the lazy dog.
Jazz LET: The quick brown fox jumped over the lazy dog.
HAZEL LET: THE QUICK BROWN FOX JUMPED OVER THE LAZY DOG.
Mona Lisa Solid OS ITC TT: The quick brown fox jumped over the lazy dog.
Jenson Old Style TT: The quick brown fox jumped over the lazy dog.
PRINCETOWN LET: THE QUICK BROWN FOX JUMPED OVER THE LAZY DOG.
Savoye LET: The quick brown fox jumped over the lazy dog.
Santa Fe LET: The quick brown fox jumped over the lazy dog.
SYNCHRO LET: THE QUICK BROWN FOX JUMPED OVER THE LAZY DOG.
Souvenir Mono ITCTT: The quick brown fox jumped over the lazy dog.
Shatter LET: The quick brown fox jumped over the lazy dog.
Type Embellishments One LET: ✺☞⚱ ☙✥⚘ ～✍～ ❧✦❀
TembleITC TT: The quick brown fox jumped over the lazy dog.
University Roman Bold LET: The quick brown fox jumped over the lazy dog.
ZiggnITC TT: The quick brown fox jumped over the lazy dog.

Add Bold to Text

You can make Web page text bold using the `font-weight` property in a style rule. The rule allows you to control the amount of boldness. Setting text to bold can help draw attention to it on a page. Adding bold formatting to colored links can give the links on your page extra emphasis. To emphasize text with italic formatting or by changing its color, see the other sections of this chapter.

Add Bold to Text

1 Click inside the tag declaration and type `font-weight:`.

Note: *To learn more about writing style sheets and rules, see Chapter 9.*

2 Type a space.

3 Type a weight value (`lighter`, `normal`, `bold`, or `bolder`).

You can use the `normal` value to remove boldness that may be inherited from previous style rules.

You can also specify a number value using a multiple of 100 from 100 to 900 to control the boldness level. Not all browsers support this feature.

The Web browser bolds all the text to which the tag is applied.

● In this example, all the paragraphs are now bold.

Note: *To learn more about how to link a style sheet to all the pages on your Web site, see Chapter 9.*

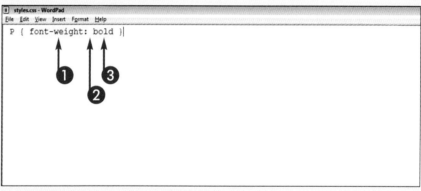

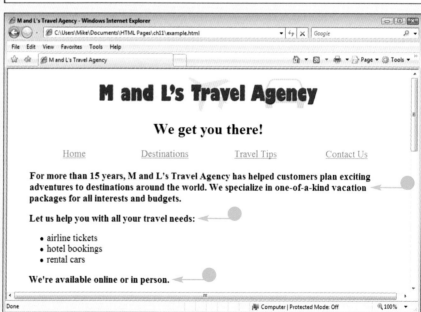

Italicize Text

You can use the `font-style` property to italicize Web page text. Applying italics is an easy way to add emphasis to text. The font-style property accepts three values: `italic`, `oblique`, and `normal`. Both the `italic` and `oblique` values apply similar slanted formatting to text whereas `normal` makes text non-italic. Use care when applying italic formatting to small text because this can make the text hard to read. To draw attention to text using bold formatting or by changing its color, see the other sections of this chapter.

Italicize Text

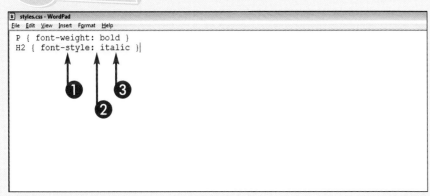

```
P { font-weight: bold }
H2 { font-style: italic }
```

① Click inside the tag declaration and type `font-style:`.

Note: *To learn more about writing style sheets and rules, see Chapter 9.*

② Type a space.

③ Type a style value (`italic`, `oblique`, or `normal`).

You can use the `normal` value to remove italics that may be inherited from previous style rules.

The Web browser italicizes all the text to which the tag is applied.

● In this example, the slogan text is italicized.

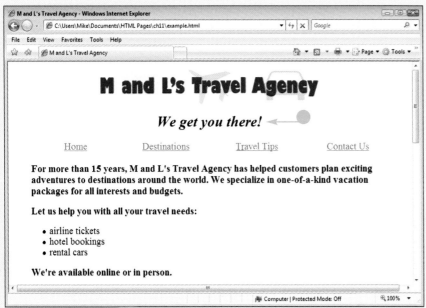

Indent Text

You can indent the first line in a paragraph using the `text-indent` property in a style rule. This can give the paragraphs on your page a more traditional look and feel. You can set the indentation as a specific measurement value or as a percentage of the overall text block width. You can create an outdent, also known as a hanging indent, by setting the `text-indent` property to a negative number.

Indent Text

① Click inside the tag declaration and type `text-indent: ?`, replacing *?* with the amount of space you want to indent, measured in pixels (px).

You can also set a size measurement in millimeters (mm), centimeters (cm), inches (in), points (pt), picas (pc), x-height (ex), or em space (em).

You can also set an indent size as a percentage of the text block width, such as 20 percent.

The Web browser indents the first line of all the text to which the tag is applied.

● In this example, all the `<P>` tags are indented.

Note: *To indent text with margins, see Chapter 11.*

Change the Font Size

You can use the `font-size` property to change the font size for a document's text. By changing font size, you can emphasize or de-emphasize different sections of text on your page. Instead of going through your document and changing each instance of a tag, you can use the style sheet rule to change the font size for all uses of the tag in your document. The `font-size` property accepts a variety of measurement units. To change the size of text using HTML, see Chapter 4.

Change the Font Size

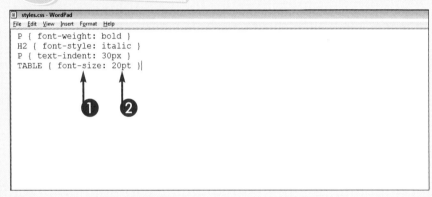

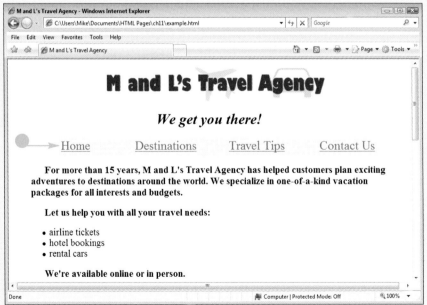

① Click inside the tag declaration and type `font-size:` and a space.

② Type a font size in points (pt), pixels (px), millimeters (mm), centimeters (cm), inches (in), picas (pc), x-height (ex), or em space (em).

You can also type a descriptive (`xx-small`, `x-small`, `small`, `medium`, `large`, `x-large`, or `xx-large`) font size.

The Web browser assigns the font size for any text to which the tag is applied.

● In this example, the style is assigned to the links inside a table.

Note: *Learn how to create tables in Chapter 7.*

Change the Font

To change the font for your HTML text, you can use the `font-family` property. You can specify a font by name. Because not all fonts are available on all computers, you can designate a second or third font choice. This way, if the computer does not have the first choice installed, the browser tries to display the next choice instead.

For best results, assign multiple font choices and be sure to include a common font, such as Arial, Verdana, Courier, or Times New Roman.

Change the Font

① Click inside the tag declaration and type `font-family:`.

Note: To learn more about writing style sheets and rules, see Chapter 9.

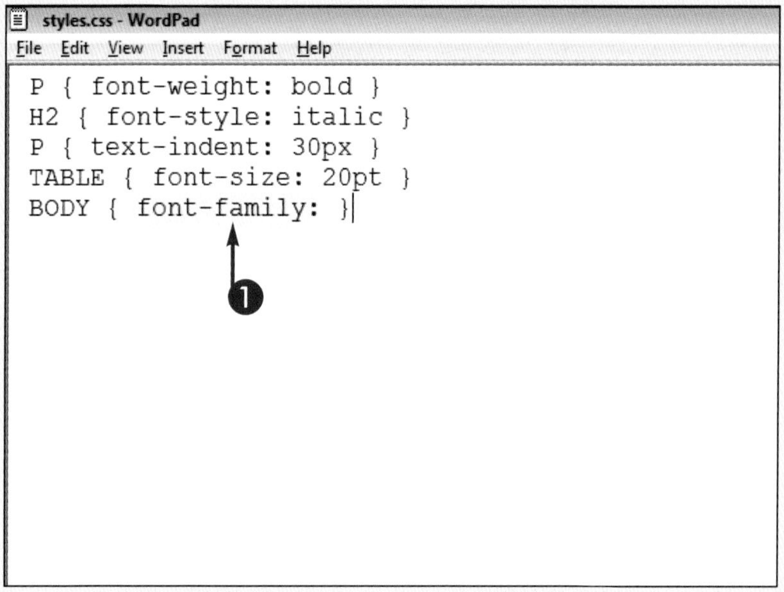

```
styles.css - WordPad
File  Edit  View  Insert  Format  Help

P { font-weight: bold }
H2 { font-style: italic }
P { text-indent: 30px }
TABLE { font-size: 20pt }
BODY { font-family: }
```

①

② Type a space and type the name of the font you want to use.

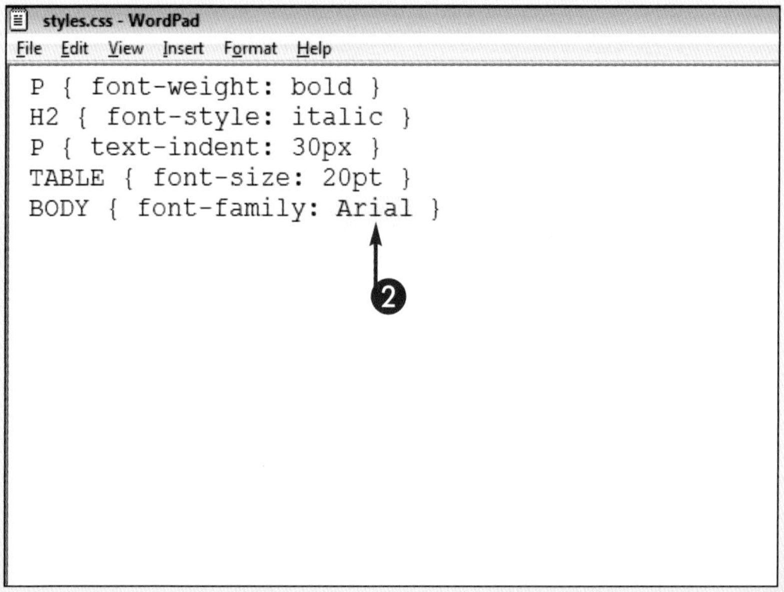

```
styles.css - WordPad
File  Edit  View  Insert  Format  Help

P { font-weight: bold }
H2 { font-style: italic }
P { text-indent: 30px }
TABLE { font-size: 20pt }
BODY { font-family: Arial }
```

②

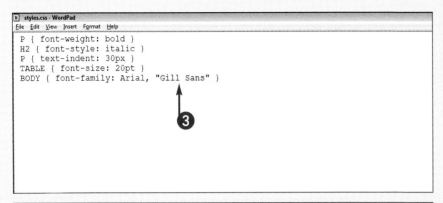

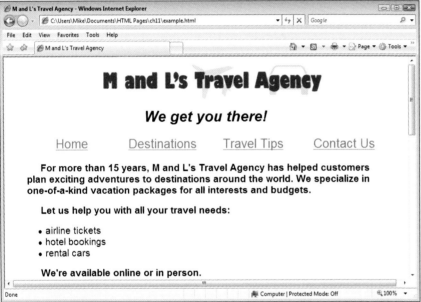

3 To designate a second font choice, type a comma, a space, and the second font name.

If the font name includes a space, surround the name in quotes.

You can repeat step **3** to assign additional fonts.

The Web browser uses the assigned font for any text to which the tag is applied.

In this example, the style rule is applied to the <BODY> tag, so all the body text is affected.

Can I apply multiple style settings to my fonts at the same time?
Yes. You can write a style rule that combines several font settings at the same time using the `font` property. For example, you can designate the font, font size, and font style for a particular tag instead of writing three different rules for the tag. Your combined rule might look like this:

```
P {font: italic 18pt "Times New Roman", Arial}
```

Some browsers may require you to type the properties in a particular order, such as font style before font size.

What are serifs?
Serifs are the small decorations that appear at the ends of some letters. Fonts can be classified by whether or not they include serifs. Common serifed fonts include Times New Roman, Georgia, and Palatino. Popular non-serifed, or *sans serif*, fonts include Arial, Verdana, and Helvetica. Sans serif fonts can be easier to read at smaller sizes on Web pages.

Change the Text Case

You can use the `text-transform` property to change the text case for a tag. For example, you may want all <H2> text to appear in all capital letters. The property controls how the browser displays the text regardless of how it was typed.

You can choose from four case values: `capitalize`, `uppercase`, `lowercase`, and `none`. Use the capitalize value if you want the first character of each word to appear capitalized. Use the `none` value to leave text as is. The `none` value cancels any case values the text may have inherited.

Change the Text Case

① Click inside the tag declaration and type `text-transform:` and a space.

② Type a text case value (`capitalize`, `uppercase`, `lowercase`, or `none`).

Note: *To learn more about writing style sheets and rules, see Chapter 9.*

The Web browser assigns the text case to the content.

● In this example, the <H2> tag appears in uppercase letters.

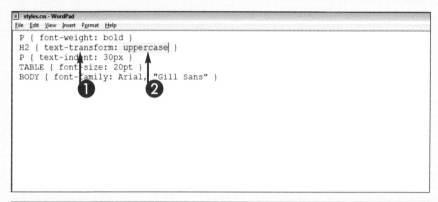

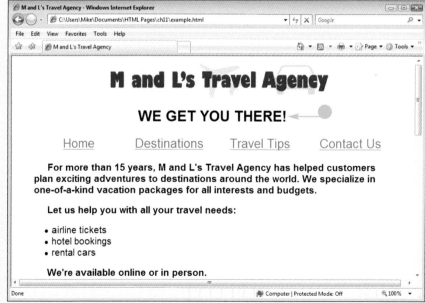

Change Text Alignment

You can control the horizontal positioning of block-level text in your page using the `text-align` property. Block-level text includes paragraphs, tables, and other elements that display a blank line before and after the element on the page. You can align text to the left or right, center the text, or create justified text. By default, most browsers align text to the left. To change the alignment of text using HTML, see Chapter 3.

Change Text Alignment

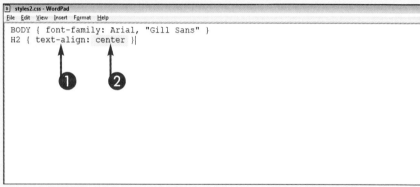

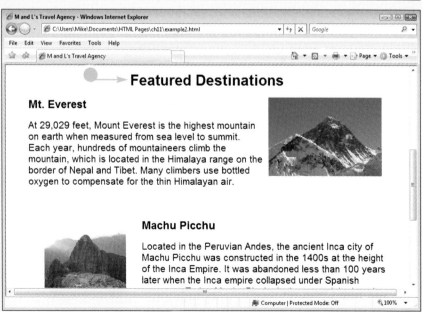

1 Click inside the tag declaration and type `text-align:` and a space.

2 Type an alignment (`left`, `center`, `right`, or `justify`).

Note: *To learn more about writing style sheets and rules, see Chapter 9.*

The Web browser assigns the alignment to the content.

● In this example, the `<H2>` tags are centered.

163

Control Line Spacing

You can use the `line-height` property to adjust the spacing, or *leading*, between lines of text. Adjusting line spacing can make your Web page text easier to read. The line spacing value can be specified as a multiple of the height of the element's font. It can also be specified as an absolute value or a percentage. Be careful when applying small values because this can result in overlapping lines. Line spacing cannot have a negative value.

Control Line Spacing

① Click inside the tag declaration and type `line-height:` and a space.

② Type a value for the spacing.

This example uses a value of 2.0 to make the spacing two times the current font height.

You can also set a percentage or an absolute value, such as 10px, for the spacing.

Note: *To learn more about writing style sheets and rules, see Chapter 9.*

The Web browser assigns the line spacing to the content.

● In this example, the <P> tags all display extra line spacing.

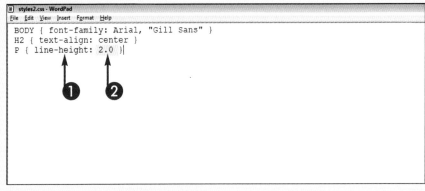

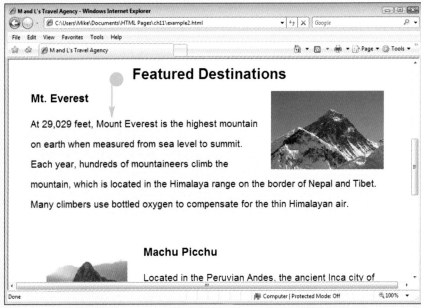

Control Letter Spacing

You can control the spacing between characters, or *kerning*, using the `letter-spacing` property. Letter spacing changes the appearance of your text by increasing or condensing the space between letters.

You can specify letter spacing in points (pt), pixels (px), millimeters (mm), centimeters (cm), inches (in), picas (pc), x-height (ex), or em space (em). The specified value is added to the default spacing that is normally inserted between letters. Negative values condense the space between letters, with high negative values causing letters to overlap.

Control Letter Spacing

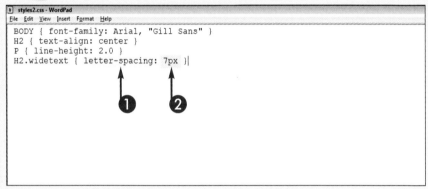

① Click inside the tag declaration and type `letter-spacing:` and a space.

② Type a value for the spacing.

Note: *To learn more about writing style sheets and rules, see Chapter 9.*

The Web browser assigns the letter spacing to the content.

● In this example, letter spacing is applied to the slogan using a style-sheet class.

Note: *See Chapter 9 to learn more about creating classes in your style sheets.*

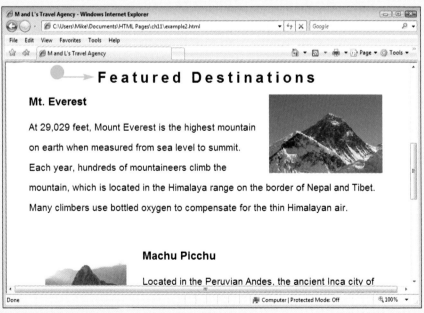

Add Color to Text

You can use the color property to change the color of text in your Web page. You can specify one of 16 predefined HTML colors, a hexadecimal color value, or an RGB value. You can change the text color to make it match the theme of your Web site. You can use color to emphasize important content, such as alert text or error messages. You can also use the color property to change other Web page elements, such as tables, borders, and horizontal rules.

Add Color to Text

1 Click inside the tag declaration and type `color:` followed by a space.

2 Type a color name, hexadecimal value, or RGB value for the color you want to assign.

Note: *To view a table of color values, see "Change the Text Color" in Chapter 4.*

The Web browser uses the assigned color for the text to which the tag is applied.

● In this example, color is assigned to the <H2> tags.

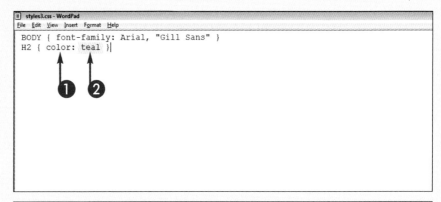

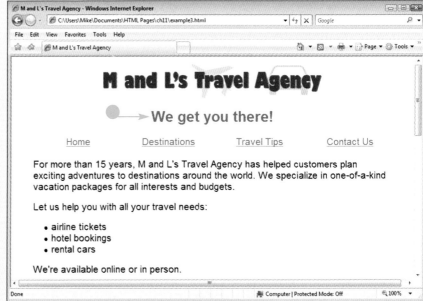

Add a Background Color to Text

You can use the `background` property to change the color that appears behind text, tables, or other elements on the page. For example, you can change the background color for a block of text or a data cell in a table. You can specify one of 16 predefined HTML colors, a hexadecimal color value, or an RGB value.

Use caution when assigning a background color to an element, taking into account the color of the text in the foreground.

Add a Background Color to Text

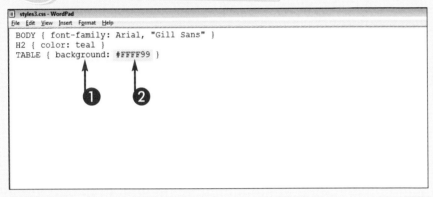

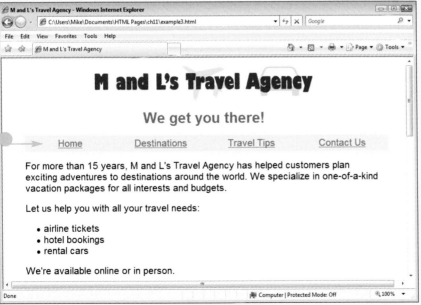

① Click inside the tag declaration and type `background:` and a space.

② Type a color name, hexadecimal value, or RGB value for the color you want to assign.

Note: *For more about color values, see Chapter 4.*

The Web browser assigns the background color to the content.

● In this example, background color is added to the `<TABLE>` element, which enclosed several text links.

Note: *See Chapter 7 to learn how to add tables.*

Add a Background Image to Text

You can add a background image to a section of text using a style sheet rule. To specify a background image, you must know the name and location of the image file. If the image is small, it repeats, or *tiles*, to fill the background area. You can control the repeat using the `repeat` values.

Be careful when assigning a background image, taking into account the color of the text in the foreground. See the section "Add Color to Text" to learn how to adjust the color of text and other content.

Add a Background Image to Text

1 Click inside the tag declaration and type `background:` and a space.

```
styles3.css - WordPad
File  Edit  View  Insert  Format  Help

BODY { font-family: Arial, "Gill Sans" }
H2 { color: teal }
TABLE { background: #FFFF99 }
DIV.machu { background: }
                        ↑
                        1
```

2 Type `url("?")` and a space, replacing *?* with the location and name of the image file you want to use as a background.

In this example, the background image is in the same directory as the style sheet so the image can be referenced with just a file name.

```
styles3.css - WordPad
File  Edit  View  Insert  Format  Help

BODY { font-family: Arial, "Gill Sans" }
H2 { color: teal }
TABLE { background: #FFFF99 }
DIV.machu { background: url("machu_bg2.jpg")| }
                                            ↑
                                            2
```

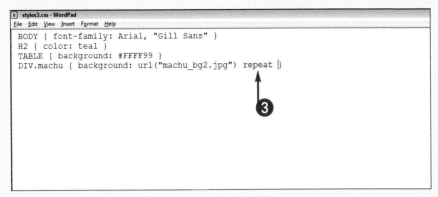

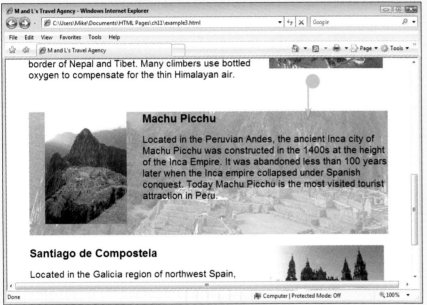

❸ Type a repeat option for the image:

`repeat` repeats the image to fill the background (default).

`repeat-x` tiles the image horizontally.

`repeat-y` tiles the image vertically.

`no-repeat` prevents a background image from repeating.

The Web browser displays the background image as designated in the style rule.

● In this example, a background image is added to a `DIV` tag surrounding one of the sections of content.

Note: *For more about applying styles with a* `DIV` *tag, see Chapter 9.*

Simplify It

Where can I find good background images to use with my Web pages?
If you do not have images to use as backgrounds, you can try finding free ones on the Web. Many sites offer texture images, such as marble backgrounds and water. For example, BackgroundCity.com (www.backgroundcity.com) and Free-Backgrounds.com (www.free-backgrounds.com) are good places to start. Try conducting a Web search on the keywords "free background images."

If users have images turned off in their browsers, can they see the background image for an element?
No. However, you can insert both a background color and a background image. While the image downloads, the browser displays the background color. If the users have images turned off, they still see the background color. Be sure to type the color property before the URL. Your style rule will look something like this:

```
P {background: yellow
url("images/wheatbg.jpg")}
```

Add a Border

You can add a border to a Web page element using the `border` property. A border can help separate the element from other Web page objects. You can designate a specific thickness value, or you can specify one of three descriptive values: `thin`, `medium`, or `thick`.

By specifying a style, you can create a border with a single, double, dotted, or other type of line. You can also assign a color value to a border. See Chapter 4 for more about color values.

Add a Border

① Click inside the tag declaration and type `border:` followed by a space.

② Type a thickness value in pixels, or specify a thickness (`thin`, `medium`, or `thick`).

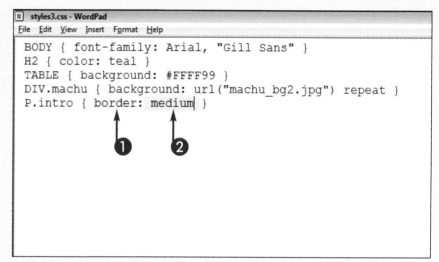

③ Type a space and then a border style (`solid`, `double`, `groove`, `ridge`, `inset`, `outset`, `dotted`, or `dashed`).

Note: *If you do not set a border style with the* `border` *property, the browser does not display a border.*

styles3.css - WordPad
File Edit View Insert Format Help

```
BODY { font-family: Arial, "Gill Sans" }
H2 { color: teal }
TABLE { background: #FFFF99 }
DIV.machu { background: url("machu_bg2.jpg") repeat }
P.intro { border: medium solid }
```
③

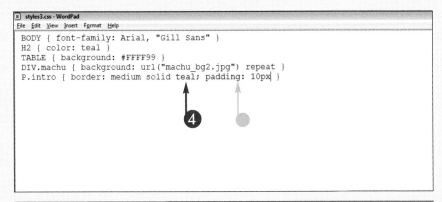

```
styles3.css - WordPad
File  Edit  View  Insert  Format  Help
BODY { font-family: Arial, "Gill Sans" }
H2 { color: teal }
TABLE { background: #FFFF99 }
DIV.machu { background: url("machu_bg2.jpg") repeat }
P.intro { border: medium solid teal; padding: 10px }
```

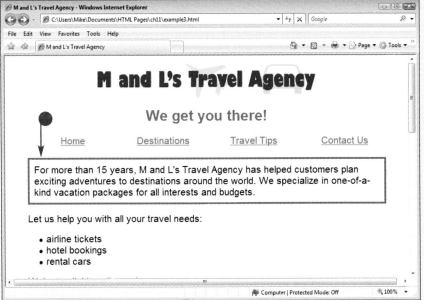

4 Type a space and then a color value.

Note: To view a table of color values, see "Change the Text Color" in Chapter 4.

In many instances, you will need to add some padding between the content and the border; you can use the `padding` property to do so.

Be sure to separate multiple property-value pairs in a rule with semicolons.

Note: See Chapter 11 to learn more about padding.

The Web browser assigns a border to the content.

In this example, a border is added to the introductory paragraph using a style-sheet class.

Note: See Chapter 9 to learn more about creating classes in your style sheets.

Simplify It

Can I add a border to certain sides of an element instead of the entire element?
Yes. You can use the `border-left`, `border-right`, `border-top`, and `border-bottom` properties to designate on which sides you want to add a border. Your code may look like this:

`H3 {border-left: double 5px;`
`border-right: double 5px}`

In this example, a double border is added to the left and right sides of the heading.

Is there a way to remove the borders from elements on my page?
Yes. To remove borders, such as those that appear by default around linked images, you can use the `border` property and set the value to `none`. Your code may look like this:

`IMG {border: none}`

Change Link Colors

You can control the appearance of links throughout your Web pages using a style rule. You can change the color of unvisited, visited, and active links to make them match the theme of your Web site. You can specify one of 16 predefined HTML colors, a hexadecimal color value, or an RGB value. You can also remove the default underlining that normally appears beneath a link using the `text-decoration` property. To change the color of a link or turn underlining on when the cursor hovers over it, see "Change Link Hover Effects."

Change Link Colors

1 Type `A:?  {}` to identify the link tag, replacing *?* with the type of link you want to change (`link`, `visited`, or `active`).

Note: *To learn more about writing style sheets and rules, see Chapter 9.*

```
styles3.css - WordPad
File  Edit  View  Insert  Format  Help

BODY { font-family: Arial, "Gill Sans" }
H2 { color: teal }
TABLE { background: #FFFF99 }
DIV.machu { background: url("machu_bg2.jpg") repeat }
P.intro { border: medium solid teal; padding: 10px }
A:link { }      ◀━━━ ①
```

2 Click between the `{ }` and type `color:` and a space.

3 Type the color name, hexadecimal code, or RGB value you want to assign.

Note: *To view a table of color values, see "Change the Text Color" in Chapter 4.*

```
styles3.css - WordPad
File  Edit  View  Insert  Format  Help

BODY { font-family: Arial, "Gill Sans" }
H2 { color: teal }
TABLE { background: #FFFF99 }
DIV.machu { background: url("machu_bg2.jpg") repeat }
P.intro { border: medium solid teal; padding: 10px }
A:link { color: #CC3300 }
              ↑         ↑
              ②         ③
```

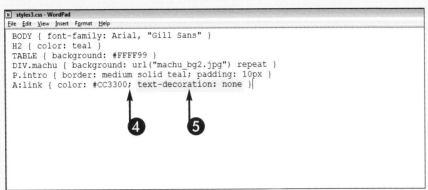

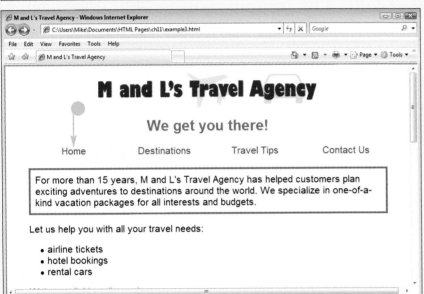

④ Type a semicolon (;) followed by a space.

⑤ Type text-decoration: none to remove the link underline.

The Web browser displays the link in the style you specified.

● In this example, the style is assigned to the navigation links.

What other style sheet properties can I apply to links?

You can use the background and font-family properties to control the appearance of your links. Here is an example of a style rule with other properties assigned:

```
A:link {background: yellow;
font-family: Arial}
```

Any time you type more than one property-value pair in a style rule, be sure to separate them with semicolons.

What is an RGB value?

An RGB value is a way of specifying a precise color in CSS. The color is defined by its mix of red, green, and blue components. You specify each color using a number between 0 and 255 or a percentage. For example, rgb(255, 255, 0) or rgb(100%, 100%, 0%) creates yellow. For more about creating colors for Web pages, see Chapter 4.

Change Link Hover Effects

You can use a style rule to control how link text appears when the mouse pointer hovers over it. For example, you can change the font style of the text, add a border, or change the background color. If you have created another rule that removes the underlining from your links, you can use a hover style to make the underlining reappear. For more about changing the color of links, see "Change Link Colors" earlier in this chapter.

Change Link Hover Effects

1 Type A:hover { } to define the hover style selector.

Note: *To learn more about writing style sheets and rules, see Chapter 9.*

styles4.css - WordPad
File   Edit   View   Insert   Format   Help

```
BODY { font-family: Arial, "Gill Sans" }
A:link { text-decoration: none }
A:hover { }
```
1

2 Click between the { } and type one or more property-value pairs that will be applied when the mouse pointer hovers over a link.

In this example, bold and border styles are defined.

styles4.css - WordPad
File   Edit   View   Insert   Format   Help

```
BODY { font-family: Arial, "Gill Sans" }
A:link { text-decoration: none }
A:hover { font-weight: bold; border: solid 2px red }
```
2

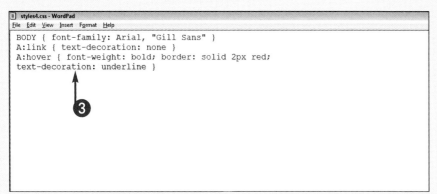

③ To add underlining, type `text-decoration: underline`.

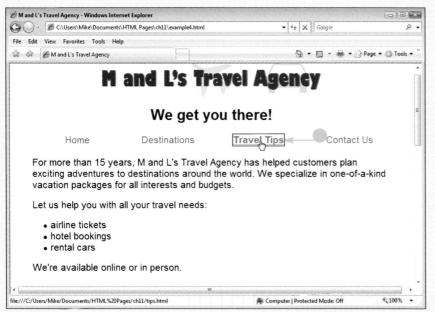

● The Web browser changes the link's style when the mouse pointer hovers over it.

Can I add other line decorations besides underline for my hover styles?
In addition to assigning the `underline` value to the `text-decoration` property, you can assign `overline` to place a line over the link text or `line-through` to place a line through the link text. You can also use these decorations to style regular, non-link text.

Why might I want to add a hover style using CSS?
With style sheets, you can customize your links so that they look more like regular text by changing their color and removing the underlining usually associated with text links. This may be stylistically appealing, but it can also hide the fact that elements on a page are hyperlinks. A hover style can give a user visual feedback that certain words on a page are clickable links.

Chapter 11

Controlling Layout with Style Sheets

Want to create complex layouts on your Web pages, beyond what is possible using HTML alone? This chapter shows you how to precisely position text, images, and other elements on your pages using style sheets. Style sheets let you place content at set coordinates within your layout. You can also control the spacing around your page elements, wrap text around images and tables, and even overlap content.

Control Layout

You can use style sheets to organize text, images, and other elements on your Web page in precise ways. This enables you to create more complicated layouts than those you can create with HTML. Style sheets allow you to specify where in a page to put different types of content by defining coordinates within the browser window. You can also precisely control the space around different elements and even overlap content on your pages.

By combining layout techniques with other CSS features covered in Chapter 10, you can produce pages that look like they were created using a page layout program.

Great Destinations

Completed in 2560 BC, the Great Pyramid of Giza is the oldest and largest of the three Egyptian pyramids located near Cairo. It is the only remaining member of the Seven Wonders of the Ancient World. The pyramid was the tallest man-made structure in the world for over 3,800 years and is believed to have been built as a tomb for Fourth dynasty Egyptian pharaoh Khufu.

The Great Wall of China is a series of stone and earthen structures built to protect the northern borders of the Chinese Empire over many centuries. It stretches over 4,000 miles along an arc along the southern edge of Inner Mongolia. At its peak, the Great Wall was guarded by more than one million men. Some written accounts state that it is the only man-made structure visible from the moon, although scientific calculations show that this is impossible.

Box Model

The key to understanding layout using style sheets is the "box model" of Web page layout, where each element on a page exists in its own rectangular box. Style sheets let you control the dimensions of the box using `height` and `width` attributes, where the box is placed on the Web page, and how the box aligns or overlaps with other boxes on the page.

HTML Block Tags

You define boxes for your content using block-level HTML tags. Block-level tags place new lines before and after the content they enclose. The `<P>`, `<H1>`, and `<TABLE>` tags are examples of block-level tags. The `<DIV>` tag is a type of generic block-level tag commonly placed around other tags to organize content when using style sheets to determine layout.

```
<H1>My Novel</H1>
<P>It was a dark and
stormy night...</P>
<DIV CLASS="illustr">
   <IMG SRC="moon.gif">
</DIV>
```

Positioning Content

You can use different types of positioning to place the boxes of content on your pages. *Relative* positioning places content on the page relative to the normal flow of the other content on the page. *Absolute* positioning places content on absolute points on the page relative to the containing block. *Fixed* positioning places content relative to the browser window and keeps it fixed as a user scrolls.

Offsetting Content

You can offset content on your Web page from its normal position using `top`, `left`, `right`, and `bottom` style sheet properties. This allows you to place content in a precise position within the browser window. You can even place content completely outside of the browser window by using a large or negative offset value. You can also overlap content in the browser window by placing an element at the same window coordinates as another element.

Padding and Margins

You can control the space that surrounds content inside each box on your page. Space outside the edge of the box is known as *margin* (⬤), whereas space inside the edge of the box is called *padding* (⬤). Style sheets let you control space on the top, left, right, and bottom of the boxes independently. You can also turn on borders, which appear where the margin and padding meet.

Floating Content

The `float` CSS property takes a box out of the normal flow of your page and moves it to the right or left side of the enclosing box. Content that follows then wraps around the floated element. Floating allows you to align images, paragraphs, tables, and other content, similar to how you can align images using the `ALIGN` attribute in HTML.

Great Pyramid of Egypt

Completed in 2560 BC, the Great Pyramid of Giza is the oldest and largest of the three Egyptian pyramids located near Cairo. It is the only remaining member of the Seven Wonders of the Ancient World. The pyramid was the tallest man-made structure in the world for over 3,800 years and is believed to have been built as a tomb for Fourth dynasty Egyptian pharaoh Khufu.

Set Width and Height for an Element

You can use the `width` and `height` properties in your style sheet to set the dimensions of your Web page elements. For example, if you want certain paragraphs to take up a fixed amount of space in your page flow, you can apply a style rule as a class. See Chapter 9 to learn more about style sheet classes.

You can also specify a size based on a percentage. Percentage sizes are measured relative to the browser window or enclosing HTML tag. You can use the `float` property to make page content wrap around a resized element. See "Wrap Text around Elements" for details.

DEFINE AN ABSOLUTE SIZE

❶ Click inside the tag declaration and type `width: ?;` `height: ?`, replacing `?` with absolute sizes for the width and height.

You can specify values in points (pt), pixels (px), millimeters (mm), centimeters (cm), inches (in), picas (pc), x-height (ex), or em space (em).

● In this example, the style is applied by assigning a class to a DIV tag. For more about using classes, see Chapter 9.

❷ Type `CLASS="?"` inside the HTML tag, replacing `?` with the class name.

● The Web browser displays the element with an absolute width and height.

In this example, borders are turned on to show the dimensions of the content boxes.

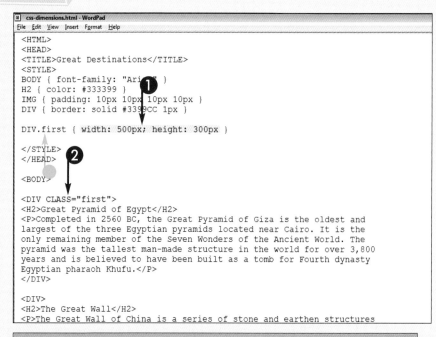

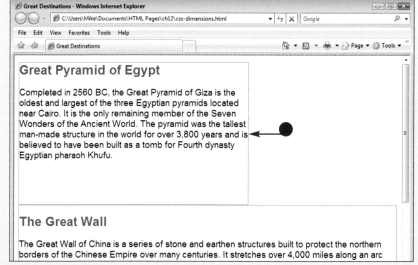

```
DIV.first { width: 40%; height: 80% }

</STYLE>
</HEAD>

<BODY>

<DIV CLASS="first">
<H2>Great Pyramid of Egypt</H2>
<P>Completed in 2560 BC, the Great Pyramid of Giza is the oldest and
largest of the three Egyptian pyramids located near Cairo. It is the
only remaining member of the Seven Wonders of the Ancient World. The
pyramid was the tallest man-made structure in the world for over 3,800
years and is believed to have been built as a tomb for Fourth dynasty
Egyptian pharaoh Khufu.</P>
</DIV>
```

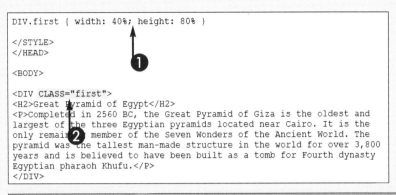

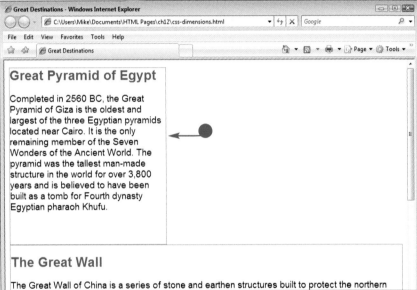

DEFINE A RELATIVE SIZE

1 Click inside the tag declaration and type `width: ?; height: ?`, replacing *?* with percentage sizes for the width and height.

2 Type `CLASS="?"` inside the HTML tag, replacing *?* with the class name.

● The Web browser displays the element with a width and height relative to the size of the enclosing box.

In this case, the enclosing box is the `<BODY>` tag, so the content is resized based on the browser window dimensions.

What are the em and ex style sheet measures?

The em and ex measures allow you to define sizes on your pages based on the size of the surrounding text. The concept comes from typography, where em represents the width of the capital letter *M* and ex represents the height of the lowercase *x*. If you set a style sheet measurement to 2 em, text will be twice the size of the normal font. If viewers adjust the font size of their browser, the content sized on your page using em also adjusts. The ex measure works similarly but on a smaller scale.

How do I control what happens to text that extends outside a CSS box?

You can control how text outside a box is handled using the `overflow` property. Setting the property to `visible` causes the text to be rendered outside the box. A `hidden` value hides the text outside the box. Both `scroll` and `auto` values display scroll bars for viewing the content, if needed. You can assign the overflow property to the DIV, P, and other block-level tags.

Use Relative Positioning

You can apply *relative* positioning to elements on your Web page to place content relative to other content on the page. If you offset a relatively positioned element using the `top`, `left`, `right`, or `bottom` property, the element is offset relative to the point where it would normally begin.

For example, setting the `left` property to `50px` adds that much space to the left side of your page content, moving it to the right. Relative is the default setting for the `position` style property.

APPLY RELATIVE POSITIONING

① Click inside the tag declaration and type `position: relative`.

● In this example, the positioning is applied to all the paragraphs on a page by defining a style for the `P` tag.

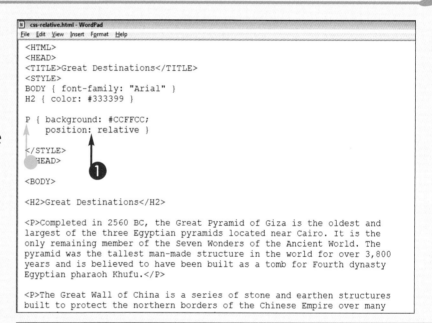

● The Web browser displays the elements with relative positioning, one after the other.

In this example, a background color is applied to the paragraphs to show the dimensions of the content boxes.

```
P { background: #CCFFCC;
    position: relati
    top: 50px;
    left: 100px }

</STYLE>
</HEAD>

<BODY>

<H2>Great Destinations</H2>

<P>Completed in 2560 BC, the Great Pyramid of Giza is the oldest and
largest of the three Egyptian pyramids located near Cairo. It is the
only remaining member of the Seven Wonders of the Ancient World. The
pyramid was the tallest man-made structure in the world for over 3,800
years and is believed to have been built as a tomb for Fourth dynasty
Egyptian pharaoh Khufu.</P>

<P>The Great Wall of China is a series of stone and earthen structures
built to protect the northern borders of the Chinese Empire over many
```

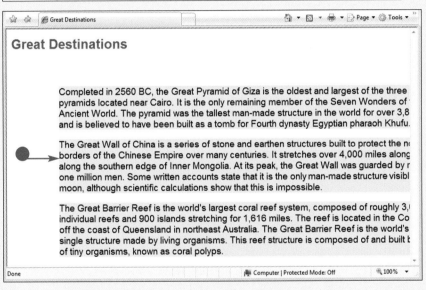

APPLY AN OFFSET

1 Click inside the tag declaration and type `top:  ?;`, replacing *?* with the amount you want to offset the elements from the top of the normal page flow.

2 Click inside the tag declaration and type `left:  ?`, replacing *?* with the amount you want to offset the element from the left of the normal page flow.

You can specify values in points (pt), pixels (px), millimeters (mm), centimeters (cm), inches (in), picas (pc), x-height (ex), or em.

● The Web browser displays elements with offsets applied. In this example, the paragraphs are offset relative to their normal position in the page flow.

Note: *You can narrow elements on your page so that they appear within the browser window by setting their dimensions. See "Set Width and Height for an Element."*

Can I offset content from the bottom or the right?
Yes, but note that offsetting from the bottom may obscure the page content above the positioned element, and offsetting from the right can move content beyond the left edge of the browser window.

How can I position content outside the browser window?
You can apply a high positive or negative positioning value to the content. For example, you could set the `left` property to −5000px to move it far to the left, outside of view. You might want to do this for descriptive content that you want search engines to see but that you want to hide from human visitors. Another way to provide descriptive information for search engines is to add metadata. See Chapter 2 for details.

Use Absolute Positioning

You can apply *absolute* positioning to place an element at exact coordinates on a page, independent of elements that came before it. The coordinates are determined relative to the box that encloses it. This allows you to precisely fit together boxes of text, images, and other content on a page, like a jigsaw puzzle. You can set the coordinates using the `top`, `left`, `right`, and `bottom` properties.

Absolute positioning removes an object from the normal flow of page content. Its size and position have no effect on the position of content that follows it.

Use Absolute Positioning

1 Click inside the tag declaration and type `position: absolute`.

Note: *In this example, absolute positioning is applied to an image using a style sheet class. For more about using classes, see Chapter 9.*

```
css-absolute.html - WordPad
File  Edit  View  Insert  Format  Help

<HTML>
<HEAD>
<TITLE>Great Destinations</TITLE>
<STYLE>
BODY { font-family: "Arial" }
H2 { color: #333399 }
P { background: #CCFFCC; width: 600px }
IMG.right-img { position: absolute }

</STYLE>
</HEAD>

<BODY>

<H2>Great Destinations</H2>

<IMG SRC="pyramid_sm.jpg">

<P>Completed in 2560 BC, the Great Pyramid of Giza is the oldest and
largest of the three Egyptian pyramids located near Cairo. It is the
only remaining member of the Seven Wonders of the Ancient World. The
pyramid was the tallest man-made structure in the world for over 3,800
years and is believed to have been built as a tomb for Fourth dynasty
Egyptian pharaoh Khufu.</P>
```

1

2 Click inside the tag declaration and type `left: ?`, replacing *?* with the amount you want to offset the element from the left.

Separate multiple style sheet rules with semicolons.

In this example, the image is offset to the left of several paragraphs of text.

```
css-absolute.html - WordPad
File  Edit  View  Insert  Format  Help

<HTML>
<HEAD>
<TITLE>Great Destinations</TITLE>
<STYLE>
BODY { font-family: "Arial" }
H2 { color: #333399 }
P { background: #CCFFCC; width: 600px }
IMG.right-img { position: absolute;
                left: 620px }

</STYLE>
</HEAD>

<BODY>

<H2>Great Destinations</H2>

<IMG SRC="pyramid_sm.jpg">

<P>Completed in 2560 BC, the Great Pyramid of Giza is the oldest and
largest of the three Egyptian pyramids located near Cairo. It is the
only remaining member of the Seven Wonders of the Ancient World. The
pyramid was the tallest man-made structure in the world for over 3,800
years and is believed to have been built as a tomb for Fourth dynasty
Egyptian pharaoh Khufu.</P>
```

2

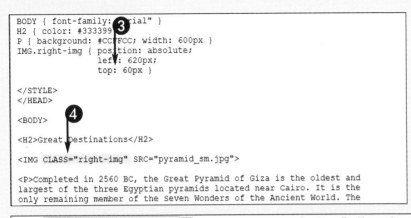

```
BODY { font-family:     rial" }
H2 { color: #333399
P { background: #CCFCC; width: 600px }
IMG.right-img { position: absolute;
                left: 620px;
                top: 60px }

</STYLE>
</HEAD>

<BODY>

<H2>Great Destinations</H2>

<IMG CLASS="right-img" SRC="pyramid_sm.jpg">

<P>Completed in 2560 BC, the Great Pyramid of Giza is the oldest and
largest of the three Egyptian pyramids located near Cairo. It is the
only remaining member of the Seven Wonders of the Ancient World. The
```

❸ Click inside the tag declaration and type `top:  ?`, replacing *?* with the amount you want to offset the element from the top.

❹ Type `CLASS="?"` inside the HTML tag to apply the style, replacing *?* with the class name.

◗ The Web browser displays the element with offsets applied.

The element is offset relative to the enclosing box, which in this example is the browser window.

In this example, the paragraphs are narrowed using a `width` style to make space for the image on the right.

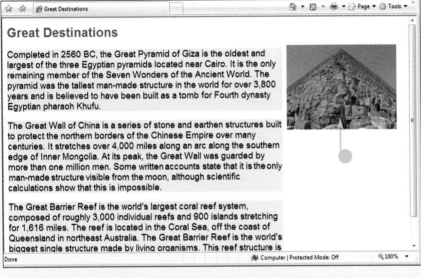

Great Destinations

Completed in 2560 BC, the Great Pyramid of Giza is the oldest and largest of the three Egyptian pyramids located near Cairo. It is the only remaining member of the Seven Wonders of the Ancient World. The pyramid was the tallest man-made structure in the world for over 3,800 years and is believed to have been built as a tomb for Fourth dynasty Egyptian pharaoh Khufu.

The Great Wall of China is a series of stone and earthen structures built to protect the northern borders of the Chinese Empire over many centuries. It stretches over 4,000 miles along an arc along the southern edge of Inner Mongolia. At its peak, the Great Wall was guarded by more than one million men. Some written accounts state that it is the only man-made structure visible from the moon, although scientific calculations show that this is impossible.

The Great Barrier Reef is the world's largest coral reef system, composed of roughly 3,000 individual reefs and 900 islands stretching for 1,616 miles. The reef is located in the Coral Sea, off the coast of Queensland in northeast Australia. The Great Barrier Reef is the world's biggest single structure made by living organisms. This reef structure is

How can I apply absolute positioning to an image and a caption?
You can apply absolute positioning to an image and caption text by surrounding both with a single `DIV` tag. Create a class that defines the absolute coordinates, and then apply it to the `DIV` tag using the class attribute. For more on using the `DIV` tag and creating classes, see Chapter 9.

How do I place an image in the bottom right corner of the browser window?
Create a class with absolute positioning similar to that in the example above, but set the `bottom` and `right` properties to 0. Apply the class to your image using a `DIV` tag.

Use Fixed Positioning

You can apply *fixed* positioning to place an element at exact coordinates on a page and have it remain fixed while a viewer scrolls. This is one way to keep navigation links visible as visitors view content on a long page. In contrast to relative and absolute positioning, fixed positioning is supported only in newer Web browsers. Using fixed positioning on some page elements but not others can result in content overlapping when the user scrolls. How the elements overlap is determined by the z-index of the page elements. For more information, see "Control the Overlap of Elements."

Use Fixed Positioning

① Click inside the tag declaration and type position: fixed.

Note: In this example, fixed positioning is applied to a box of navigation links using a class. For more about using style sheet classes, see Chapter 9.

```
css-fixed.html - WordPad
File  Edit  View  Insert  Format  Help

<!DOCTYPE HTML PUBLIC "-//W3C//DTD HTML 4.01 STRICT//EN"
"HTTP://WWW.W3.ORG/TR/REC-HTML4/STRICT.DTD">
<HTML>
<HEAD>
<TITLE>Great Destinations</TITLE>
<STYLE>
BODY { font-family: "Arial" }
H2 { color: #333399; position: relative; width: 600px; left: 170px }
P { position: relative; width: 600px; left: 170px }
DIV.left-nav { position: fixed }
</STYLE>
</HEAD>

<BODY>

<DIV>
<A HREF="adventure.html">Adventure Travel</A><BR>
<A HREF="aquatic.html">Aquatic Travel</A><BR>
<A HREF="historical.html">Historical Travel</A><BR>
<A HREF="great.html">Great Destinations</A>
</DIV>

<H2>Great Destinations</H2>
```

② Click inside the tag declaration and type left: ?, replacing *?* with the amount you want to offset the element from the left.

Separate multiple style rules with semicolons.

```
css-fixed.html - WordPad
File  Edit  View  Insert  Format  Help

<!DOCTYPE HTML PUBLIC "-//W3C//DTD HTML 4.01 STRICT//EN"
"HTTP://WWW.W3.ORG/TR/REC-HTML4/STRICT.DTD">
<HTML>
<HEAD>
<TITLE>Great Destinations</TITLE>
<STYLE>
BODY { font-family: "Arial" }
H2 { color: #333399; position: relative; width: 600px; left: 170px }
P { position: relative; width: 600px; left: 170px }
DIV.left-nav { position: fixed; left: 10px }
</STYLE>
</HEAD>

<BODY>

<DIV>
<A HREF="adventure.html">Adventure Travel</A><BR>
<A HREF="aquatic.html">Aquatic Travel</A><BR>
<A HREF="historical.html">Historical Travel</A><BR>
<A HREF="great.html">Great Destinations</A>
</DIV>

<H2>Great Destinations</H2>
```

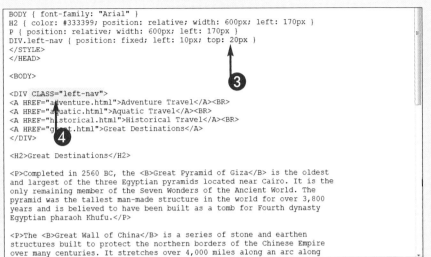

```
BODY { font-family: "Arial" }
H2 { color: #333399; position: relative; width: 600px; left: 170px }
P { position: relative; width: 600px; left: 170px }
DIV.left-nav { position: fixed; left: 10px; top: 20px }
</STYLE>
</HEAD>

<BODY>

<DIV CLASS="left-nav">
<A HREF="adventure.html">Adventure Travel</A><BR>
<A HREF="aquatic.html">Aquatic Travel</A><BR>
<A HREF="historical.html">Historical Travel</A><BR>
<A HREF="great.html">Great Destinations</A>
</DIV>

<H2>Great Destinations</H2>

<P>Completed in 2560 BC, the <B>Great Pyramid of Giza</B> is the oldest
and largest of the three Egyptian pyramids located near Cairo. It is the
only remaining member of the Seven Wonders of the Ancient World. The
pyramid was the tallest man-made structure in the world for over 3,800
years and is believed to have been built as a tomb for Fourth dynasty
Egyptian pharaoh Khufu.</P>

<P>The <B>Great Wall of China</B> is a series of stone and earthen
structures built to protect the northern borders of the Chinese Empire
over many centuries. It stretches over 4,000 miles along an arc along
```

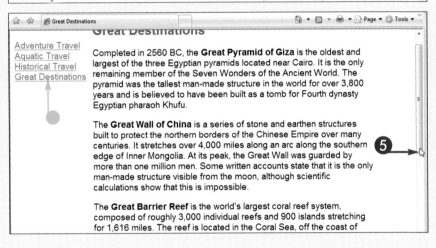

③ Click inside the tag declaration and type top: ?, replacing ? with the amount you want to offset the element from the top.

④ Type CLASS="?" inside the HTML tag to apply the style, replacing ? with the class name. In this example, the style is applied to a DIV tag.

In this example, navigation links are fixed to the left of several paragraphs of text. The paragraphs of text are shifted to the right using relative positioning.

The Web browser displays the element with offsets applied. The element is offset relative to the enclosing box, which in this example is the browser window.

⑤ Scroll down the page.

⬤ The fixed content stays in the same place while the rest of the page content moves.

Simplify It

How can I ensure that as many browsers as possible display fixed content correctly?
Many earlier versions of Web browsers, such as Internet Explorer 6, do not support fixed positioning. Later versions of Internet Explorer support it, but only if the page has a document type set to strict. (See Chapter 2 for more about document types.) You can set the document type to strict by putting the following code at the top of your page:

```
    <!DOCTYPE HTML PUBLIC "-//W3C//
DTD HTML 4.01 Strict//EN" "http://
www.w3.org/TR/html4/
strict.dtd">
```

Set Margins

You can control the margins of your Web page elements using the margin properties. You can set margin values for the top, bottom, left, and right margins around a Web page element. The margin is the spacing on the outside of a page element's border, whether or not the border is visible. To control the spacing inside the border, see "Add Padding."

You can set margin sizing using points (pt), pixels (px), millimeters (mm), centimeters (cm), inches (in), picas (pc), x-height (ex), or em space (em).

Set Margins

1 Click inside the tag declaration and type `margin-?:` and a space, replacing *?* with the margin you want to adjust (`top`, `bottom`, `left`, or `right`).

2 Type a value for the margin spacing.

Typing `margin:` and then a spacing value adds that spacing around all sides of an element.

The Web browser assigns margins to the Web page element.

● In this example, margins are assigned to the paragraphs on a page.

In this example, borders are turned on. Margin spacing exists outside an element's border.

Note: *See "Add Padding" to learn how to add spacing inside borders.*

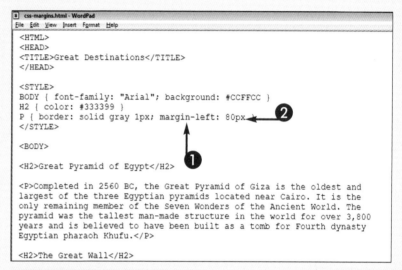

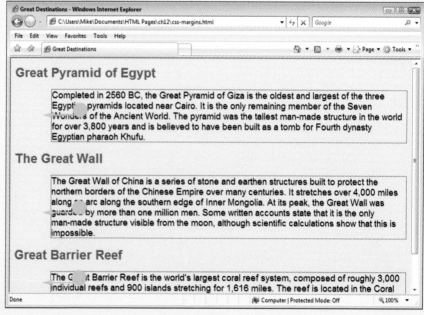

Add Padding

You can use the `padding` property to add space around Web page content. Adding padding can be useful for making text elements readable when they abut one another in a page layout. Padding is the spacing on the inside of a page element's border, whether or not the border is visible. To control the spacing outside the border, see "Set Margins."

You can specify padding in points (pt), pixels (px), millimeters (mm), centimeters (cm), inches (in), picas (pc), x-height (ex), or em space (em).

Add Padding

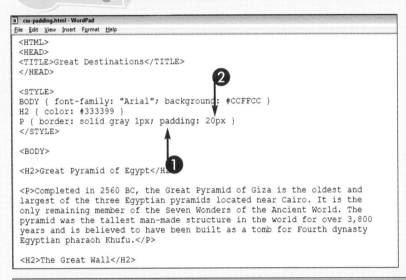

① Click inside the tag declaration and type `padding:` and a space.

② Type a value for the spacing.

To add padding to just one side, you can type `padding-?:`, replacing `?` with `top`, `bottom`, `left`, or `right`.

The Web browser uses the assigned padding for the element to which the tag is applied.

● In this example, padding is assigned to the paragraphs on a page.

In this example, borders are turned on. Padding spacing exists inside an element's border.

Note: *See "Set Margins" to learn how to add spacing outside borders.*

189

Wrap Text around Elements

You can use the `float` property to control how text wraps around the elements on your Web page. The `left` value floats an element to the left side of the browser window or containing HTML tag, and the `right` value floats an element to the right side. To ensure proper text wrapping, place the floating element right before the text you want to wrap. By floating several similarly sized elements to the same side, you can achieve the same effect as elements placed in a row of table cells. The `float` property does not work with elements for which you have assigned an absolute or fixed position.

① Click inside the tag declaration you want to control and type `float:` and a space.

② Type `left` to set the element to the left side of the text, or type `right` to set the element to the right side of the text.

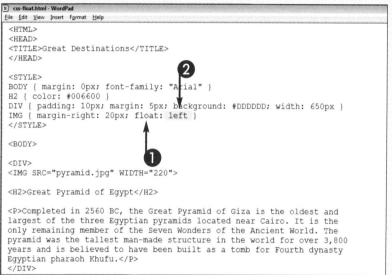

The Web browser floats the element as directed.

● In this example, the `<IMG>` elements float to the left of the headings and paragraphs.

Margins have been added to the `<IMG>` elements to separate them from the text.

Note: *See "Set Margins" for details about setting margins.*

Change Vertical Alignment

You can control the vertical positioning of elements on your page using the `vertical-align` property. You can choose from six vertical alignments: `baseline`, `text-top`, `text-bottom`, `middle`, `top`, `bottom`, `sub`, and `super`. When applied to inline elements in your page, the `vertical-align` property controls how the elements appear relative to the text or other content that comes before and after it. This can be useful for adding text captions to images. When assigned to a table cell, the `vertical-align` property has an effect similar to the `VALIGN` HTML attribute. See Chapter 7 for more about `VALIGN` and tables.

Change Vertical Alignment

```
css-vertical.html - WordPad
File  Edit  View  Insert  Format  Help

<HTML>
<HEAD>
<TITLE>Great Destinations</TITLE>
</HEAD>

<STYLE>
BODY { font-family: "Arial" }
DIV { padding: 10px; margin: 5px; background: #DDDDDD }
IMG { vertical-align: middle }
</STYLE>

<BODY>

<DIV>
<IMG SRC="reef.jpg" WIDTH="200">
The Great Barrier Reef is the world's largest coral reef system.
</DIV>


</BODY>
</HTML>
```

1 Click inside the tag declaration and type `vertical-align:  ?`, replacing *?* with the vertical alignment option you want to assign (`baseline`, `text-top`, `text-bottom`, `middle`, `top`, `bottom`, `sub`, or `super`).

The Great Barrier Reef is the world's largest coral reef system.

The Web browser displays the element using the assigned vertical alignment.

● In this example, the style sheet causes the text following the image to be middle-aligned.

Note: *Learn how to add images in Chapter 5.*

Control the Overlap of Elements

You can use style sheets to overlap elements on your pages by positioning them at similar coordinates. You can then control the stack order of those elements, adjusting the `z-index` property for each element. An element with a higher z-index value appears above an element with a lower z-index value. z-index values can be positive, negative, or zero.

See the "Use Absolute Positioning" section for more about setting the coordinates of a page element.

① Create style sheet classes for the overlapping elements.

② Use absolute positioning to arrange the elements on the page.

③ Apply the classes to the elements by typing `CLASS="?"` inside the HTML tags, replacing ? with the class names.

In this example, two images are overlapped.

Note: *For more about creating style sheet classes, see Chapter 9. For more about absolute positioning, see "Use Absolute Positioning."*

④ Inside the class declaration for the element you want on the bottom, type `z-index: ?`, replacing ? with a number.

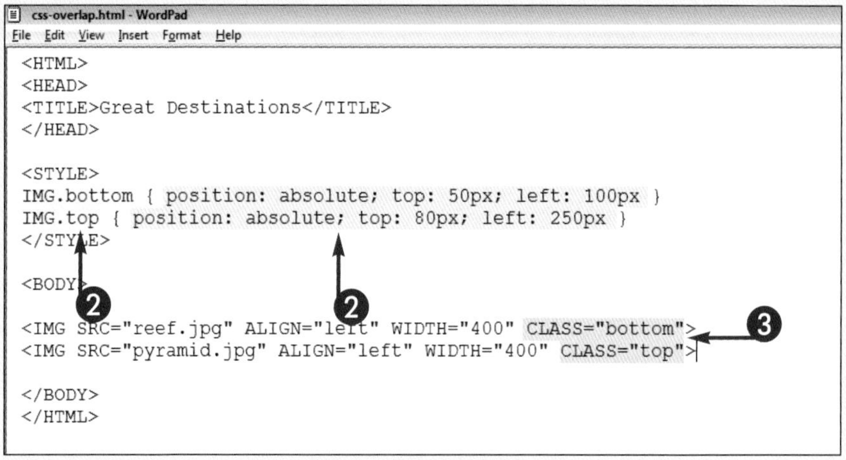

```
css-overlap.html - WordPad
File  Edit  View  Insert  Format  Help

<HTML>
<HEAD>
<TITLE>Great Destinations</TITLE>
</HEAD>

<STYLE>
IMG.bottom { position: absolute; top: 50px; left: 100px }
IMG.top { position: absolute; top: 80px; left: 250px }
</STYLE>

<BODY>

<IMG SRC="reef.jpg" ALIGN="left" WIDTH="400" CLASS="bottom">
<IMG SRC="pyramid.jpg" ALIGN="left" WIDTH="400" CLASS="top">

</BODY>
</HTML>
```

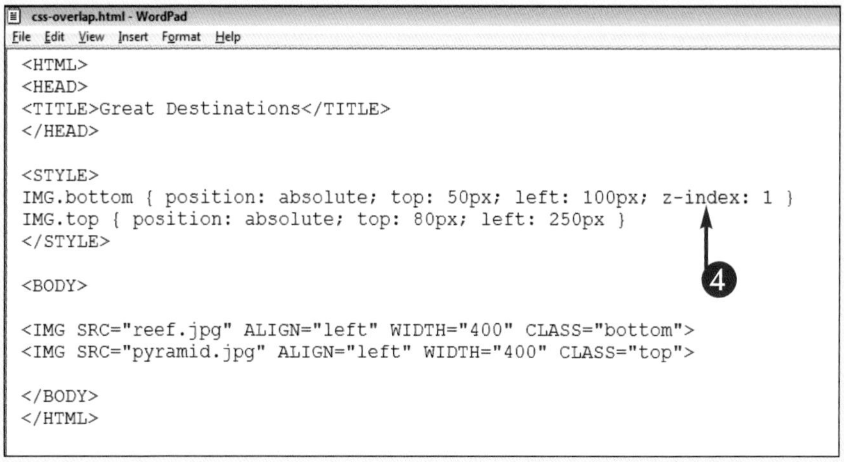

```
css-overlap.html - WordPad
File  Edit  View  Insert  Format  Help

<HTML>
<HEAD>
<TITLE>Great Destinations</TITLE>
</HEAD>

<STYLE>
IMG.bottom { position: absolute; top: 50px; left: 100px; z-index: 1 }
IMG.top { position: absolute; top: 80px; left: 250px }
</STYLE>

<BODY>

<IMG SRC="reef.jpg" ALIGN="left" WIDTH="400" CLASS="bottom">
<IMG SRC="pyramid.jpg" ALIGN="left" WIDTH="400" CLASS="top">

</BODY>
</HTML>
```

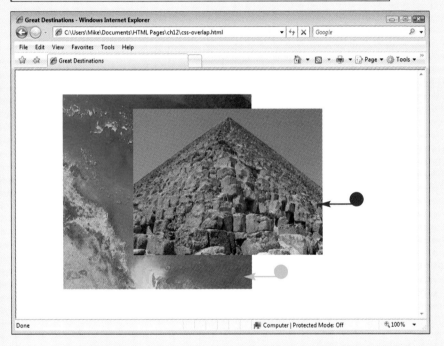

```
css-overlap.html - WordPad
File  Edit  View  Insert  Format  Help

<HTML>
<HEAD>
<TITLE>Great Destinations</TITLE>
</HEAD>

<STYLE>
IMG.bottom { position: absolute; top: 50px; left: 100px; z-index: 1 }
IMG.top { position: absolute; top: 80px; left: 250px; z-index: 2 }
</STYLE>

<BODY>

<IMG SRC="reef.jpg" ALIGN="left" WIDTH="400" CLASS="bottom">
<IMG SRC="pyramid.jpg" ALIGN="left" WIDTH="400" CLASS="top">

</BODY>
</HTML>
```

5 Inside the class declaration for the element you want on top, type `z-index: ?`, replacing *?* with a number greater than the number in step **4**.

The Web browser displays content with stack order determined by the z-index values.

● In this example, the image with the z-index of 1 is on the bottom.

● The image with the z-index of 2 is on top.

How can I make an element transparent so that elements below it show through?
You can make content on your Web page transparent by changing its opacity. However, different browsers recognize different style sheet commands for changing opacity. For Internet Explorer, you can type `filter: alpha(opacity=?)` in your style rule, replacing *?* with a value from 0 to 100. For other popular browsers, you can type `opacity: ?` in your style rule, replacing *?* with a fractional number from 0.0 to 1.0. You can put both properties in a declaration to make the effect compatible with as many Web browsers as possible.

Customize a Background Image

You can place an image as a background on your Web page using style sheets and control how the image repeats. You can make it repeat only horizontally to create a border across the top of your page, or make it repeat only vertically to create a border down the left side.

You can also make it not repeat at all. See the tip on the next page for customizing the placement of a nonrepeating background image.

A background image normally repeats both horizontally and vertically to fill the entire page.

Customize a Background Image

1 Place the image you want to use as your background in the same directory as your HTML file.

2 Type BODY { } to create a style rule for the BODY HTML tag.

```
css-background2.html - WordPad
File  Edit  View  Insert  Format  Help
<TITLE>Great Destinations</TITLE>
</HEAD>

<STYLE>
BODY { }
H1 { color: #FFFF66; font-family: "Arial" }
H2 { color: #006600 }
DIV { padding: 10px; margin: 5px; background: #DDDDDD; font-family:
"Arial" }
IMG { margin: 10px; float: left }
</STYLE>

<BODY>

<H1>Great Destinations</H1>

<BR><BR><BR><BR>

<DIV>
<IMG SRC="reef.jpg" ALIGN="left" WIDTH="200">
<H2>Great Barrier Reef</H2>
<P>The Great Barrier Reef is the world's largest coral reef system,
composed of roughly 3,000 individual reefs and 900 islands stretching
```

3 To insert the image as a background, type `background-image: url('?');`, replacing *?* with the image file name.

```
css-background2.html - WordPad
File  Edit  View  Insert  Format  Help
<TITLE>Great Destinations</TITLE>
</HEAD>

<STYLE>
BODY { background-image: url("reef_bg.jpg"); }
H1 { color: #FFFF66; font-family: "Arial" }
H2 { color: #006600 }
DIV { padding: 10px; margin: 5px; background: #DDDDDD; font-family:
"Arial" }
IMG { margin: 10px; float: left }
</STYLE>

<BODY>

<H1>Great Destinations</H1>

<BR><BR><BR><BR>

<DIV>
<IMG SRC="reef.jpg" ALIGN="left" WIDTH="200">
<H2>Great Barrier Reef</H2>
<P>The Great Barrier Reef is the world's largest coral reef system,
composed of roughly 3,000 individual reefs and 900 islands stretching
```

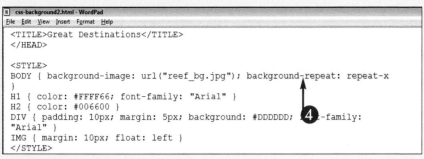

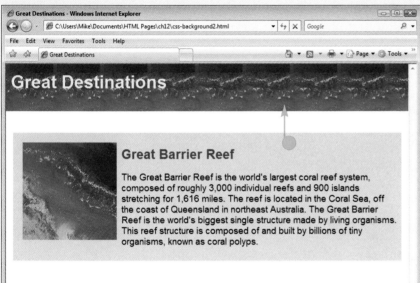

4 To control how the image repeats, type `background-repeat: ?`, replacing *?* with `repeat`, `repeat-x`, `repeat-y`, or `no-repeat`.

The `repeat-x` value tiles the image horizontally, whereas `repeat-y` tiles the image vertically.

The `repeat` value, which is the default, tiles the image in both directions.

The `no-repeat` value displays the image once.

● The Web browser displays the image as a background with the specified repeat style.

In this example, text formatted with H1 tags in the body of the page overlays the background.

Note: *To add a background image using HTML, see Chapter 5.*

Simplify It

How do I create a background image that appears once in the center of my page?
You can assign a `no-repeat` value to the `background-repeat` property to place the image once in the background. Then you can specify the location of the image using the `background-position` property. A `center center` value places the image in the center of the Web page. You can use percentage values to place the image relative to the entire height and width of the window or numeric values to place it at pixel coordinates. The first value is always the horizontal position, whereas the second value is the vertical.

How do I keep a background image from scrolling with the page?
To control whether or not your background image scrolls with the page content, you can assign a `background-attachment` property. Assigning a `scroll` value, which is the default, allows the background image to scroll, whereas `fixed` keeps the background image fixed as the page content moves. This feature works with the different repeat and positioning settings described in this task.

Chapter 12

Adding Multimedia and Other Features

Do you want to add multimedia to your Web pages? Multimedia offers interesting ways to tell stories, describe products, and provide interactivity to your viewers. This chapter shows you how to integrate video, audio, Java applets, and more to enliven your pages and attract users to your site. It also teaches you what users need to have installed in order to view these advanced features.

Understanding Multimedia Elements

The term *multimedia* encompasses all kinds of dynamic visual and audio data, including graphics, sound, animation, and movies. Multimedia can create an ambiance for the site, enhance your site's message, illustrate a product or service, or simply entertain. You can incorporate your multimedia elements into your HTML pages in a variety of ways, but you should first understand how such elements work on the Web.

Delivering Media Files

You can deliver multimedia files to your Web site visitors in several ways. You can link to an external media file, embed the file into your page, or stream the file. The method you choose depends on the way in which you want the user to interact with the file. This chapter covers linking to external files and embedding files. Regardless of the method, you must specify the location of the file — either on your Web server, where the multimedia files are stored with your HTML, or on an external host. When choosing a media file and format to add to your page, always consider your target audience. It is usually a good idea to include information about the multimedia elements in case the user needs to install special programs or plug-ins to view them.

External Media Files

One way to incorporate a multimedia element into your page is to supply a link to an external media file. For example, you might allow a visitor to click a link and download a PDF slide show of your vacation pictures or an MP3 music file of your latest song. If the user decides to access the file, the browser helps him or her determine how to download it and where to store it. After downloading the file, the user can play the file in a separate window using the appropriate media player or program.

Embedded Files

You can integrate a multimedia file directly onto your page by embedding the file. When the user accesses the page, the file plays as part of the page content. For example, you might embed a video file to play in an area on the Web page. The file could be located on your server or on an external host such as YouTube. Depending on the file type and setup, the file may play immediately when the user displays the page or when the user clicks a button or other feature on the page.

Dueling HTML Elements

Establishing standards for Web page development is an ongoing task for the World Wide Web Consortium (W3C). Currently, two popular HTML tags exist for showing multimedia files on Web pages: EMBED and OBJECT. Netscape created the nonstandard EMBED element, whereas the W3C introduced the standard OBJECT element. Microsoft added ActiveX controls to the OBJECT element; today's browser versions support them to varying degrees. For the widest support, many developers combine the OBJECT element with the nonstandard EMBED element. See "Embed an Audio File" for details.

Embed with ActiveX Controls

Another way you can embed multimedia content into your pages is by using ActiveX controls along with the `OBJECT` tag. ActiveX uses a `CLASSID` attribute control number to define which data type the browser loads for playback. The `CLASSID` attribute for QuickTime, for example, is a different number than that for Windows Media Player. Once you define the proper player, you can set the parameters for the clip's playback. For an example, see the section "Embed a Flash Movie."

Plug-ins

Plug-ins are specialized applications that work with the browser to play media files, typically focusing on a particular file format. If users do not have the right plug-in to play your file, they can download the plug-in, install it, and use it as part of their Web browser. First introduced by Netscape, plug-ins are now popular among all the browsers. For example, you can install a Flash Player plug-in to allow your browser to play Flash multimedia files.

Media Players

Media players are separate programs designed to handle many types of media files. Often called *all-in-one players*, media players can work both separately and alongside browsers to play multimedia files encountered on and off the Web. Popular media players include Windows Media Player from Microsoft, QuickTime player from Apple, and RealPlayer from RealNetworks. Users can download copies of these popular media players from the Internet. You can help your users by providing links to download locations.

Finding Media Players and Plug-ins

Player	Web Site
Windows Media Player	www.microsoft.com/downloads
Apple QuickTime	www.apple.com/quicktime
Adobe Flash Player	www.adobe.com/products/flashplayer
Adobe Shockwave Player	get.adobe.com/shockwave
Adobe Reader	www.adobe.com/products/acrobat
RealPlayer	www.real.com

Link to Audio or Video Files

You can insert links on your Web page that, when clicked, download and play an audio or video file. When you link to a file, the file may open within the Web browser or in a separate application window, depending on the configuration of your computer. Linking is the least complicated way to deliver multimedia files to your Web page visitors.

If you are hosting the multimedia content yourself, make sure you upload the audio or video file along with the HTML document when publishing your content.

Link to Audio or Video Files

1 Type the text you want to use as a link.

2 Type `<A HREF="?">` in front of the link text, replacing *?* with the location and name of the audio or video file to which you want to link.

Note: See Chapter 6 to learn more about creating HTML links.

```
extras-linkto.html - WordPad
File  Edit  View  Insert  Format  Help

<HTML>
<HEAD>
<TITLE>M and L's Travel Agency</TITLE>
<STYLE>
BODY { font-family: "Arial"; background: #FFFFFF }
DIV#search { text-align: center }
</STYLE>
</HEAD>
<BODY LEFTMARGIN="200" RIGHTMARGIN="200">

<P ALIGN="center"><IMG SRC="mltravel.gif"></P>

<P ALIGN="center"><I>We get you there!</I></P>

<P>For more than 15 years, M and L's Travel Agency has helped customers
plan exciting  adventures to destinations around the world. We
specialize in one-of-a-kind vacation  packages for all interests and
budgets. Let us help you with your airline tickets, hotel bookings, and
rental cars, either online or in person.
</P>

<P>Here's what our <A HREF="testimonial.mp3">customers are saying.</P>
```

3 Type `</A>` at the end of the link text.

● You can optionally describe the multimedia file. You can include the file format and file size.

```
extras-linkto.html - WordPad
File  Edit  View  Insert  Format  Help

<HTML>
<HEAD>
<TITLE>M and L's Travel Agency</TITLE>
<STYLE>
BODY { font-family: "Arial"; background: #FFFFFF }
DIV#search { text-align: center }
</STYLE>
</HEAD>
<BODY LEFTMARGIN="200" RIGHTMARGIN="200">

<P ALIGN="center"><IMG SRC="mltravel.gif"></P>

<P ALIGN="center"><I>We get you there!</I></P>

<P>For more than 15 years, M and L's Travel Agency has helped customers
plan exciting  adventures to destinations around the world. We
specialize in one-of-a-kind vacation  packages for all interests and
budgets. Let us help you with your airline tickets, hotel bookings, and
rental cars, either online or in person.
</P>

<P>Here's what our <A HREF="testimonial.mp3">customers are saying</A>
(MP3 format, 1.7 MB).</P>
```

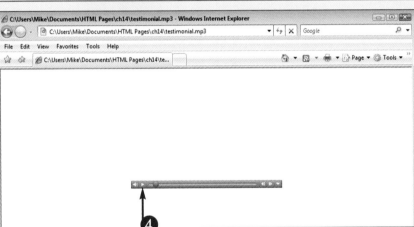

When you open the HTML document, the Web browser displays the link on the page.

● When the user clicks the link, the Web browser attempts to play the audio or video file.

Note: *See Chapter 2 to learn more about viewing your HTML document as an offline Web page.*

In this example, a QuickTime player is displayed within the Web browser to play the audio file.

④ Click the **Play** button (▶) to play the file.

Simplify It

Does my page need to include information about the multimedia file to which I am linking?
It is always good practice to give your Web page visitors all the information they need to know in order to download and view any type of multimedia file. For example, you can include a brief description of the file, list the file format and size, and provide a link to any plug-ins or media players the user might need to play the file.

How can I add background music to my page?
You can assign an audio clip to play in the background while users visit your page using the BGSOUND tag. The tag is not part of the official HTML standard; it works in Internet Explorer but does not work in some other browsers such as Firefox. You reference the audio file using the SRC attribute, such as <BGSOUND SRC="audio.mp3">.

Embed a Video File

You can use the `<EMBED>` tag to add an embedded video clip to your HTML page. Embedded videos play directly on your page. Playback controls also appear on the page, allowing the user to start and stop the video.

You can control the size of the window in which an embedded video appears. You can also control whether the video starts automatically when the page loads and whether the video repeats, or *loops*, after it finishes. To add embedded sound to your page, see "Embed an Audio File."

Embed a Video File

1 Type `<EMBED SRC="?">` where you want to insert the video window on the page, replacing *?* with the location and name of the video file.

Popular video file formats include Audio/Video Interleaved (.avi), QuickTime (.mov), and Windows Media Video (.wmv).

```
extras-video.html - WordPad
File  Edit  View  Insert  Format  Help
<HTML>
<HEAD>
<TITLE>M and L's Travel Agency</TITLE>
<STYLE>
BODY { font-family: "Arial"; background: #FFFFFF }
DIV#search { text-align: center }
</STYLE>
</HEAD>
<BODY LEFTMARGIN="200" RIGHTMARGIN="200">

<P ALIGN="center"><IMG SRC="mltravel.gif"></P>

<H2 ALIGN="center">Machu Picchu</H2>

<P ALIGN="center">
<EMBED SRC="machu.avi">          ①
</P>

</BODY>
</HTML>
```

2 Within the `<EMBED>` tag, type `WIDTH="?"` `HEIGHT="?"`, replacing *?* in both attributes with the width and height values for the size of the window.

```
extras-video.html - WordPad
File  Edit  View  Insert  Format  Help
<HTML>
<HEAD>
<TITLE>M and L's Travel Agency</TITLE>
<STYLE>
BODY { font-family: "Arial"; background: #FFFFFF }
DIV#search { text-align: center }
</STYLE>
</HEAD>
<BODY LEFTMARGIN="200" RIGHTMARGIN="200">

<P ALIGN="center"><IMG SRC="mltravel.gif"></P>

<H2 ALIGN="center">Machu Picchu</H2>

<P ALIGN="center">
<EMBED SRC="machu.avi" WIDTH="320" HEIGHT="280">
</P>                                          ②

</BODY>
</HTML>
```

```
extras-video.html - WordPad
File  Edit  View  Insert  Format  Help
<HTML>
<HEAD>
<TITLE>M and L's Travel Agency</TITLE>
<STYLE>
BODY { font-family: "Arial"; background: #FFFFFF }
DIV#search { text-align: center }
</STYLE>
</HEAD>
<BODY LEFTMARGIN="200" RIGHTMARGIN="200">

<P ALIGN="center"><IMG SRC="mltravel.gif"></P>

<H2 ALIGN="center">Machu Picchu</H2>

<P ALIGN="center">
<EMBED SRC="machu.avi" WIDTH="320" HEIGHT="280" AUTOSTART="true"
LOOP="true">
</P>

</BODY>
</HTML>
```

● If you want the video to play immediately when the page loads, type AUTOSTART="true" in the EMBED tag.

● If you want the video to play continuously, type LOOP="true" in the EMBED tag.

When you open the HTML document, the Web browser displays the embedded video window and playback controls on the page.

● The embedded controls enable the user to play, pause, stop, rewind, and fast-forward the video.

Simplify It

How do I embed a video hosted on YouTube?
You can embed a video from YouTube (www.youtube.com) on your Web page by inserting HTML from the video's Embed text box. The video owner must have embedding enabled for this box to be available. To add the video, click the Embed box on the YouTube page for the video to select the HTML. Then click **Edit** and then **Copy** in your browser to copy the code for pasting into your HTML document. You can edit the WIDTH and HEIGHT attribute values in the code to change the dimensions of the inserted video.

Embed an Audio File

You can add an embedded sound to your HTML page using the `<EMBED>` tag. You can surround the `<EMBED>` tag with `<OBJECT>` tags to make your code compatible with more Web browsers. The `OBJECT` tag requires class ID information that tells the browser what type of multimedia file is being played.

You can adjust the space in which the sound controls appear on the page. To add embedded video to your page, see "Embed a Video File."

Embed an Audio File

① Type `<EMBED SRC="?">` where you want to insert sound controls on the page, replacing *?* with the location and name of the audio file.

② Within the `<EMBED>` tag, type `WIDTH="?" HEIGHT="?"`, replacing *?* in both attributes with the width and height values you want to use for the size of the controls.

You can experiment with the values to make the controls the right size for your page.

③ Before the `EMBED` tag, type `<OBJECT CLASSID= "clsid: ?"`, replacing *?* with the class ID for a multimedia plug-in.

In this example, the QuickTime plug-in is specified with a class ID of `02BF25D5-8C17-4B23-BC80-D3488ABDDC6B`.

You can perform a Web search to find the class IDs for other popular plug-ins.

④ Type `WIDTH="?" HEIGHT="?">`, replacing *?* in both attributes with width and height values.

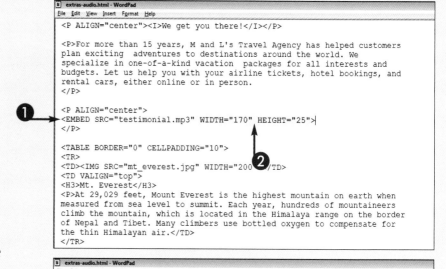

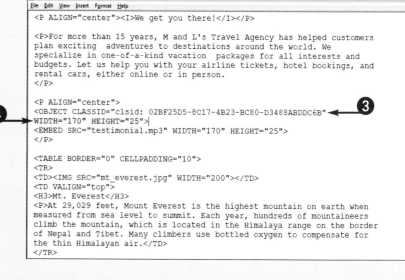

```
<P>For more than 15 years, M and L's Travel Agency has helped customers
plan exciting  adventures to destinations around the world. We
specialize in one-of-a-kind vacation  packages for all interests and
budgets. Let us help you with your airline tickets, hotel bookings, and
rental cars, either online or in person.
</P>

<P ALIGN="center">
<OBJECT CLASSID="clsid: 02BF25D5-8C17-4B23-BC80-D3488ABDDC6B"
WIDTH="170" HEIGHT="25">
<PARAM NAME="filename" VALUE="testimonial.mp3"/>
<EMBED SRC="testimonial.mp3" WIDTH="170" HEIGHT="25">
</OBJECT>
</P>
```

⑤

⑥

⑤ Type `<PARAM NAME= "src" VALUE="?" />`, substituting the location and name of the audio file for *?*.

⑥ Type a closing `</OBJECT>` tag after the EMBED tag.

When you open the HTML document, the Web browser displays the sound controls on the page.

● The user can click the **Play** button () to start the sound.

The embedded sound controls allow you to play, pause, and stop the sound as well as control the volume.

M and L's Travel Agency

We get you there!

For more than 15 years, M and L's Travel Agency has helped customers plan exciting adventures to destinations around the world. We specialize in one-of-a-kind vacation packages for all interests and budgets. Let us help you with your airline tickets, hotel bookings, and rental cars, either online or in person.

Mt. Everest

At 29,029 feet, Mount Everest is the highest mountain on earth when

Simplify It

What audio file formats are common on the Web?
Here is a list of common audio formats supported by most browsers, plug-ins, and media players:

Audio Formats	
Format	**File Extension**
MP3 (MPEG-1, Layer III)	.mp3
MIDI (Musical Instrument Digital Interface)	.mid
AIFF (Audio Interchange File Format)	.aif
WAV (RIFF WAVE)	.wav
WMA (Windows Media Audio)	.wma
RA (RealAudio)	.ra

Embed a Flash Movie

You can add a Flash movie to your Web page. Introduced in 1996, Flash is a popular method for adding animations, interactive games, and movies to Web pages. Using an ActiveX class ID along with the `OBJECT` element, you can instruct the browser with the necessary information to load and play the Flash file. Flash movies usually have a file extension of .swf, which stands for Shockwave Flash, or .flv, which stands for Flash Video.

Embed a Flash Movie

① Click where you want to insert the Flash movie and type `<OBJECT CLASSID= "clsid:D27CDB6E-AE6D-11cf-96B8-444553540000".`

② Type `CODEBASE= "http://download. macromedia.com/pub/ shockwave/cabs/ flash/swflash. cab#version=6,0, 40,0".`

③ Type `WIDTH="?" HEIGHT= "?">`, replacing ? in both attributes with the width and height values for the movie.

④ Type `<PARAM NAME= "movie" VALUE="?">`, substituting the Flash file name for *?*.

⑤ Type `</OBJECT>`.

● In Flash-enabled browsers, the Flash movie plays when the page is displayed.

Add a
Java Applet

You can add Java applets to your Web pages to add animation and interactivity. Java applets are programs written in the Java programming language. Many applets are available for downloading on the Web. The Java Boutique (www.javaboutique.internet.com) and JavaShareware.com (www.javashareware.com)

are good places to start. You can also conduct a Web search to find more free Java applets. To view Java applets, viewers must be using a Java-enabled Web browser. A browser plug-in is included with the Standard Edition of Java, which can be downloaded at www.java.com.

Add a Java Applet

① Click where you want to insert the applet and type <APPLET CODE="?">, replacing *?* with the location and name of the applet.

● Optionally, to control the size of the applet window, type WIDTH="?" HEIGHT="?" within the <APPLET> tag, replacing *?* with width and height values.

● You can also add alternative text for browsers that do not run Java applets.

② Type </APPLET>.

● In Java-enabled browsers, the Java applet runs when the page is displayed.

Chapter 13

Publishing Your Web Pages

Are you ready to place your HTML document on the Web? This chapter shows you how to find a Web host and transfer your files to a server using FTP client software. After the files are transferred, users can view your pages with a Web browser. This chapter also explains how to register a domain name for your Web site and fix common problems on your pages.

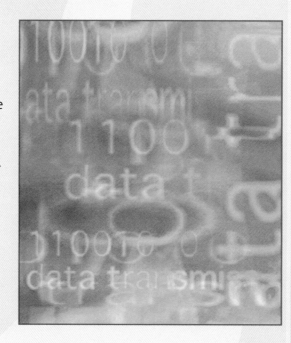

Understanding Web Page Publishing

The final phase of creating a Web site is publishing your pages. When it comes to building Web sites, the term *publishing* refers to all the necessary steps you must take to make your HTML documents, images, and other content available to others. This includes finding a service provider to host your pages and registering a domain name. The final step is to transfer the files for your pages from your local computer to a Web server at your service provider.

Web Hosts

To place your pages on the Web, you need a Web server — an Internet-connected computer specifically set up to store and manage Web pages. Unless you have your own Web server, you need to find a service provider that will give you access to one. These companies are commonly called *Web hosts* because they provide the computers that host your HTML documents and other files. Sometimes the same company that you receive Internet access from also includes hosting services as part of the package. Checking with them first could save you money.

Determine Your Needs

Before you start looking for a Web host, first determine what features and services you need. For example, how much storage space do you anticipate using for your Web site? Although HTML documents are generally small in size, images and multimedia files included with Web pages can consume large amounts of space. Does your site require e-commerce features such as an online shopping cart or a secure server for handling confidential information? How about advanced Web technologies such CGI scripts, PHP, and database access? Do you need to keep track of Web statistics, such as who visits your site and how often? Knowing your needs beforehand can help find the right host.

Finding a Web Host

The best place to start looking for a host is with your existing Internet service provider. If it does not offer Web hosting services, you can look for a Web host on the Internet. For example, *Web Host Magazine & Buyer's Guide* (www.webhostmagazine.com) can help you compare offerings. Also consider asking friends and family for recommendations. When publishing your first Web site, technical support is often important, so you might consider paying extra for a host that has a good track record in that area.

Acquire Your Own Domain Name

An Internet domain name, such as wiley.com, can give your Web site a personalized address that is easy for users to remember. You can register for a domain name through a domain name registrar, of which there are hundreds. Your Web host may also offer domain registration services, sometimes for a reduced fee because you are already a customer. Once you acquire a domain name, you can associate the name with your Web site by setting up domain name service, or *DNS*, with your Web host. This allows you to use your custom domain name rather than the host's in the Web addresses for your pages. For more information, see "Look Up a Domain Name." After you register a domain name, you can also use it for e-mail.

Transfer Files

After you set up an account with a Web host, you can transfer your HTML files, images, and other content to the server to set up your Web site. Transferring files from your computer to a Web server is called *uploading*. Depending on your server, you can transfer files using FTP (File Transfer Protocol) or a Web interface provided by your hosting service. More often than not, you use FTP to upload your files.

FTP Programs

FTP is a standard method for transferring files over the Internet. To transfer files with FTP, you need an FTP program, also called a *client*. You can find free and inexpensive FTP clients on the Internet. Popular FTP programs include WS_FTP (www.ipswichft.com) and CuteFTP (www.globalscape.com/cuteftp). Also, check your Web host to see what FTP clients or file-uploading tools it recommends. See the section "Transfer Files to a Web Server with WS_FTP" for more information.

Maintain Your Site

After you upload your pages, you can view and test your site. One of your chores as a Web developer is to maintain your Web site. It is up to you to keep your information and links current. Regularly testing your site for broken links is good practice. See the section "Troubleshoot Your Web Pages" to learn more about fixing page problems. It is also good practice to update your content on a regular basis or give it a fresh look from time to time. Stale data can keep visitors from returning to your site.

Look Up a Domain Name

Registering a custom domain name gives viewers an easy-to-remember way to get to your Web site. You can look up the status of a domain name at a *domain name registrar*, which is a company that provides domain registration services. If the domain name is available, you can register it. If it is not available, you can check who owns it and when the registration expires via a WHOIS search. Domain names are classified by the characters that follow the dot in their names, also known as *extensions*. Although the .com, .net, and .org extensions are the most popular, you can also choose from dozens of other extensions.

CHECK AVAILABILITY

① Visit the Web site of a domain name registrar.

This example uses Network Solutions at www.network solutions.com. Most registrars have a similar lookup process.

② Type a name in the search box.

③ Click one or more extensions to check (☐ changes to ☑).

A domain name can have up to 63 characters and can include letters, numbers, and hyphens.

④ Click **Search**.

The domain name registrar looks up the availability of the domain name and returns the results.

● Typically, a registrar offers multiple domain extensions and checks the availability of all of them.

⑤ Select one or more extensions to register (☐ changes to ☑).

⑥ Click **Add Domain(s) to Order** to begin the registration process.

The registration process includes submitting contact information, paying for the registration, and possibly adding related services.

212

CHECK REGISTRATION INFORMATION

❶ Visit a Web site that offers WHOIS lookup services.

WHOIS is an Internet protocol for checking domain name information.

This example uses the Network Solutions WHOIS service at www.networksolutions.com/whois.

❷ Type a domain name.

❸ Click **Domain** (◎ changes to ◉).

❹ Click **Search**.

The service returns the registration information for the domain name.

● Scroll down the page to view contact and expiration information.

How do I associate my domain name with my Web site?
You can associate the domain name with your Web site by setting up domain name service, or *DNS*. To do this, first find out your Web host's DNS information, which will be in the form of two or more server addresses. You can then submit the information, usually via an online form, to the registrar where you registered the domain name. If you ever switch your site to a different Web host, you can submit new DNS information to move the domain name.

How do I renew my domain name registration?
When you register a domain name, you choose a registration period of one or more years. At the end of the registration period, you must renew the domain name if you want to continue to use it. If you do not renew the registration, the name becomes available to others for registration. For this reason, it is important to keep the contact information at your registrar current so you can receive renewal notices.

Transfer Pages to a Web Server with WS_FTP

You can transfer your Web page files to a Web server using FTP software. FTP stands for *File Transfer Protocol*, which is a method for moving files on the Internet. In this section, you learn how to transfer files using Ipswitch WS_FTP, a popular program for transferring Web files. If you use another FTP program, your steps may differ. Once you transfer your HTML files, images, style sheets, and other supporting files to the Web server, you can view your pages on the Internet using a Web browser.

SET UP YOUR CONNECTION

① Open the WS_FTP program window.

The first time you use the program, the Connection Wizard appears to help you set up your server connection.

Note: *If you have not downloaded and installed the program, visit www.ipswitch.com. This example uses the Home version of WS_FTP.*

② Type a descriptive name for your connection. This can be the name of your Web site.

③ Click **Next**.

④ Select a connection type.

The default and most common type for transferring files is FTP.

⑤ Click **Next**.

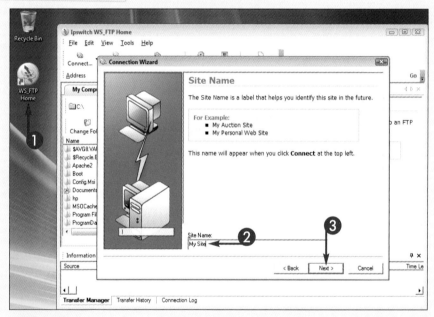

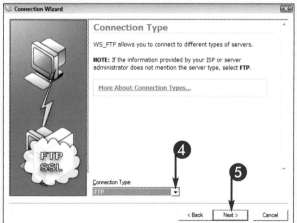

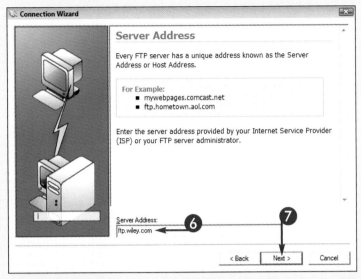

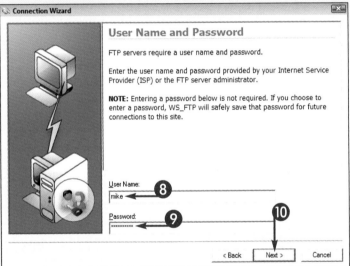

6 Type your host name or IP address. This information will be several words or numbers separated by periods (.).

If you do not know the host name or IP address, contact your service provider for more information.

Typically, you receive this information when you sign up for an account.

7 Click **Next**.

8 Type your user name.

9 Type your user password.

If you do not know your user ID or password, contact your service provider.

Again, you typically receive this information when you sign up for an account.

10 Click **Next**.

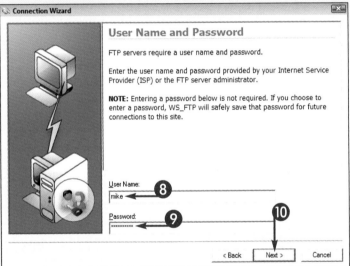

Where can I find an FTP program?
You can find a variety of downloadable FTP programs on the Internet, including freeware and shareware programs. Download.com (www. download.com) is a popular site for obtaining such programs. Many programs offer a free trial version you can experiment with to see if you want to purchase the full version. You can find a trial version of Ipswitch WS_FTP at www. ipswitch.com.

What information do I need to connect to my server with an FTP program?
Most servers ask you for a server address, a user name, and a password. When you create an account with a Web host provider, you are assigned this information, including a destination folder on the server's directory. You can use this folder to store your HTML files, along with any image and multimedia files you include with your Web page.

Transfer Files to a Web Server with WS_FTP *(continued)*

After you establish your server connection, you can start transferring files. The WS_FTP program window shows two panes, one displaying the files on your computer and the other displaying files on the Web server. You can move files between the two using the Upload and Download buttons.

You can upload a single file or multiple files. Any time you need to update your site, you can transfer more files from your computer to the server.

Transfer Files to a Web Server with WS_FTP *(continued)*

● You can click this option if you immediately want to open your connection once you complete the Connection Wizard (☐ changes to ☑).

⑪ Click **Finish**.

Your connection information is saved and the program window remains open and ready for any file transfer activities you want to perform.

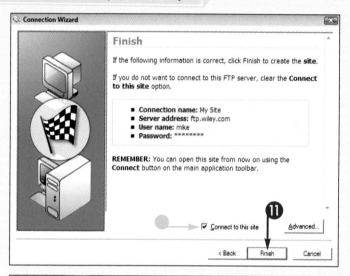

TRANSFER FILES

① If you have not connected to your server, click **Connect**.

Note: You must connect to the Internet before transferring files.

② Click your connection name from the list.

③ Click **Connect**.

WS_FTP connects your computer to the server.

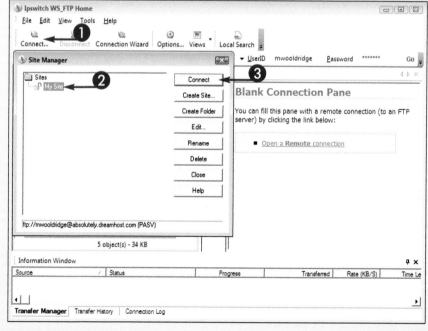

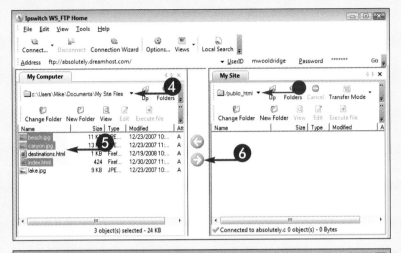

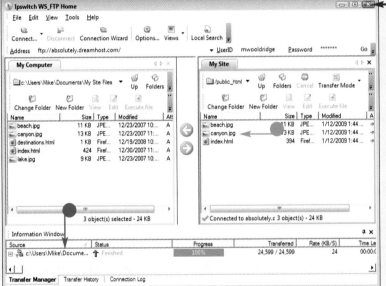

4 Navigate to the folder on your computer that contains your HTML and other site files.

● You may need to navigate to a special folder on the server where Web site files are stored. Check with your Web host for details.

5 Click the files to transfer.

To select multiple files, press and hold `Ctrl` while clicking the file names.

6 Click the **Upload** button (▣).

● WS_FTP shows status messages as it transfers the files. The transfer may take several minutes.

● The transferred files appear in the list of server files.

7 Click **Close** (☒) to exit the program when you finish transferring files.

You can now use your browser to view the pages.

Simplify It

How do I remove a file from my Web site?
Open your connection to the server, select from the Web server pane the file you want to delete, and press `Delete`. A prompt box appears asking if you really want to remove the file. Click **Yes** to remove the file from the server.

What address do I use to access my newly published page?
The address you type in your browser to access your page depends on the domain name for your site, the name of your HTML file, and the location of the file on the server. If your domain name is example.com, your HTML file is page.html, and you uploaded the file to the main HTML folder on the server, your address might be something like http://www.example.com/page.html. Contact your service provider for more details. For more about Web addresses, see Chapter 6.

Troubleshoot Your Web Pages

No matter how carefully you create your pages, errors can creep in. If your Web page does not display properly in a browser, you must track down the problem. In most situations, you can track the problem to a common coding error. If you cannot find the error even after a thorough check, you can share your document with another Web developer for feedback or submit your code to an HTML validator.

Typing Errors

Typing errors are the most common mistake in HTML documents. Web browsers ignore tags they do not recognize, so always start your troubleshooting process with a careful proofread of your document. Read each line in your document, paying close attention to tags and attributes. One mistyped character, quotation mark, or bracket can cause a browser to display a broken page. Many Web editors color-code HTML to help you find such errors.

Invalid Paths and Extensions

Typing the wrong path to a file can cause an error on your pages. This can occur in hyperlinks, image and multimedia tags, and references to CSS and scripts. If a server cannot locate a file on the Web server, it cannot access or display the corresponding content. When page content does not appear as expected, double-check your text for the correct paths. It is also essential to use the correct file extensions when specifying files, such as .css for style sheets.

Broken Links

Even if the paths to your links are syntactically correct, that does not guarantee that the file on the corresponding server is still there. Nothing is more frustrating to Web page visitors than clicking a nonfunctioning link, so test your links on a regular basis. Because pages come and go on the Web, make it a regular practice to check your links.

Missing Image Files

If the Web browser cannot display your images, you may have entered the wrong file name. Verify your image name, making sure you typed the correct upper- and lowercase letters for the file name. It is also common to type the wrong file extension for an image file, such as typing .gif instead of .jpg. Remember, not all browsers support all kinds of image files. Be sure to stick with formats commonly found on the Web. See Chapter 5 to learn more.

HTML Code Appears

If the browser displays your HTML code instead of the Web page, you probably saved the file as a TXT file instead of an HTML file. Also double-check to see if your <HTML> tag appears at the top of the page. If this tag is missing, the browser may not read your page as an HTML document.

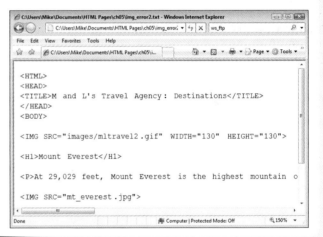

HTML Validators

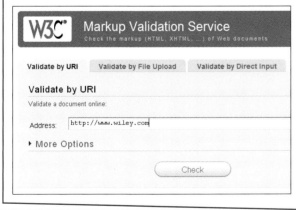

After you upload your pages, you can access an HTML validator and have it automatically download and process your page content. Because most validators reference the official HTML specification, they can point out syntax errors and tell you if you are coding to the latest official standard. The W3C, which maintains HTML specifications, offers a validation service at http://validator.w3.org. To ensure that a validator checks your code correctly, make sure you HTML includes a document declaration. See Chapter 2 for details.

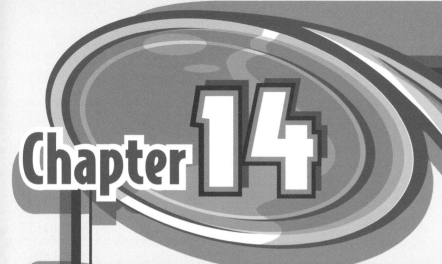

Chapter 14

Creating a Google Site

Services such as Google Sites allow you to create pages using a visual interface that you access through a Web browser. This saves you from writing HTML by hand and having to upload site files yourself. Although you do not have as much control over your design as you do when you create and publish pages on your own, this option is a great choice when you do not need a lot of

customization and want to create something fast. This chapter gets you up to speed with publishing a Google Site.

Understanding Google Sites

Google Sites is a free online service for building and managing Web sites. You choose a name and style for your site and then add Web pages one at a time. You can create your pages using button- and menu-based commands or, if you prefer, by writing HTML. All page creation is done inside your Web browser on the Google servers, so there is no uploading required to publish your site. You can also control the accessibility of your site, making your site visible to the public or to only a select group of users.

Making It Your Own

With Google Sites, you do not have complete control over your pages as you would if you were building them from scratch and hosting them yourself. However, you can still customize the look and feel to match your personal taste or your company's style. You can add a banner image to the top of your pages and customize the colors of your text, borders, and page backgrounds. You can also attach a custom domain name to your Google Site.

Page Templates

This chapter covers how to add Web pages to your Google Site using the service's basic Web page template. You can also add other types of pages using different templates. A Dashboard is a page featuring one or more Google gadgets, which are interactive modules such as maps or slide shows. A File Cabinet page makes available text documents, spreadsheets, and other files from your computer. Announcement pages let you post a chronological list of news and events. For more about these and other page types, see the Google Sites online help documentation.

Collaboration

One of the big advantages of Google Sites is its collaborative features. Using the sharing settings, you can enable multiple users to sign in and edit your site. You can assign users one of three different user levels — owner, collaborator, and viewer. Each level has a different set of permissions. Google Sites keeps track of the changes each user makes to your pages so mistakes can be rolled back if they occur. For more information, see "Share Your Site."

A Google Sites Page

Each page on a Google Site has a similar organization. The page includes a header with a title and search box, a sidebar with navigation links, and a body where most of the content lives. You can make adjustments to the layout such as changing the width and height of sections in the site settings.

Web Address

Because Google Sites are hosted on Google's Web servers, your site starts out with a sites.google.com Web address. If you have your own domain name, you can attach it to your Google Site. See the Google Sites help documentation for details. To register a domain name, see Chapter 13.

Title

You choose a title for your Google Site when you first create it. By default, the title appears in text on the top of all of your pages and in the browser title bar. You have the option to replace the title with a banner image, as shown here.

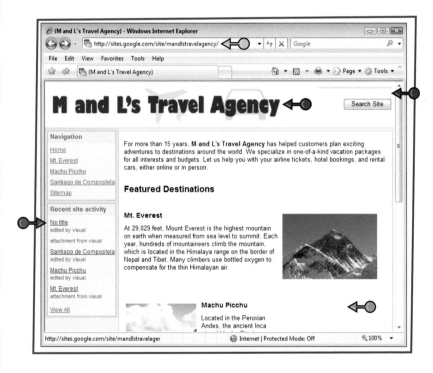

Sidebar

Links to your site pages are organized in a navigation area on the left side of your pages. You can choose which pages you want to list in the sidebar and the order in which they are listed. You can also display other information such as links to recently edited pages. For more information, see "Manage Navigation."

Page Body

You can add text, images, tables, and other HTML content to the main body of your pages. Google Sites gives you an easy-to-use, menu-based interface for changing the size and color of text, inserting images and tables, and more. You can also switch to an HTML interface if you want to make changes to your pages using techniques covered in earlier chapters. See "Edit a Page" for more information.

Search

As you might expect from a Google service, every Google Site includes a search feature at the top of all pages. Viewers can submit keywords to search the pages that you have published.

Create a
Google Account

You can create a Google account to get access to a variety of online services from Google, including Google Sites. Creating an account involves submitting your e-mail address, password, and other basic information. After confirming your account details, you can log in to your new Google account and start using Google Sites. Creating a Google account also allows you to use the Blogger service to create a personal Web blog. Blogger is covered in Chapter 15.

Create a Google Account

1 Visit the Google Create an Account page at www.google.com/accounts/newaccount.

2 Type your e-mail address.

3 Type a password.

A good password includes at least eight characters, letters, numbers, and punctuation.

4 Retype your password.

● You can optionally turn on Web History, which keeps track of the pages you browse (changes to).

● You can optionally set your browser home page to Google. This option may not be available in all browsers (changes to).

5 Select your location.

6 Type the letters shown in the verification box. This ensures a human is creating the account.

7 Click here to accept the terms of service and create an account.

If you set your browser home page to Google, a pop-up window may appear asking you to confirm the setting.

● Google displays a confirmation page and sends a confirmation e-mail to the address you submitted for the account.

⑧ Access the Web address included in the confirmation e-mail to confirm that you have access to the e-mail address.

Your e-mail address is confirmed and Google creates your account.

⑨ You can click here to manage your new account.

How do I associate more than one e-mail address with my Google account?	I forgot my password. How do I log in?
Log in to your account at www.google. com/accounts and then click **Edit** in the e-mail section of the page that appears. Here, you can add more e-mail addresses to your account.	On the log-in page at www.google. com/accounts, click **I cannot access my account**. Google displays a page that lets you reset your password. The page also helps you if you forgot your user name or if you think someone else is using your account and you want to report it.

Set Up a Google Site

Creating a new Google Site involves choosing a name for the site, choosing a public or private setting, and selecting a theme. When you choose a name, Google uses the characters of the name to generate a Web address for the site. The Web address must not conflict with any existing Google sites. If it conflicts, you can either try changing the name or editing the Web address directly. A site theme is a prepackaged combination of layouts, colors, and images that is applied to your pages. Google currently offers 24 themes ranging from subdued to flashy. You can change the theme later on in your site settings.

Set Up a Google Site

① Visit the Google Sites home page at sites.google.com.

② Type the e-mail address associated with your Google account.

Note: To create a Google account, see "Create a Google Account."

③ Type your password.

④ Click **Sign in**.

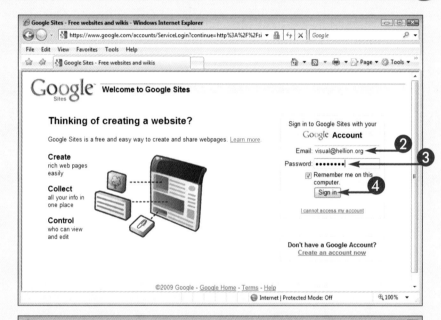

Google signs you in to Google Sites.

● You can click here to access Google Sites tutorials and example sites.

⑤ Click **Create site**.

If you have already created a site, this page lists it. You can click **Create new site** to create a new one.

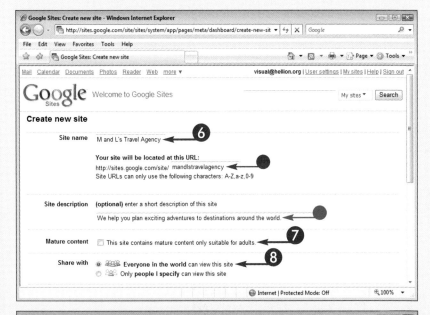

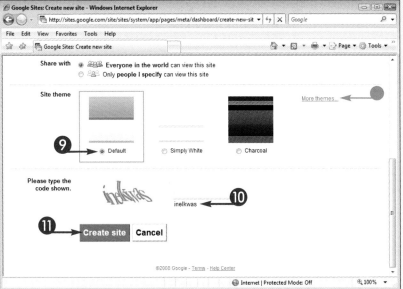

The Create New Site page appears.

⑥ Type a name for your site. This name appears on the top of all your site pages.

● Google converts the name to create a Web address for the site.

● You can type an optional site description.

⑦ Click here if your site contains adults-only content (☐ changes to ☑).

⑧ Select who can see your site (◎ changes to ◉).

⑨ Select a theme to determine the colors and style for your site (◎ changes to ◉).

● You can click here to view more themes.

⑩ Type the distorted letters. This ensures a human is creating the site.

⑪ Click **Create site**.

Google creates your site and displays it. To add Web pages and make other additions, see the other tasks in this chapter.

How can I add a banner image?
When you first create your site, Google places the text of your site name at the top of every page. You can optionally replace that text with a banner image. Click **Site settings** and then **Change appearance** in the menu that opens. On the Appearance page, click **change logo** to add a banner image.

Can I change the home page for my site?
Your home page is the landing page that the user sees when visiting the site's Web address. To change it, click **Site settings** and then **Other stuff** in the menu that opens. Then click **Change** next to Landing Page.

227

Create a Page

You can add content to your Google Site by creating a page. A page can include most of the content discussed in the earlier chapters of this book, including text, images, tables, and more. Although Google does not specifically limit the number of pages you can create, it does have a storage limit — 100MB. You can increase this limit by subscribing to a Google Premier account. This chapter discusses creating pages using the regular Web page template in Google Sites. Additional page templates are offered that allow you to display announcements, manage documents, integrate maps, and more. See the Google Sites help documentation for details.

Create a Page

① Log in to Google Sites at sites.google.com.

Google displays a list of your sites.

② Click a site name.

Google displays the site in a new browser window.

● If you just created a new site, a blank Home page appears.

Note: For details on editing the Home page or other pages, see "Edit a Page."

③ Click **Create new page**.

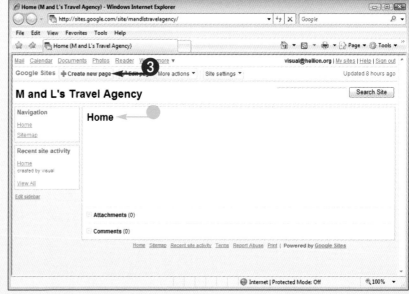

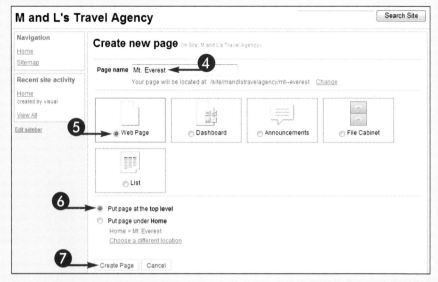

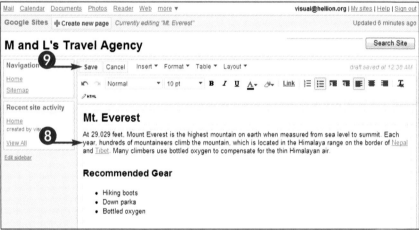

The Create New Page page appears.

4 Type a name for the page.

5 Select a page type (◎ changes to ◉).

Note: See "Understanding Google Sites" for a description of the page types.

6 Select a location in the page hierarchy for the new page (◎ changes to ◉).

Note: See "Manage Navigation" to control how links to pages appear.

7 Click **Create Page**.

Google creates the new page and displays the editor.

8 Type and edit your content in the editor window.

Note: For more about adding and editing content, see "Edit a Page."

9 Click **Save**.

Google saves the page.

Simplify It

How can I attach other documents to a page?
You can attach documents such as word processing files, spreadsheets, and PDF files to a page using the Attachments feature at the bottom of each page. Click the plus sign (⊞) to open the section and then click **Browse** to locate on your computer the file to attach. Attached files appear as links on the bottom of the page and also include file size, date uploaded, and other information.

How do I adjust site colors?
The theme you choose when you set up your site determines what colors appear initially. You can make adjustments by clicking **Site settings** and then **Change appearance**. On the page that appears, click **Colors and Fonts**. You can change the color of site text and backgrounds. You can also add background images.

Edit
a Page

You can edit a page on your Google Site to add, change, or delete content. Google Sites allows you to edit your content similar to how you would edit it in a word processor. You can change text in an editable text box. You click buttons or select commands from menus to

make text bold, create headings and bulleted lists, change the size and color of text, and more. You can insert a table to organize content into rows and columns. You can also switch to an HTML view to make changes not available in the editor commands.

Edit a Page

SELECT A PAGE TO EDIT

1 View your Google Site.

Note: See "Create a Page" for more about signing in and viewing a site.

2 Click **Edit page** to edit your page.

● You can click the navigation and other links to view and edit a different site page.

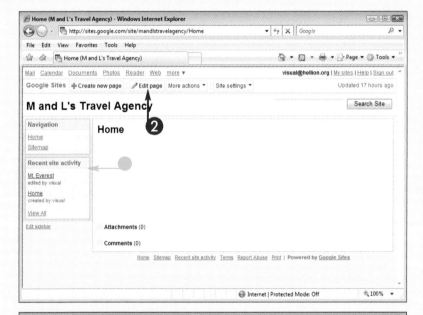

EDIT TEXT

Google displays the editor.

This example shows how to edit a regular Web page.

3 Type here to edit the page title.

4 Type here to add or edit content in the page body.

5 Click and drag to select some text.

6 Click a menu and select an option.

In this example, color is applied to text.

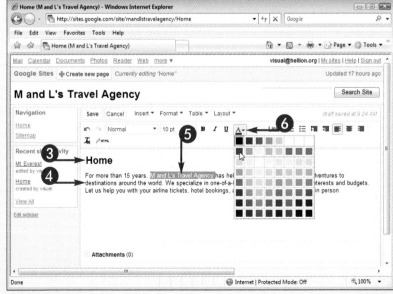

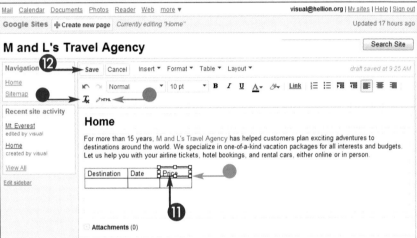

● Google applies the formatting.

INSERT A TABLE

⑦ Click where you want to insert a table.

⑧ Click **Table**.

⑨ Click **Insert table**.

⑩ To select the size of the table to insert, click the grid that appears.

● As you move your mouse cursor over the grid, the dimensions appear here.

Google inserts a table.

⑪ Click inside the table cells and type to add content.

● You can click and drag the handles (□) to resize the rows and columns.

● To remove formatting, select text and then click ⊼.

● You can click ⌗HTML to edit the page as HTML.

⑫ Click **Save** to save the edited page and close the editor.

Simplify It

How do I align page content?
You can select the page content, such as a paragraph, and click the ▤, ▤, or ▤ buttons to align it. To align content inside a table cell, click inside the cell and then click an alignment button. To align an entire table, position your cursor immediately before or after the table and click an alignment button.

How can I create a two-column layout?
In the editor, click **Layout** and then click **Two-column**. Google changes the editor to display side-by-side boxes for adding content. You can switch back to a one-column layout by clicking **Layout** and then **One-column**. Any content in the right-hand column is moved below the left-hand content.

Create a Link

You can insert links in your pages to connect related content within your site or to give viewers access to pages on external sites. To create a link, you select the content on your page that you want as the link and then choose a destination from a list of existing pages.

Alternatively, you can type an external Web address. Another way to offer links to other pages on your site is to display them in the sidebar as navigation. For details, see "Manage Navigation."

Create a Link

1. View your Google Site.

   Note: See "Create a Page" for more about signing in and viewing a site.

2. Click **Edit page** to edit your page.

   ● You can click the navigation and other links to view and edit a different site page.

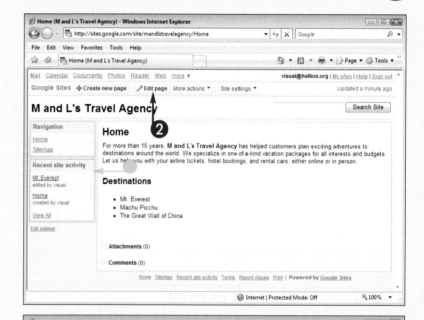

   Google displays the editor.

3. Click and drag to select the content you want to turn into a link.

4. Click **Link**.

   ● You can also click **Insert** and then **Link** from the menu that appears.

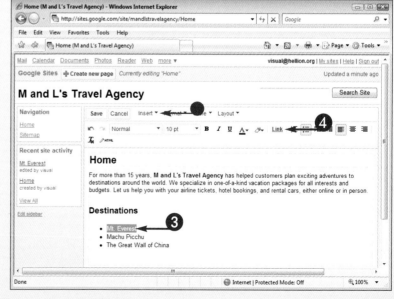

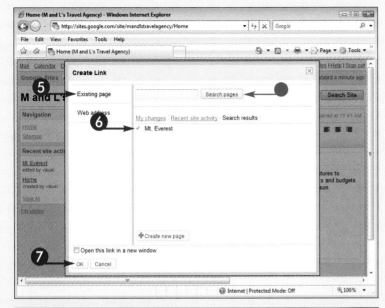

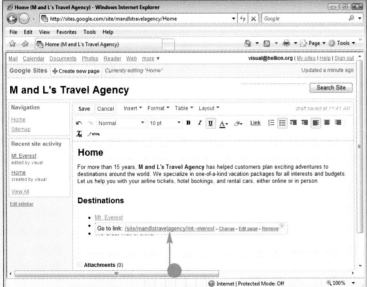

The Create Link dialog box appears.

5 If it is not selected, click **Existing page**.

Google displays the pages in your site.

● You can type a keyword and then click **Search pages** to filter the list.

6 Click the page to which you want to link.

Google displays a ☑ next to the selection.

7 Click **OK**.

Google creates the link and displays editing options.

● You can click the address to test the link.

8 Press **Alt** to close the options box.

How do I remove a link?
In the editor, click the linked content. A blue box appears showing the link address and other options. Click **Remove** to remove the link from the content.

How do I link to a page on an external site?
In the Create Link dialog box, click **Web address**. In the text box that appears, type or paste the Web address for the external page. Click **OK** to create the external link.

Insert
an Image

You can display images in your Google Site pages just as you can in other types of Web pages. When you insert an image in Google Sites, Google first uploads the image from your computer and stores it in a content repository for your site. Then it adds the HTML code that references the uploaded photo. Google offers shortcuts for resizing and aligning your inserted images. These shortcuts appear when you are in the editor and click an image. For more about Web images, see Chapter 5.

Insert an Image

① View the page into which you want to insert an image and click **Edit page**.

Note: For more about opening and editing a page, see "Edit a Page."

② Click where you want to insert an image.

③ Click **Insert**.

④ Click **Image**.

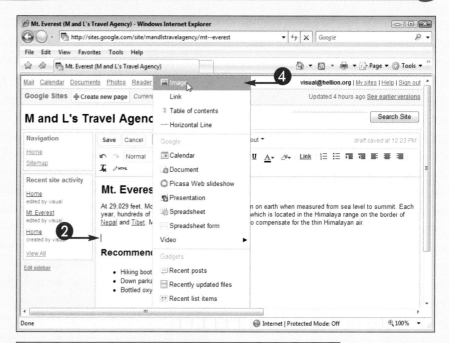

The Add an Image dialog box appears.

● The dialog box displays any images you have previously uploaded. You can click an image to insert it.

⑤ Click **Browse**.

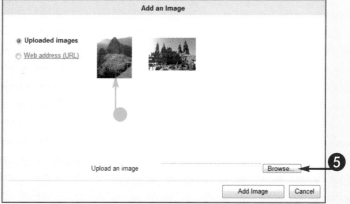

The Choose File dialog box appears.

⑥ Navigate to the folder on your computer where your image is located.

⑦ Click the image.

⑧ Click **Open**.

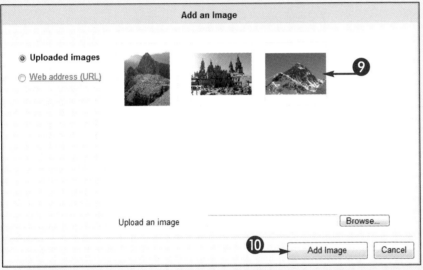

Google uploads the image and displays it.

⑨ Click the image.

⑩ Click **Add Image**.

Google inserts the image on the page.

Simplify It

How do I resize an inserted image?
In the editor, click the inserted image to display a blue options box. The box includes four size options: S for small, M for medium, L for large, and Original for the actual size of the uploaded image. Click a size option to resize the photo. To resize the image precisely, you can click [HTML] and edit the HTML on the page. See Chapter 5 for more about changing the size of an image with HTML.

How do I align an inserted image?
In the editor, click the inserted image to display a blue options box. The box includes three alignment options: L for left, C for center, and R for right. Click an alignment option to align the photo. You can wrap text around a left- or right-aligned photo by clicking the **Wrap on** option.

Manage Navigation

You can make it easy for users to access important pages on your Google Site by placing links to them in the sidebar. The sidebar appears on the right side of all your site pages and can include navigation, a list of recent updates, and more. You can also give users access to different content on your site by putting links in the body of your pages. See "Create a Link" for more information.

Manage Navigation

① View your Google Site.

The default view shows navigation and recently updated pages in the sidebar.

② Click **Edit sidebar**.

● You can also click **Site settings** and then **Change appearance**.

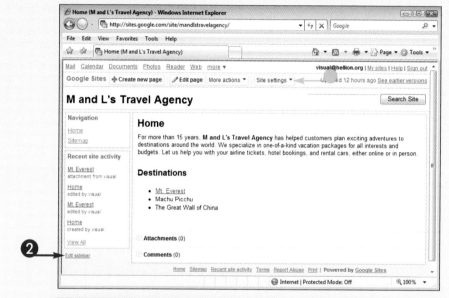

Google displays the Appearance page with the Site Elements tab selected.

③ Click **edit**.

The Configure Navigation dialog box appears.

● You can click a page and then click ⊠ to delete it from the Navigation.

④ Click **Add page to sidebar navigation**.

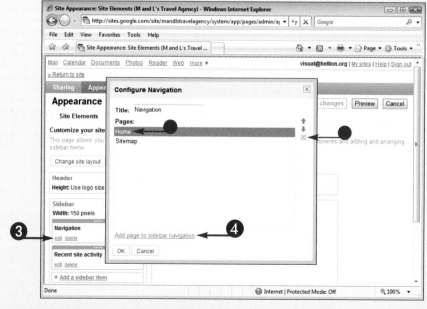

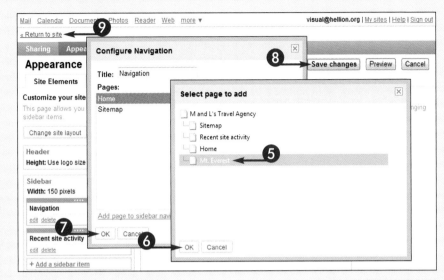

The Select Page to Add dialog box appears.

5 Click the title of the page to add.

6 Click **OK**.

7 Click **OK**.

8 Click **Save changes**.

9 Click **Return to site**.

● Google displays your site page with the updated navigation.

What types of content can I add to the sidebar?
By default, your Google Site displays navigation links and links to recently updated pages in the sidebar. You can also add a text item, a countdown item, and an item that shows your site activity. To add a new item, click **Add a sidebar item** on the Appearance page.

Can I adjust the layout of the site?
Yes, to some extent. On the Appearance page, click **Change site layout**. A dialog box appears that lets you hide or display the header and sidebar and adjust the dimensions of different elements. You can also rearrange the order of items in the sidebar by clicking and dragging the title bars of the items up and down.

Share
Your Site

You can share your Google Site with other users so that they can create and edit pages, change page styles, and perform other tasks. This makes a Google Site useful for managing a project among a dispersed group of people. You can set user permissions to one of three levels — owner, collaborator, or viewer — depending on the amount of access you want a user to have. When you set up new users, Google sends an invitation to the users informing them of their status.

Share Your Site

① View your Google Site.

② Click **Site settings**.

③ Click **Share this site**.

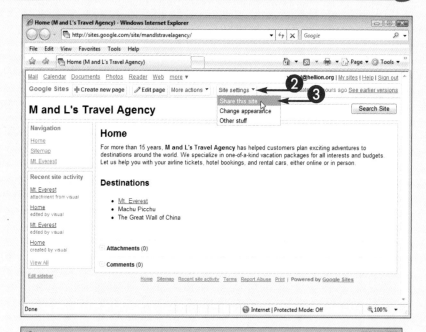

Google displays the Sharing page.

When you first create a site, you are the Owner.

④ Select a permission level for the invitees (◎ changes to ◉).

Owners can make major changes to the site, including changing the name and deleting it.

Collaborators can make lesser changes, including creating, editing, and deleting pages.

Viewers cannot make changes to the site.

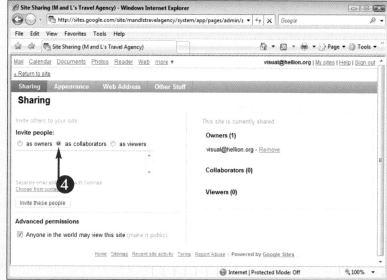

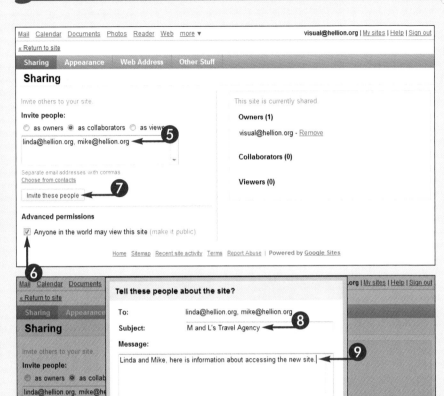

⑤ Type the e-mail addresses of the people with whom you are sharing. Separate multiple addresses with commas.

⑥ You can click here to make the site private (☑ changes to ☐).

⑦ Click **Invite these people**.

Google displays a message window.

⑧ You can edit the subject here.

⑨ Type a message.

⑩ You can click here to send a copy of the message to your own e-mail address (☐ changes to ☑).

⑪ Click **Send**.

Google sends the invitations and lists the invitees on the Sharing page.

How do I revert a change made to a page?
Google keeps track of every change made to your site so you can roll back a page to an earlier version in the event of a mistake. To revert a change, visit the page you want to roll back and click **See earlier versions**. Google displays a list of versions of that page. Both owners and collaborators can perform this task.

How do I receive automatic notifications of changes to pages on my site?
After signing in to Google Sites, visit the page for which you want notifications. Click **More actions** and then **Subscribe to page changes**. You will receive an e-mail notification when the page is updated by a user.

Chapter 15

Creating a Blog on Blogger

Want an easy, inexpensive way to record your thoughts and opinions and make them available to everyone on the Web? This chapter shows you how to start a blog, which is a Web site where you can regularly post information for others to view and comment on. You will find out how to set up an account on Blogger, which is a popular service for creating and maintaining blogs.

Understanding Blogs

A *blog*, which is short for Web log, is basically an online written journal. You type your thoughts into a Web form and click a submit button, and the content appears at the top of your blog with previous entries listed below. Blogs can also include images, videos, and other media as well as links to related online resources. Setting up a blog is great for people who want their opinions known because a blog can be accessed by anyone with an Internet connection. The blog search engine Technorati estimates that as of 2009 more than 100 million blogs are on the Web.

Ways to Blog

There are a variety of popular blogging platforms that make setting up a blog relatively easy. Some of the platforms exist as software that you download and install yourself on your Web server. These platforms include WordPress and Movable Type. There are also Web-based services that you sign up for online and where content is hosted by the service. Hosted options include Blogger, LiveJournal, and WordPress.com. Most social networking Web sites also offer a blog component. This chapter describes the Blogger service, which is owned by Google. For more blog options, visit http://wikipedia.org/wiki/Weblog_software.

Blog Posts

A blog entry is known as a *post*. In its simplest form, a blog is a series of dated posts listed in reverse chronological order. A post can be a short comment about what one did that day or a long essay illustrated with images and videos that tackles a complicated subject. Usually you log in to your blog to add a post. Some services also let you add posts by sending messages to an e-mail address. If you want to save a partially written post without publishing it, you can save it as a draft and come back to it later. On most blogs, you can search for posts on a particular subject by performing a search or browsing an archive.

Social Aspect

Although a blog is usually the work of one person or at most a small group, many blogs also have a strong social aspect. Viewers who have helpful tips related to a post can add them as comments, and those comments appear below the post. The audience can also compliment or disagree with the blog owner using the comments feature. Blog owners can recommend other blogs by linking to them on their blog pages. A list of related blogs is known as a *blogroll*.

A Blogger Page

Most blogs share a common structure. The main component is a list of posts, which are dated entries that the blog owner has submitted. There may also be additional features, such as comment areas, archives for browsing past posts, and lists of links to related blogs. When you create a blog on Blogger, you choose a theme that determines the colors and layout of the blog. The example below shows one of the simpler Blogger themes.

Title

On Blogger, the title of the blog appears at the top of every page. You can click the title to return to the blog's home page.

Blog Post

Each entry an owner submits to a blog is called a *post*. Posts appear in reverse chronological order in the blog. Blog posts can include text, images, videos, and more. See "Create a Post" for more information.

Timestamp

Every post includes the date showing when the post was created. The date determines the order in which the post appears on the blog. You can edit the date when you create a post.

Extra Information

Text at the bottom of each post tells who made the post and at what time of the day. If comments are turned on, a post includes a link for viewing or adding comments. For more information, see "Manage Comments."

Gadgets

You can add extra features to your blog by installing *gadgets*. Gadgets are modules that appear to the side of your posts. They let you add slideshows, videos, advertisements, and more to your blog. See "Add a Gadget" for more information.

Blogger Tools

Blogger adds a search box and links to the top of your blog. The search box enables you to search your blog by keyword, whereas links allow you to visit other blogs on the Blogger network, create a new blog, or sign in to your account. You can hide these features in your blog settings.

Set Up a Blog on Blogger

Blogger is a popular online service for creating and maintaining a blog. It provides a Web-based system for creating new posts, editing existing posts, managing user comments, and more. Blogger is owned by Google, and you use a Google account to sign in and create a blog. Blogger offers a variety of thematic templates that determine the color scheme and layout of your blog.

Set Up a Blog on Blogger

① Set up a Google account.

Note: *For details about setting up an account, see Chapter 14.*

② Visit the Blogger home page at www.blogger.com.

③ Type the e-mail address associated with your Google account.

④ Type your password.

⑤ Click **Sign In**.

A Sign Up page appears.

⑥ Type a display name. This name will appear on your blog posts.

⑦ Click here to accept the terms of service (☐ changes to ☑).

⑧ Click **Continue**.

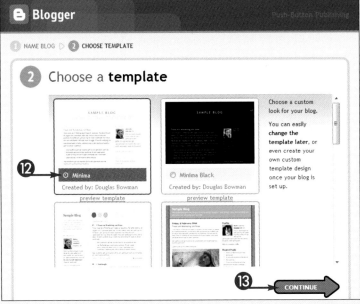

A Name Your Blog page appears.

9 Type a name for your blog.

10 Type a Web address for your blog. The address can include letters, numbers, and hyphens.

● You can click here to check the availability.

11 Click **Continue**.

A Choose Template page appears.

12 Click a template (◎ changes to ◉).

You can change your blog's template later, if needed.

13 Click **Continue**.

Google creates your blog and displays a confirmation page (not shown).

14 Click **Start Blogging** to create your first post (not shown).

What are the advanced options for hosting?
You can have Blogger store its content on your server rather than on the Google servers. During setup, click **Advanced Blog Setup** on the Name Your Blog page. A page appears enabling you to enter FTP information for your server.

How do I import a blog to Blogger?
You can import content that you have previously exported from another blog in Blogger. During setup, click **Import Blog Tool** on the Name Blog page. A page appears allowing you to upload the exported blog's XML file.

Create a Post

A *post* is a dated entry in your blog. It might describe what you have been doing over the past week if you are keeping a personal blog. Or it might be your opinion on some recent news item, product, or event if your blog focuses on a specific subject. A post usually contains text, and can also include images, videos, and other media. Your most recent post appears at the top of your blog's home page. Viewers can scroll down to see previous posts. Viewers can also comment on a post, and other viewers can see those comments.

Create a Post

① Sign in to Blogger.

Note: *See "Set Up a Blog on Blogger" for details on signing in.*

Blogger displays the Dashboard.

● You can click here to view your blog.

The Dashboard also lists information about blogs you are following.

② Click **New Post**.

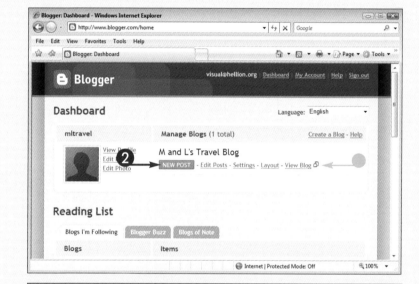

A posting form appears.

③ Type a title for your post.

④ Type the content of your post.

● You can use buttons to change text size, change color, add images, and more. See "Edit a Post" for more information.

⑤ Click **Post Options**.

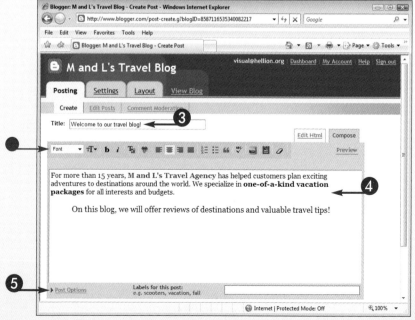

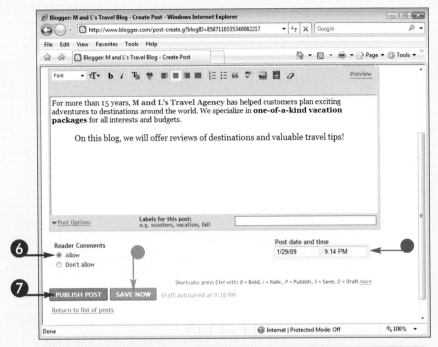

Blogger displays more options.

6 Click here to turn viewer comments on or off (◎ changes to ◉).

● You can edit the time associated with your post. Posts are listed in reverse chronological order on your blog.

● You can click here to save your work without publishing it. Unpublished posts are marked as drafts in the management screens.

7 Click **Publish Post**.

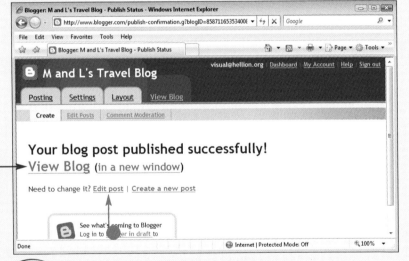

Blogger publishes the post to your blog.

● You can click here to view your blog.

● You can click here to edit the post.

Simplify It

How do I turn comments off by default?
On the new post page, click the **Settings** tab, and then click **Comments** on the page that appears. In the Comments Default for Posts menu, select **New Posts Do Not Have Comments**. Scroll to the bottom of the page and click **Save Settings**. Comments will be turned off when you create new posts.

How do I follow another blog?
Blogger can keep track of other blogs that you are interested in and display them on your Dashboard. Visit the blog you want to follow and click the **Follow This Blog** link. Recent posts to followed blogs show up in the Reading List section of your Dashboard. You can follow only other blogs on the Blogger network this way.

Edit a Post

You can customize your posts to suit your tastes and the subject you are writing about. The Blogger post editor includes buttons and commands that allow you to add HTML formatting without typing HTML. You can change text size, color, and alignment. You can also switch to an HTML view if you want to fine-tune the code by writing the tags yourself. Posts can include images and videos uploaded from your computer. You can also display images hosted on another Web server — for example, on an image hosting service such as Flickr.

Edit a Post

1 Sign in to Blogger.

Note: See "Set Up a Blog on Blogger" for details on signing in.

Blogger displays the Dashboard.

● You can click here to set up another blog. Blogger allows users to manage multiple blogs.

2 Click **Edit Posts**.

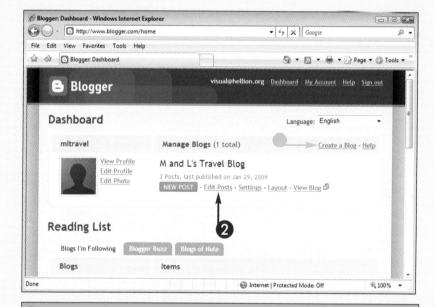

Blogger lists your blog posts.

● You can click here to filter the list.

● You can click here to delete a post.

● You can click here to view a summary of a post's content (▶ changes to ▼).

3 Click **Edit**.

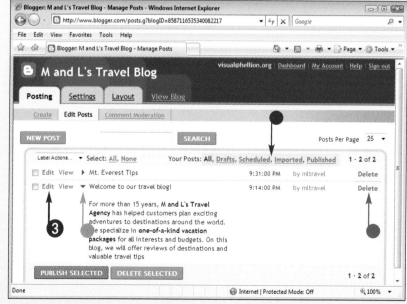

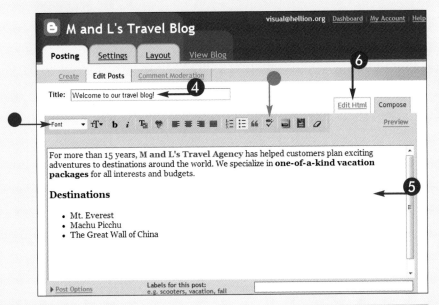

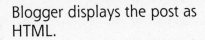

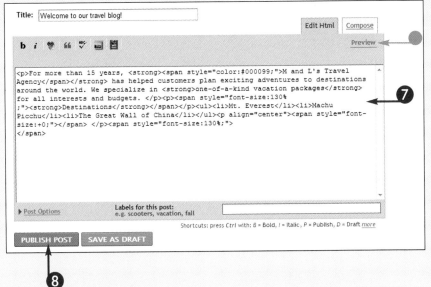

The post appears in an editing window.

④ Type here to edit the title.

⑤ Type here to add, edit, or delete content.

● You can click editing buttons to format selected text.

● You can click 🔲 to check spelling.

⑥ Click **Edit HTML**.

Blogger displays the post as HTML.

⑦ Edit the HTML.

***Note:** For more about editing HTML, see the previous chapters in this book.*

● You can click **Preview** to view the post as it appears on the blog.

⑧ Click **Publish Post**.

Blogger publishes the post to your blog.

Simplify It

How do I insert an image?

In the post editor, you can click 🔲 to insert an image. A dialog box appears allowing you to upload an image from your computer or reference an image on the Web. You can also choose an alignment and size.

How do I insert a video?

In the post editor, you can click 🔲 to insert video. A dialog box appears allowing you to upload an AVI, MPEG, QuickTime, Real, or Windows Media file. Videos can be up to 100MB in size.

Change the Layout

You can customize the layout of your blog to organize how sections are displayed. In the blog header, you can edit the title and description or replace the title with the logo of your organization. In the blog posts section, you can control how many posts are shown on a page, change the date format, and even turn on advertising. Most of the fonts and colors in your blog design are configurable, and you can also change the theme of your blog if you want a quick, wholesale change.

Change the Layout

1 Sign in to Blogger.

Note: *See "Set Up a Blog on Blogger" for details on signing in.*

Blogger displays the Dashboard.

2 Click **Layout**.

Blogger displays the Layout page.

● You can click here to update the font styles and backgrounds that appear in your blog.

● Sections that are shaded can be rearranged on the page. Blogger calls these sections *gadgets*.

3 Click and drag a gadget to a new location.

4 Release the mouse button.

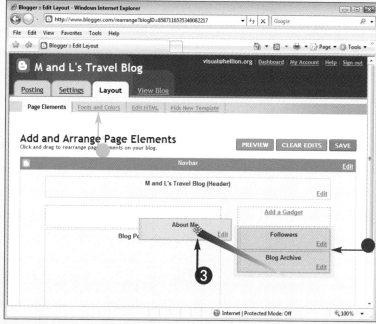

B M and L's Travel Blog

Posting Settings **Layout** View Blog

Page Elements | Fonts and Colors | Edit HTML | Pick New Template

Add and Arrange Page Elements
Click and drag to rearrange page elements on your blog.

PREVIEW CLEAR EDITS SAVE

Navbar   Edit

M and L's Travel Blog (Header)   ⑤ → Edit

About Me   Add a Gadget
           Edit
                                          Followers
Blog Posts   Edit

                                          Blog Archive
                                                   Edit

B Configure Header   ? Help

Blog Title M and L's Travel Blog
Blog Description

Image   ● From your computer:
              Browse...
        ○ From the web
           http://   ⑥

Placement
        ● Behind title and description
        ○ Instead of title and description
        ☐ Shrink to fit
        Image will be shrunk to 660 pixels wide.

                        CANCEL SAVE ⑦

● Blogger moves the gadget to the new location.

⑤ Click an **Edit** link for a section.

Blogger displays an editing window.

⑥ Edit the section using the form fields.

In this example, you can change the text in the blog header or add an image.

⑦ Click **Save**.

⑧ On the Layout page, click **Save** (not shown).

Blogger saves the layout changes.

Simplify It

How do I edit the code of a template?
When you create your blog, you choose a design template to define the appearance of the blog. If you want to make changes to the look and feel, Blogger lets you edit the template HTML. On the Layout page, click the **Edit HTML** tab. An HTML editing box appears where you can add and change the code for the blog. Blogger templates are written in XHTML, which is a version of HTML that conforms to the stricter standards of a language called XML. For more information about XML, see http://wikipedia.org/wiki/XHTML. An alternative to editing the HTML is simply to switch Blogger templates. To do this, click **Pick New Template** on the Layout page.

Add a Gadget

You can customize your blog design to add slideshows, videos, advertisements, and more. Blogger calls these features *gadgets*, and you can access a library of available gadgets from the Layout page. When you create a new blog, Blogger adds several standard gadgets to the layout of your blog. These default gadgets include a list of followers of your blog, links to archived posts, and profile information. You can remove these default gadgets as well as add new gadgets from the library.

Add a Gadget

1 From your Blogger Dashboard, click **Layout** to view the Layout page for your blog.

Note: See *"Change the Layout"* for more about accessing the Layout page.

2 Click **Add a Gadget**.

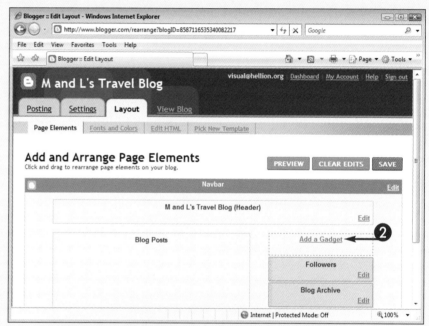

The Add a Gadget page appears.

● You can click categories to view different gadgets.

● You can search for gadgets by keywords.

3 Click 🞣 to add a gadget.

The Configure page for the gadget appears.

④ Use the form fields to configure the gadget.

● You can click **Back** to return to the Add a Gadget page.

⑤ Click **Save**.

● Blogger inserts the gadget into your layout.

Note: *To rearrange the layout, see "Change the Layout."*

● To remove a gadget, you can click an **Edit** link and then **Remove** in the page that appears.

⑥ Click **View Blog** to access your updated blog.

Simplify It

What is a blogroll?
A *blogroll* is a list of blogs that you like and want to recommend to others. You can add a blogroll in Blogger using the Blog List gadget. You need to know the Web addresses of the blogs you want to add.

How can my audience subscribe to my blog?
Experienced viewers often keep track of their favorite blogs by using programs to automatically check the RSS feeds of the blogs. Blogger includes RSS feeds for all its blogs. You can add a Subscription Links gadget to your page to help viewers subscribe to your feed. For more about RSS feeds, see http://wikipedia.org/wiki/RSS.

Manage Comments

By allowing comments, blog owners can turn their blogs into interactive forums where viewers can submit additional tips about a post or give kudos when they think a post is particularly interesting. The blog settings page enables a blog owner to customize how comments work. By turning on moderation, a blog owner can review submitted comments before they appear on the blog. This allows owners to screen for offensive or irrelevant comments. Comments can also be turned off completely.

Manage Comments

1 View the Dashboard for your blog.

2 Click **Settings**.

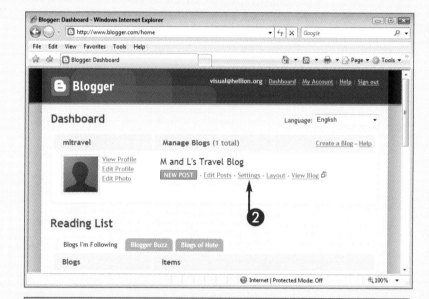

The Settings page appears.

3 Click **Comments**.

Blogger displays the Comments settings.

4 Click here to show or hide comments on all posts (⊙ changes to ⦿).

Note: Hiding comments does not delete them from the system.

5 Click here to specify who can comment on posts (⊙ changes to ⦿).

6 Click here to specify how to display the comment form (⊙ changes to ⦿).

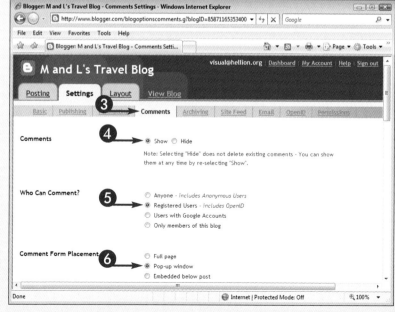

254

Comments Timestamp Format	January 31, 2009 6:34 PM ▼ ⑦
Comment Form Message	We welcome your comments!
	You can use some HTML tags, such as <b>, <i>, <a>
Comment moderation ⑧	◉ Always
	○ Only on posts older than 14 days
	○ Never
	Review comments before they are published. A link will appear on your dashboard when there are comments to review. Learn more
	Email address
	We will email you at this address when a non-member leaves a comment on your blog. Leave blank if you don't want to receive these emails.

Show word verification for comments? ⑨	◉ Yes ○ No
	This will require people leaving comments on your blog to complete a word verification step, which will help reduce comment spam. Learn more
	Blog authors will not see word verification for comments.
Show profile images on comments?	◉ Yes ○ No
Comment Notification Email	visual@hellion.org ⑩
	Choose from contacts
	You can enter up to ten email addresses, separated by commas. We will email these addresses when someone leaves a comment on your blog.

SAVE SETTINGS ⑪

⑦ Select a time format for comments.

● You can type optional instructions to appear above the comment box here.

⑧ Click here to turn moderation on or off (◎ changes to ◉).

Moderation allows you to preview and approve comments before they appear on your blog.

⑨ Click here to turn on word verification to keep automated programs from submitting comments (◎ changes to ◉).

⑩ Type one or more e-mail addresses here to be notified of new comments.

⑪ Click here to save your settings.

Blogger saves the settings.

Simplify It

What are backlinks?
A *backlink* is a link from an external Web site to a blog post. Monitoring backlinks can help you keep track of who is interested in your blog. You can choose to show or hide backlinks in your posts on the Comments setting page. Backlinks for a post appear below the comments.

What is comment spam?
Comment spam occurs when humans or automated programs leave comments on your blog for the sole purpose of promoting commercial services. You can cut down on comment spam by adding word verification to your blog's comment form in step **9**. This keeps automated programs from posting comments. You can read more about comment spam at http://wikipedia.org/wiki/Spam_in_blogs.

Chapter 16

Creating a Facebook Page

Do you want to connect with friends and family online? Social network Web sites let you stay in touch with your social circle by exchanging messages, viewing status updates, sharing images and videos, and more. You can get started with Facebook, one of the world's most popular social networks, by signing up for an account, adding some information to your online profile, and then connecting with other users by marking them as "friends." This chapter shows you how.

Understanding Social Networks

Social networks offer a fun and convenient way to communicate with distant friends and make new connections with people who share similar interests. You can exchange messages, share photos, and keep tabs on the activities of your friends all in one place. Most social networks are free to join. Once you sign up, you can create a profile page that displays basic information about yourself and then connect with other people you know. This chapter covers using Facebook, which is currently the most popular online social network in the United States.

Social Networking Web Sites

Use of social networking Web sites has increased dramatically since the launch of Friendster, the first widely popular site, in 2002. Facebook and MySpace are currently the most popular sites in the U.S., both with more than 100 million active users. Sites outside the U.S. with high activity include Friendster and Cyworld in Asia, Bebo in Europe, and Orkut in South America. For a comprehensive list of social networking sites, see http://wikipedia.org/wiki/List_of_social_networking_websites.

Personal Profiles

Mike Wooldridge

Wall   Info   Photos   +

Basic Information

Sex: Male
Birthday: June 19
Hometown: Concord, CA
Relationship Status: Married
Looking For: Friendship
                        Networking

Personal Information

Activities: Writing computer books
Interests: Creating Web pages
Favorite Books: Teach Yourself Visually Photoshop

When you sign up at a social networking site, you typically create an online profile page to represent yourself to other users. The profile can include your name or nickname, a picture, location, education and work history, and interests. It may also include a current status that you can update periodically to let other users know what you are doing. You create this page by filling in forms; you do not need to know any HTML. For more about profiles on Facebook, see "View and Edit Your Profile." Typically, users with whom you have not made a formal connection on the site can see only a limited version of your profile. To see complete profiles and use all the communication features of the service with another user, you must become that user's *friend*.

Making Friends

On social networks, a *friend* is a person you know and trust, and with whom you are interested in communicating. Many people connect with one another on social networks when they have an existing connection in the real world, such as through work, school, or family relations. Other times they connect because they find they have common interests based on the profiles they have created. You can usually search for friends on social networks by name or e-mail address, or by an affiliation such as a high-school graduation year or company name. On Facebook, both parties must confirm a friend request to become friends. After confirmation, the friends can see each other's full profile and can view each other's ongoing activity on the site. For more about adding a friend on Facebook, see "Add a Friend."

Communicating

Most social networks offer users a variety of ways to communicate with their network of friends. On Facebook, users can share text messages, photos, links, and other content to their friends' Walls. A *Wall* is a list of recent activity on Facebook that appears in your personal profile. Sharing to a Wall is a semipublic way of communicating because all friends can see what is written on one another's Walls. If you want a more private way to communicate, you can send a friend a message, which is similar to sending an e-mail. Messages appear in a user's inbox and can be viewed only by the sender and recipient. Facebook also offers instant messaging for users who are online at the same time and want to chat.

Sharing Media

In recent years, social networking sites have integrated many photo- and video-sharing features. Users can share memories by sharing old pictures of friends and stay up to date by uploading new pictures. On Facebook, users can organize uploaded photos into virtual albums. Friends can comment on uploaded photos and tag the photos with the names of people that appear in them. If the tagged people are Facebook friends, those photos also become linked to those friends' accounts.

Facebook Applications

One feature that has distinguished Facebook is the many add-on programs that users can add to their personal profiles. Users can add third-party applications that let them compare taste in movies with friends, keep track of birthdays, compete with other users in word games, and more. You can search for applications by typing keywords in the Facebook search box. For developers, Facebook applications have become lucrative enterprises because the applications can include advertisements.

Set Up a Facebook Account

You can set up a Facebook account to establish a personal page on the site and start connecting with people you know who are also on Facebook. Anyone over the age of 13 who has an e-mail address can register for a Facebook account. The registration process involves submitting some basic information about yourself, including your name, e-mail address, birth date, and password. Facebook sends a confirmation message to your e-mail address to ensure the address is valid. After you have validated your e-mail address, you can start customizing your Facebook profile and adding friends.

Set Up a Facebook Account

1. Visit the Facebook home page at www.facebook.com.

2. Type your full name.

3. Type your e-mail address.

4. Type a password. It must be at least six characters in length.

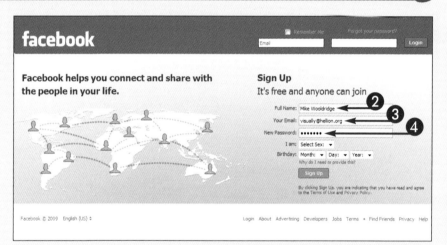

5. Select your sex.

6. Select your birth date. You must be at least 13 years old to register for a Facebook account.

● You can click here to view the site's Terms of Service and Privacy Policy.

7. Click **Sign Up**.

● To confirm you are a real person, Facebook displays a pair of distorted words.

⑧ Type the words, separating them with a space.

● If the words are too hard to read, you can click here to display a new pair.

● You can click here to hear an audio clip of voices reciting numbers, which you must type.

⑨ Click **Sign Up**.

Facebook displays a confirmation page and sends a confirmation e-mail to the address you submitted for the account.

⑩ Access the Web address included in the confirmation e-mail to confirm that you have access to the e-mail address.

Will my birth date appear on my Facebook profile?
You can choose whether or not to display your birth date on Facebook in the profile settings. You can also choose to display the day and month of your birth but not the year. Facebook uses birth dates to display upcoming birthdays of friends on your home page. For more about profile settings, see "View and Edit Your Profile."

How do I log in after I set up my account?
Type your e-mail address and password at the top of the home page at www.facebook.com, and then click **Login**. You can click **Forgot your password?** to have Facebook send a link to your e-mail address allowing you to reset your password.

Set Up a Facebook Account *(continued)*

During the registration process, Facebook offers a variety of ways to search for friends who are already on Facebook. Facebook can automatically search through your e-mail contact list. Facebook can connect directly to many popular online e-mail services and can also use a contact list that you have uploaded from an e-mail program such as Microsoft Outlook. You can also search for friends by joining networks for your school, company, or geographic region. Once you have joined a network, you can view many of the detailed profiles of other users in that network.

Set Up a Facebook Account (continued)

Facebook creates your new account.

If you use a popular online e-mail service such as Yahoo Mail or Gmail, Facebook can automatically search for your friends using your e-mail address book.

● You can optionally type your e-mail address and password and click **Find Friends** to search for friends.

● Click here to optionally search for friends using your instant messaging contacts.

⓫ Click here to skip this step.

Facebook can help you search for friends using your education and work information. This information is also added to your account profile.

● You can optionally type and select your education and work information here and click **Save**.

⓬ Click here to skip this step.

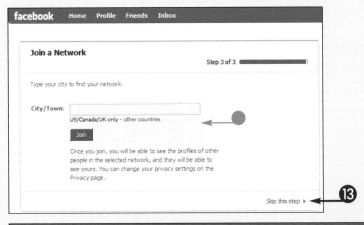

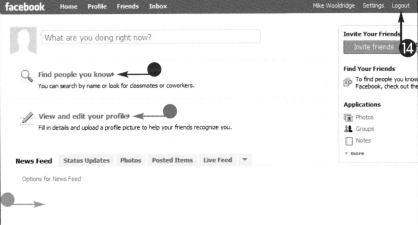

You can associate your account with a regional network. Users in a regional network can see one another's profile information.

● You can optionally type your city or town to look up a regional network. Facebook displays relevant networks and you can select one and click **Join** to join the network.

⓭ Click here to skip this step.

Facebook displays your account home page.

● Click here to search for friends. For more information, see "Add a Friend."

● Click here to customize your Facebook profile. For more information, see "View and Edit Your Profile."

● Once you have added friends, a summary of their recent activities appears here on your home page.

⓮ Click **Logout**.

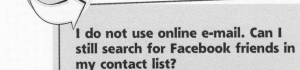

I do not use online e-mail. Can I still search for Facebook friends in my contact list?
You can upload your contacts from various e-mail programs such as Microsoft Outlook, Mozilla Thunderbird, and Entourage. On the home page, click **Find people you know** and then click **Upload Contact File**. A page appears allowing you to automatically import contacts from Outlook or upload a contact file from other programs.

How do I hide my profile from users in my networks who are not friends?
After you join a network, be it a regional network or one associated with your school or company, everyone in that network can see your profile by default. To hide your profile from one or more of your networks, click **Settings** at the top of the page and then click **Privacy Settings**. Then click **Profile** on the Privacy page that appears.

View and Edit Your Profile

Your profile is your online representation on Facebook. It is what your friends see when they visit your Facebook page. When you first sign up on Facebook, your profile displays the basics: your sex, birth date, and e-mail address. You can edit your profile to display your educational background, the name of the company you work for, your favorite TV shows and movies, your religious and political preferences, and more. Your profile also includes a Wall that shows your recent site activity. By default, only your friends and users in your networks can see your complete profile.

View and Edit Your Profile

VIEW YOUR PROFILE

1 Log in to your Facebook account at www.facebook.com. For details, see "Set Up a Facebook Account."

Your Facebook home page appears.

● The home page lists activity from your friends.

● You can click the side links to filter the information to view just status updates, photo updates, and more.

2 Click **Profile**.

Facebook displays your profile.

● Facebook displays your Wall, which lists your site activity in reverse chronological order.

● You current status appears here. See "Update Your Status" for more information.

3 Click **Info**.

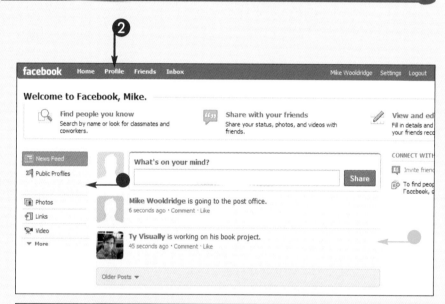

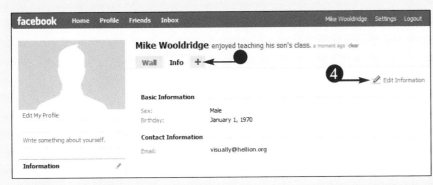

Facebook displays details about you.

● You can click the plus sign to see other content, such as videos and applications.

EDIT YOUR PROFILE

④ Click **Edit Information**.

Facebook displays fields for editing your profile.

⑤ Add to or edit your personal information.

⑥ You can scroll down to edit more details, including your contact, education, and work information.

⑦ Click **Save Changes** to save your edits.

⑧ Click **Done Editing** to switch back to your public profile.

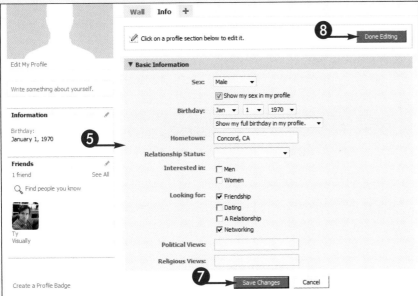

Simplify It

What are Facebook groups?
Facebook groups are communities within Facebook that enable users who share common interests to post comments and upload related photos and videos. There are thousands of Facebook groups devoted to a wide range of interests, including celebrities, hobbies, causes, and more. Groups can be public or private. To join a private group, a group administrator must approve your membership. To search for a group, type keywords in the Facebook search box.

What are Facebook fan pages?
Facebook fan pages are similar to Facebook groups in that they are forums devoted to some common interest that Facebook users can join. Many popular subjects have both groups and fan pages devoted to them. Fan pages are more open in that they can be visited by unregistered users and cannot be made private. Just like groups, you can search for fan pages using the Facebook search box.

Add a Profile Picture

You can add a face to your Facebook presence by uploading a picture to appear on your profile page. Facebook supports the three most common Web file formats: JPEG, GIF, and PNG. Uploaded photos must be no more than 4MB in file size. For your profile page, Facebook resizes the dimensions of your picture so that it is 200 pixels wide. A small, square version of your profile photo, also known as a *thumbnail*, appears next to status updates and other activities in News Feeds and on Walls. To make your photos look their best before uploading, you can use image-editing software such as Paint for Windows, iPhoto for Mac, or Adobe Photoshop Elements.

Add a Profile Picture

① Log in to your Facebook account at www.facebook. com. For details, see "Set Up a Facebook Account."

Your Facebook home page appears.

● The home page lists activity from you and your friends.

② Click **Profile**.

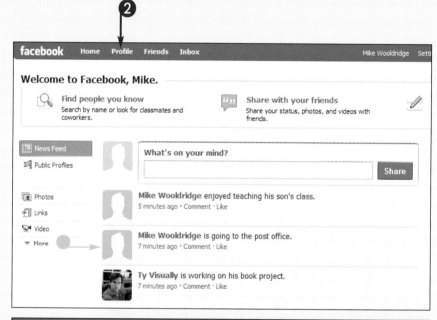

Facebook displays your profile.

③ Move the cursor over the default profile picture and click the **Change Picture** link that appears.

④ In the menu that appears, click **Upload a Picture**.

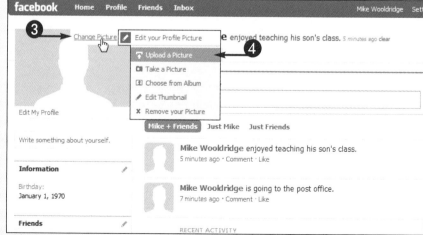

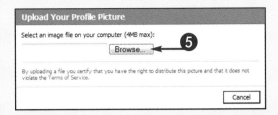

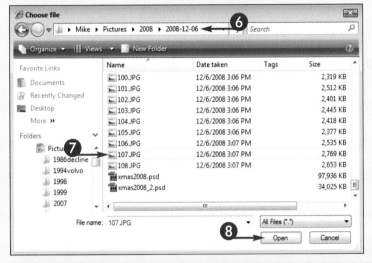

Facebook displays an Upload Your Profile Picture dialog box.

⑤ Click **Browse**.

A Choose File dialog box appears.

⑥ Navigate to the folder on your computer where you saved your picture.

⑦ Click to select your picture file.

⑧ Click **Open**.

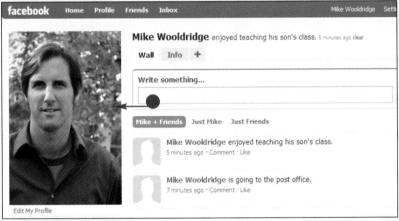

Facebook uploads the picture.

● The picture appears on your profile page.

Simplify It

Can I edit the thumbnail version of my profile picture that appears next to my updates?
You can adjust how the thumbnail picture is cropped. On your profile page, position your mouse cursor over your profile picture, click the **Change Picture** link that appears, and then click **Edit Thumbnail**. A dialog box appears enabling you to click and drag the thumbnail to adjust the cropping.

How can I access past profile photos?
Each profile photo you upload is stored in a Profile Pictures album in your account. To view the album, visit your profile page and click the **Photos** tab. When viewing a photo from one of your albums, you can set the photo as your profile picture by clicking the **Make Profile Picture** link.

Update Your Status

You can let your Facebook friends know what you are doing, where you are going, or what you are thinking by posting a status message to your Facebook page. A status message can include up to 160 characters and appears at the top of your profile page and home page. It also appears as an entry in the News Feeds of your Facebook friends. Friends can comment on your status updates. Making regular status updates to your Facebook account is known as *microblogging*. This is in contrast to blogging, where people post much longer descriptions of what they are doing that can include photos and other media.

Update Your Status

1 Log in to your Facebook account at www.facebook.com. For details, see "Set Up a Facebook Account."

Your Facebook home page appears.

2 Type a new status here.

3 Click **Share**.

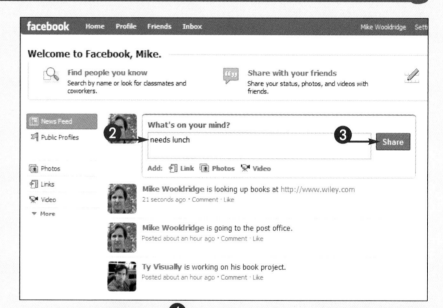

● Your status update appears in the News Feed.

● If you include a Web address in your status, it appears as a clickable link in the News Feed.

4 Click **Profile**.

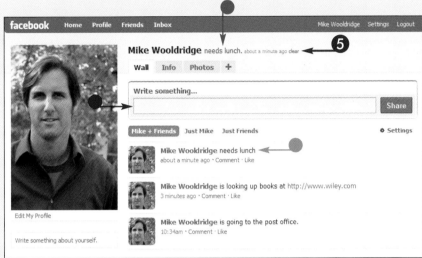

● Facebook also displays the status on your profile page.

● Your status update appears on your Wall.

● You can update your status from your profile page by typing in the box and clicking **Share**.

⑤ Click **clear**.

● Facebook removes your status.

Simplify It

Where else can I add personal details on my profile page?
You can add a caption below your profile picture. Click **Profile** to view your profile page and then click the **Write something about yourself** link. This is a convenient place to add a short description of yourself, an inspirational message, or a favorite quote.

How do I comment on someone's status?
In the News Feed on your home page, you can click the **Comment** link next to a user's status update to make a comment. You can comment on friend statuses or your own status. Multiple comments can be left on a status, and those comments appear as a list below the status. Comments on your status also appear on your Facebook Wall.

Add a Friend

Facebook becomes much more interesting after you establish connections to other Facebook users by making them your friends. You can see a friend's full profile, and his or her site activity appears in the News Feed on your Facebook home page. You can find friends to add by searching on a name or e-mail address. You can also have Facebook search your e-mail address book for people who are on Facebook. In the friend search results, Facebook shows you a thumbnail profile picture and a list of the networks to which a user belongs to help you pick out friends that you know. After a user confirms your friend request, you become connected on Facebook.

Add a Friend

1 Log in to your Facebook account. For details, see "Set Up a Facebook Account."

Your Facebook home page appears.

2 Position your mouse cursor over **Friends**.

A list of links appears.

3 Click **Find Friends**.

To view a list of your current friends, you can click **Friends**.

The Find People Your Know on Facebook page appears.

● If you use a popular online e-mail service such as Yahoo Mail or Gmail, you can find friends by typing your e-mail address and e-mail password and clicking **Find Friends**.

4 Type the name or e-mail address of a friend.

5 Click 🔍 to search.

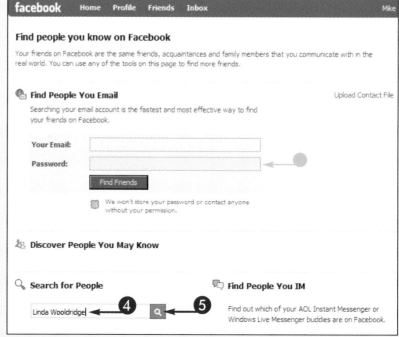

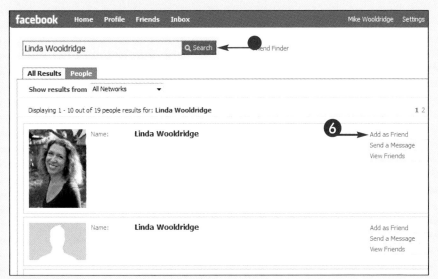

Facebook performs a search and displays names, profile pictures, and networks in the results.

Facebook takes into account nicknames and common misspellings in its search.

● You can revise your search here.

❻ Click **Add as Friend**.

A pop-up dialog box appears.

● You can click here to add a personal message to the default note that Facebook sends.

● You can click here to group this user in a Friend List. See the tip below for details

❼ Click **Add Friend**.

Facebook sends the user a friend request by e-mail.

If the user confirms the request, you are sent an e-mail confirmation. A message about the new friendship is also posted to your Wall.

How do I respond to a friend request?
When another user adds you as a friend, Facebook sends you an e-mail to alert you of the request. Facebook also displays a link on the top of your home page showing the number of your pending friend requests. You can click the link in the e-mail or on the home page to confirm or ignore requests.

I have lots of Facebook friends. How can I organize them?
You can group your Facebook friends into lists to make them easier to manage. You might create separate lists for your high school friends, work friends, and family members. After you create a list, you can easily send messages to all the friends in the list at once. You can also apply different privacy settings to different friend lists. To create a list, click **Friends**. Then click **Make a New List** on the page that appears.

Share to a Wall

On Facebook, your Wall shows a summary of your site activity. It is also a place for friends to share publicly visible notes, links, and other content to you. Entries on your Wall appear in reverse chronological order. When a friend adds a message to your Wall, a dated entry for that message appears at the top of the Wall. Recent activity that appears on the Walls of your friends also appears in the News Feed on your home page.

Share to a Wall

SHARE A TEXT MESSAGE

1 View the profile of a Facebook friend.

You can click a friend name on your home page News Feed or on your Friends page to view the profile.

2 Type a message.

3 Click **Share**.

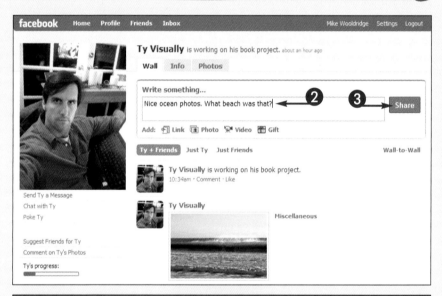

● Facebook displays the message at the top of the friend's Wall.

● A thumbnail of your profile picture appears next to the message.

● If you have exchanged multiple messages on each other's Walls, you can click **Wall-to-Wall** to see the exchange.

SHARE A LINK

1 In the Write Something box, click **Share Link**.

The Link box appears.

2 Type or paste a Web address.

3 Click **Attach**.

Facebook retrieves the linked page and displays a summary.

● You can click here to display a specific image from the linked page.

● You can type an optional message here.

4 Click **Share** to share the link and the summary to the Wall.

Simplify It

How do I send a private message?
Wall comments are for all friends of a user to see. To communicate privately, click **Inbox** and then **Compose Message**. In the form that appears, you can type one or more friend names in the To: field, or type the name of a friend list to send a message. Messages on Facebook are similar to e-mail correspondence. You can view messages that you have sent and received by clicking **Inbox**.

How can I have my activity from other Web sites shown on my Wall?
You can automatically share links to your activity on sites such as Flickr, YouTube, Digg, and others to your Wall. This can save you from having to update your Facebook account after you have already made an update elsewhere. Click the **Settings** link on your Wall to see what sites are supported. The sites appear in the Stories Posted By You section.

Index

Index

Index

Index

Index

Index

Index

Read Less–Learn More®

There's a Visual book for every learning level...

Simplified®

The place to start if you're new to computers. Full color.

- Computers
- Creating Web Pages
- Mac OS
- Office
- Windows

Teach Yourself VISUALLY™

Get beginning to intermediate-level training in a variety of topics. Full color.

- Access
- Bridge
- Chess
- Computers
- Crocheting
- Digital Photography
- Dog training
- Dreamweaver
- Excel
- Flash
- Golf
- Guitar
- Handspinning
- HTML
- Jewelry Making & Beading
- Knitting
- Mac OS
- Office
- Photoshop
- Photoshop Elements
- Piano
- Poker
- PowerPoint
- Quilting
- Scrapbooking
- Sewing
- Windows
- Wireless Networking
- Word

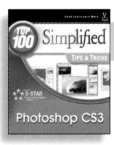

Top 100 Simplified® Tips & Tricks

Tips and techniques to take your skills beyond the basics. Full color.

- Digital Photography
- eBay
- Excel
- Google
- Internet
- Mac OS
- Office
- Photoshop
- Photoshop Elements
- PowerPoint
- Windows

Wiley, the Wiley logo, the Visual logo, Master Visually, Read Less-Learn More, Simplified, Teach Yourself Visually, Visual Blueprint, and Visual Encyclopedia are trademarks or registered trademarks of John Wiley & Sons, Inc. and or its affiliates. All other trademarks are the property of their respective owners.

...all designed for visual learners—just like you!

Master VISUALLY®

Your complete visual reference. Two-color interior.

- 3ds Max
- Creating Web Pages
- Dreamweaver and Flash
- Excel
- Excel VBA Programming
- iPod and iTunes
- Mac OS
- Office
- Optimizing PC Performance
- Photoshop Elements
- QuickBooks
- Quicken
- Windows
- Windows Mobile
- Windows Server

Visual Blueprint™

Where to go for professional-level programming instruction. Two-color interior.

- Ajax
- ASP.NET 2.0
- Excel Data Analysis
- Excel Pivot Tables
- Excel Programming
- HTML
- JavaScript
- Mambo
- PHP & MySQL
- SEO
- Vista Sidebar
- Visual Basic
- XML

Visual Encyclopedia™

Your A to Z reference of tools and techniques. Full color.

- Dreamweaver
- Excel
- Mac OS
- Photoshop
- Windows

Visual Quick Tips

Shortcuts, tricks, and techniques for getting more done in less time. Full color.

- Crochet
- Digital Photography
- Excel
- iPod & iTunes
- Knitting
- MySpace
- Office
- PowerPoint
- Windows
- Wireless Networking

Visual
An Imprint of ⊕WILEY
Now you know.

For a complete listing of Visual books, go to wiley.com/go/visual